ADVANCE PRAISE FOR

# *Ageing of the Oppressed*

Silvia Perel-Levin, a highly respected international expert and leading advocate on human rights and ageing, has brought together contributors from around the world and from different disciplines to reflect on ageing, human rights, and oppression in its many forms. The book offers provocative, moving, and powerful stories and analyses of marginalization in older age and the interaction of age and other forms of discrimination in the denial of human rights. The book demands of its readers that they reflect deeply on their own ageism, prejudices, and complacency. A must-have for anyone interested in ageing, human rights, law, and structures of power in our societies.

—Andrew Byrnes, Emeritus Professor of Law, University of New South Wales,
Sydney, Australia

As an eminent global advocate for the improvement of human rights of all citizens and most especially older people, Silvia Perel-Levin is well qualified to bring together leading experts in their field to convey through storytelling the manifest urgency for formal recognition and collective action against unjust treatment in all its forms. Each narrative will leave an imprint on your soul of the pain of being human yet most importantly the innate power in voice and meaningful engagement.

—Jane Barratt, Secretary General, International Federation on Ageing

# Ageing of the Oppressed

# COUNTERPOINTS

# Studies in Criticality

Shirley R. Steinberg
*General Editor*

Vol. 542

Silvia Perel-Levin

# Ageing of the Oppressed

## A Pandemic of Intersecting Injustice

PETER LANG

Lausanne • Berlin • Brussels • Chennai • New York • Oxford

**Library of Congress Cataloging-in-Publication Control Number**: 2023024629

Bibliographic information published by the **Deutsche Nationalbibliothek.**
**The German National Library** lists this publication in the German
National Bibliography; detailed bibliographic data is available
on the Internet at http://dnb.d-nb.de.

Cover design by Blake Calderwood

ISSN 1058-1634 (print)
ISBN 9781433195310 (paperback)
ISBN 9781433195303 (hardback)
ISBN 9781433195280 (ebook)
ISBN 9781433195297 (epub)
DOI 10.3726/b21013

© 2023 Peter Lang Group AG, Lausanne
Published by Peter Lang Publishing Inc., New York, USA
info@peterlang.com - www.peterlang.com

This publication has been peer reviewed.

To Norma Frontini, Alfredo Díaz, Horacio García Gastellú, Oscar Ledesma Medina, and to all those who were murdered because they wanted a better world.

To the memory of Eva Piwowarski. We "discovered" together *Pedagogy of the Oppressed* and shared many years of renewed friendship.

# Contents

# Figure

# Acknowledgments

This book would not have been written without the encouragement of my dear cousin and writing mentor, Judith Pearl Summerfield. She managed to instill in me confidence to embark on this project. She is always there to read my drafts, provide useful feedback and solid advice, and always finds the words to make me want to continue.

I would also like to thank:

The series editor, Shirley Steinberg, who understood me and gave me a stage.

All the writers who engaged with me in multiple dialogues to achieve meaningful chapters. I thank them for their time, and their trust: Alex Kalache, Bette Moskowitz, Adolf Ratzka, Michael Adams, Kate Swaffer, María Soledad Cisternas Reyes, Liat Ayalon, Claudia Mahler, Larraine j. Larri and Alanna Armitage.

Those behind the scenes, who helped with translations, editing, copy-editing and more: Paul Faber, Delories Dunn de Ayuso, Abigail Harris-Culver, Mary Murphy and Marcela San Martín.

Blake Calderwood for designing the cover.

And always my family: My man Mark Levin, who has read, edited, provided feedback and also cooked, brought me tea and coffee to the desk and went out for walks on his own so that I could concentrate on the task at hand. And to my remarkable adult children: Gal, Assaf and Aviv Levin, who never tire of listening to my stories.

# Ageing of the Oppressed: A Pandemic of Intersecting Injustice

Silvia Perel-Levin

## Introduction

### A Personal Introduction

*Pedagogy of the Oppressed* by Paulo Freire and *Theatre of the Oppressed* by Augusto Boal have shaped my ideological and professional life through all its twists and turns.[1,2,3]

I was introduced to Paulo Freire's work circa 1974–75 when, every afternoon after school, my friend Eva and I used to go to the small wooden school shack with its corrugated metal roof that an evangelist group had built in the shanty town, *La Carcova*, on the outskirts of Buenos Aires. Our mission, as part of our militancy in the *Union de Estudiantes Secundarios* [Union of Secondary Students], was to help children with their school homework. We soon realized that these kids couldn't read and sometimes, they just needed something to eat. Often, their parents couldn't read either. These children from the *Villa Miseria* (shanty town) were always at the back of the class in schools. They rarely got the teachers' attention, except for disciplinary measures. Eva and I didn't know how to help to make a difference, how to rescue them from the never-ending cycle of controlling behavior that instilled discipline and imposed punishments that these children were used to.

Our UES chief or team leader, *El Gallego* [the Galician; his militant nom de guerre], contacted a professor of early childhood education, a friend of his mother, so that she could advise us. For this connection, El Gallego gave us his real name. We never used our real names, but that is how this woman knew him: Horacio García Gastelú. The military took him by force from his girlfriend's house and he "disappeared" a few months after the military coup of March 1976. His remains were found years later in the common grave of the *Massacre of Fátima*, the same massacre where 30 young people, including my friend Norma and The Paraguayan Oscar, were murdered and dynamited in Fatima, north of Buenos Aires, on August 20, 1976.[4] Horacio was featured in the 2014 documentary El Futuro es Nuestro [*The Future is Ours*].[5] His mother, one of the founders of the *Mothers of Plaza de Mayo*, passed away recently as I was writing these lines.

This professor commended our efforts and proposed we use corners of the shack for different activities as was done at the time in kindergartens. She gave us simple play tips. But this was not a kindergarten and we had no resources. This is when another schoolmate or *compañero* introduced us to *Pedagogy of the Oppressed* by Paulo Freire as an example of educational techniques used for adult literacy that could help us, as Freire himself had used his method with his maid and illiterate poor people.

We didn't have much success with our educational enterprise. The task was clearly too ambitious for us, two teenagers. At the time, the work of literacy for poor people was a *subversive* activity and therefore a dangerous one. The violence of the months before the military coup, the military-led dictatorship that started in 1976, the disappearances, the persecutions, and the deep fear, not only drew me away from the *Villa*, but also from the country.

A few years later, during my studies in Social and Educational Theatre at Tel Aviv University, I deeply connected with Augusto Boal's *Theatre of the Oppressed*, obviously building on Freire's work. I wrote essays on his theories and used his techniques—the Forum Theater, Invisible Theater, and theater games—in the Community Theater Project I coordinated in a neighborhood in south Tel-Aviv and in the theater and puppetry workshops I ran for teachers and community leaders from Israel and developing countries.[6] I wanted to make theater meaningful for everyone, to mobilize communities away from being just passive *spectators* to being *spect-actors* toward social change. Boal's view of catharsis is not to create equilibrium, as normally understood, but rather to create a "disequilibrium" which prepares the way for action. Individuals, and by extension society itself, can be changed by a catharsis that is not the sole province of the controlling group; as a removal of blocks, the purification is in the action.[7,8]

When I moved to Geneva in the late 1990s and started working with United Nations agencies and international non-governmental organizations (NGOs), I continued to apply Boal's approach to promote health and social justice. Making the voices of people in vulnerable situations heard has always been part of my life.

I have been a defender of the human rights of older persons for over 20 years at the UN, in its specialized agencies including several years at the

World Health Organization (WHO) and the UN Human Rights mechanisms, mostly the Human Rights Council.

## Human Rights of Older Persons, Oppression, and Intersectionality

Human rights are universal, inalienable, indivisible, and interdependent.[9] We all have rights simply because we are human beings regardless of nationality; ethnic, social, or economic background; religion; gender; age or any other status. All rights are equally important, whether it is the right to life, food, education, adequate housing, work, health, liberty, and more, as set out in the International Bill of Human Rights (Universal Declaration of Human Rights (UDHR); the International Covenant for Civil and Political Rights; and the International Covenant for Economic, Social, and Cultural Rights) and all international human rights treaties.[10,11]

We are all, in principle, covered by the international human rights system. However, the current international human rights framework does not include explicit guarantees against ageism, or an explicit obligation for States to take active measures to eliminate ageism and its discriminatory consequences.[12] Older persons are very rarely mentioned in human rights treaties. The UDHR does not explicitly include age. Article 2 of the UDHR stipulates:

> Everyone is entitled to all the rights and freedoms set forth in this Declaration, without distinction of any kind, such as race, colour, sex, language, religion, political or other opinion, national or social origin, property, birth or other status.[13]

*Other status* should in principle include everyone, but the reality is that generally neither governments nor the Committees that examine the human rights situations in the reporting countries consider the human rights situation of older persons in their reports or ask about older persons.

Furthermore, existing monitoring mechanisms have not dealt with intersectionality where age would intersect with other grounds of discrimination. In fact, intersectionality is not much of a part of the system. Discrimination is often examined with components of accumulation of discrimination, i.e., women and race, migration and poverty, and while "intersection" is mentioned in human rights mechanisms, the concept is contested by some governments ignoring the interlocking relationships and the different experiences that result from "intersectional discrimination," reinforcing the silos. Virginia May describes "lived identities, structural systems, sites of marginalization, forms of power and modes of resistance that 'intersect' in dynamic, shifting, ways."[14,15] *Other status* is clearly not enough to include and meaningfully discuss either the discrimination suffered in older age or the privileges that some enjoy across the life course, systemic structures, and relationships of power.

The degree of resistance by governments to recognize older persons as full human rights holders is striking. The root source of most injustices suffered by older people is widely attributed to *ageism*. The term ageism was coined by the American Gerontologist Robert Butler in 1968 to describe the systemic discrimination of older persons and equate it to sexism or racism.[16] It was only in 2021 that a Human Rights Council included Ageism for the first time in the text of the first substantive resolution on the human rights of older persons.[17] *Structural ageism* is the systematic stereotyping, attitudes, actions, and language that we find in laws, policies, practices, or culture.[18] Ageism is manifested at all levels of society including in families, health care settings, the media, and entertainment industries. When policymakers, our elected representatives, or international donors claim that ageing or older persons are not a priority for public policy, when UN agencies claim the same, they are complicit in probably one of the deepest, although not universally recognized and sometimes invisible, forms of social injustice: discrimination against older persons.

Ageism and age-based discrimination intersect with other forms of biases, discrimination, and inequalities based, for example, on disability, gender, gender identity and sexual orientation, ethnic background, and socioeconomic status, to name a few. The longer we live, the more our identities and life conditions intersect, creating often unique barriers and challenges in the exercise of our human rights. Ageism and racism combined create aggravating forms of discrimination and dehumanization that are rarely addressed—or admitted—by policymakers or service providers.[19] During the COVID-19 pandemic, older ethnic minorities were physically attacked and were victims of online hate speech, blamed for the virus and denied access to health care or adequate information, which compounded and aggravated the effects of both ageism and racism during the pandemic.[20]

Older women are particularly and negatively affected by social, economic, and cultural norms and discriminatory laws in almost all countries, suffering *gendered ageism*.[21] Women's low quality of life in older age is a culmination of a life course of inequalities, lack of access to education, lack of adequate work, or lower salaries and interrupted careers with a *motherhood penalty* resulting in pension gaps and further disadvantages. Older women's situations in later life have been regarded as a litmus test for the quality of women's economic and social life.[22] Older women are too often ignored by feminist organizations and scholars,[23] and by research on violence against women that generally focuses on women and girls below the age of 49, described as the "reproductive years" with the baseless assumption that women beyond reproductive age are free of violence.[24] Older women who spend decades in the shade of a male culture, absorbing male-dominated media messages, find themselves in old age in the shade of their male offspring. In some cultures, older widows are subjected to harmful rituals and accusations of witchcraft and are dispossessed of their land.[25] Those who have been feminists through-out their younger and adult lives, often with great sacrifice, may suddenly realize that the feminist movement is ageist and that older women are either not taken seriously or are completely ignored.[26] Silvia Gascón, a friend, shared with me the story of her life as a lifetime feminist, activist, community organizer, expert on ageing, and at times a government official in Argentina. On Sunday, January 1, 2023 she sent me her story by email, and complemented by a Zoom call the following day, she told me:

> Of course, looking after the children was the exclusive task of women. We sang revolutionary songs to them; we fell asleep hugging each other. We wanted to make a better world for them. That they wouldn't have to go through what we went through. And we *broke our backs* to give them opportunities for education, connections, political awareness, and essential values. Being a woman, mother, daughter, militant, worker, friend, partner and student were shaping an identity that eventually enabled me to feel free of ties. I could choose who to be and how.

She also reminisced about an eye-opener workshop she once organized with local and provincial ministers of social development programs who were all women, whereas almost all governors were men:

> Committed and courageous women, who worked in very difficult situations and who in many cases were the wives of high-ranking officials. Those tireless hard-working women, with a very high political commitment, who made daily important decisions and helped men win the elections, seemed like girls waiting for *Prince Charming* to grant them a key place in politics. The underlying idea was that *real* aspirations belonged to men whereas ours, were *pure love and militancy*.

Some older women are saying *enough*. Organizations of older women are emancipating; they have had enough of being told what to do, how to behave, and what to wear. They are radicalizing, coming out of the shadows, showing their strengths, using technologies, and managing their finances. The Knitting Nannas in Australia, featured in this book, are one good example. *La Revolución de las Viejas* [The Old Women's Revolution] is a book by an Argentinean journalist, writer, and politician Gabriela Cerruti, claiming emancipation and mobilization of a generation of women that grew under military and male oppression.[27] But language is important. While many older women, including myself, are happy to identify as *vieja*, many see this word as offensive: *Viejos son los trapos* [*Old are the rags*]. During our conversation, Silvia Gascón told me about the many lasting successes of the *Red Mayor (Older Network)* she created in her city *La Plata*[28] and also some of the challenges:

> Economic resources were scarce, so we supplemented with a lot of voluntary work from the older women who were interested. A second challenge was that many older women, even those who had been active militants in the women's network, did not join (as I had expected) because they did not want to belong to a group of *viejas*.

In English, many professionals and the media tend to use the word "elderly" to describe an older person. Most older persons would reject being generalized under such a term that assumes all older people are the same, defined with an adverb that determines a specific way of being, in this case, *frail*. The UN Independent Expert on the enjoyment of all human rights by older persons and other experts on ageism have clearly expressed the view that the word "elderly" is, in fact, ageist.[29,30] To engage in a meaningful dialogue that can lead to increased *conscientização* [*consciousness*], we need to consider seriously the language, and the words we use. According to Freire, the word is much more than just a tool for dialogue. The word has two dimensions that interact with each other. One dimension is "reflection," and the other one is "action," and no one dimension can be sacrificed. The radical interaction between the two dimensions is such that if we sacrifice one, we are also compromising the other.[31] The words we use to describe older persons have a direct impact on the perceptions, attitudes, and actions that are taken in the public domain, policies, and discourse.

Older persons and persons with disabilities are generally left behind in emergency situations and conflicts.[32,33] Amnesty International reports that following the invasion of Ukraine in 2022, older people appeared to make up a disproportionate number of civilians remaining in areas of active hostilities, in harrowing conditions, and at greater risk of injury and death and that support for older people who have disabilities is rarely provided in temporary shelters.[34]

The exclusion is so perverse that it is, in fact, oppression.[35] It is not a case of ignorance, or cultural blindness. It is often a calculated decision, based on prejudice. Ageism is used as a political tool. Denying people the autonomy to decide where and with whom they want to live, denying them the self determination to decide whether they can or want to work, depriving them of the support to live independently and be included in the community, denying the support to exercise their wishes and legal capacity, depriving them of liberty, denying their choice of type of care and palliative care, denying them access to information or to justice, is plainly oppression. The use of discriminatory language and narratives that portray population ageing as a danger to society, and older persons as objects that need to be taken care of, segregated from the public eye and perhaps not worthy of investment, operationalizes ageism as a violent, political, and oppressive tool. As Freire says:

> Any situation in which "A" objectively exploits "B" or hinders his and her pursuit of self-affirmation as a responsible person is one of oppression. Such a situation in itself constitutes violence, even when sweetened by false generosity, because it interferes with the individual's ontological and historical vocation to be more fully human.[36]

While some of us in the world are lucky enough to live longer and healthier lives and find older age to be a time of emancipation, many more endure lifelong oppression. The oppression intersects with the ageism and age-based discrimination that most of us experience daily in older age. How can we move away from the *false generosity* of viewing older persons as a homogenous group in need of charity and pity, into a recognition that all human beings— whatever their birthplace, race, gender, socioeconomic status, or *age*—must enjoy their individual and collective human rights? How can we move away from fatalistic, determinist thinking that assumes that at a certain age, it is too late to learn, start a business, get credit, migrate, or simply enjoy family life and cultural, travel, or leisure activities?

*Social exclusion* considers the interlinkages between different levels of risk factors, processes, and outcomes at the societal, community, and individual levels. It also considers the different forms and complexities that may be amplified in older age leading to "inequities in choice and control, resources and relationships, and power and rights in key domains of neighborhood and community; services, amenities and mobility; material and financial resources; social relations; socio-cultural aspects of society; and civic participation."[37] Discourse about social exclusion implies that there must be an *inclusion*. But inclusion in what? Once people are outside the world of work, not admitted to educational institutions because they are *too old*, or do not have access to frameworks or social clubs because they may live in remote areas without proper transport, they are excluded from opportunities to learn and grow. Freire says:

> The truth is, however, that the oppressed are not "marginals," are not people living "outside" society. They have always been "inside"—inside the structure

which made them *beings for others*. The solution is not to *integrate* them into the structure of oppression, but to transform that structure so that they can become beings for themselves.[38]

The concept of oppression in the context of ageism is not new. Carroll Estes places social policy within power struggles and the "interlocking systems of oppression" of race, class, gender, and age.[39] Maggie Kuhn, founder of the social movement Gray Panthers,[40] defined ageism as a problem of alienation and oppression and aligned it with racism as both deprive people of their own choices and control over their lives. She also aligned ageism with ableism since persons with disabilities—young and old—are discriminated against and marginalized.[41] Kuhn was a loud critical voice against the *neutral* researchers, calling on gerontologists to take the side of the oppressed rather than the oppressive establishment.

Kuhn, like Freire, lived decades ago. It may seem anachronistic for some to try to revive *old* theories of people who fought capitalism at a time when there seems to be no way out of it. However, as we witness big pushbacks in human rights, a shrinking of civil society space, and an increased *normalization* of extreme right-wing and dictator-like regimes, I claim that we need to remind ourselves that humanistic theories and *praxis* still prevail so that we all can age with dignity.

## *About the Book*

The idea of this book was born in the early stages of COVID-19 while we were witnessing, and experiencing, different levels of discrimination, stigmatization, and demonization of older persons. Older persons have been particularly affected by COVID. It was not just the virus that was killing us but also the rampant, staggering neglect and ageism that became more apparent than ever as older persons—mainly in institutions—were dying in big numbers and we had to listen to the patronizing, harmful, discriminatory language used in the media and everywhere. Discrimination was experienced in triage and the lack of admissions to hospitals, in the cancelation of vital treatments and services, and in stricter lockdown rules based on arbitrary age limits. We saw shocking media reports of institutions that had been abandoned by their staff, leaving their old residents to die.[42,43,44,45,46] While initially older activists were pushed into a corner as we were not allowed in many places to leave our homes or to volunteer or attend public places, a new active online community of older activists was born with global cafés, webinars, and online discussions taking place daily around the world for those who had access to technology. Many older persons who had previously not attended virtual events, learned how to. I spent time teaching several people how to access and use the different virtual meeting tools. A growing body of reports, books, and academic articles on ageism and social exclusion have been recently published, which is a welcome trend.[47,48,49] We were naïve enough to expect that ageing and older persons would, from that point onwards, be more visible in public discourse.

There is a disconnect between the academic literature dispersed across disciplines and public policies, but there also often seems to be a disconnect between what older persons feel, experience, want, or demand and what academics publish. Social policies and legal frameworks do not include older persons in their designs and implementations. So, why do we not react? Some research would explain that older persons themselves are self-ageist, having internalized the ageist attitudes and stereotypes, and are convinced that their time is up and that they need to cede their place to younger people.[50]

To approach older persons as full agents of change and to instill in them the confidence that society belongs to *all* its members, we need to use all the tools available to us: legal and human rights, education, and conscientization. Macedo claims that the goal of *Pedagogy of the Oppressed* is to awaken in the oppressed the knowledge and critical reflection "to unveil, demystify, and understand the power relations responsible for their oppressed marginalization and, through this recognition, begin a project of liberation."[51] There needs to be a real dialogue with older people to reach the level of *conscientização* that can lead to their full recognition in society.

Let us make the invisible, visible. Let us name oppression when we see it. Let us listen to the voices of older persons who want to have a say in how to lead their lives until the end of their lives. Let us challenge the narratives that paint older persons as useless, unproductive, and ugly. Let us make the connections between the individual, the relationships, and the bigger social issues that have an impact on us all.

This book is a modest attempt to raise some of these issues. It does not pretend to be a global representation of all the complexities of ageing. It is, however, a timely snapshot of certain types of daily oppression that when accumulated and intersected in older age, become so overwhelming, complex, and painful, that many prefer to close their eyes and not see what they themselves could become in their future selves. It showcases some personal testimonies from some parts of the world, without pretending to represent all regions or all types of oppression. It links some legal background and some gerontological, demographic and human rights theories with lived experiences and fiction.

Before I describe the chapters that follow, I would like to make a note about spelling and terminology. I use "ageing" with an "e," which is the UN spelling. However, U.S. spelling uses "aging." I did not change the spelling chosen by the authors.

*Chapter 1: Growing Old Among Inequalities in Brazil, by Alexandre Kalache.* Brazil is rapidly ageing. There are already 33 million Brazilians over 60 and this number will more than double by 2050. By this time, Brazilians over the age of 60 will represent 30 percent of the overall population, double the proportion of children under 15. Living a long life, and surviving a long life, are not the same thing. Since records began, Brazil has consistently ranked as one of the most unequal countries in the world. Tens of millions of Brazilians are ageing in the context of unmet needs, threatening environments, invisibility, disempowerment, and outright exclusion. The fast ageing of the country is occurring on top of historic failures to address basic structural inadequacies in health, education, sanitation, housing, transport, and labor market participation. Brazil is missing opportunities to address the causes of vulnerability; to reinforce preparedness and capacity in all groups; to incorporate such components as cultural safety into policy actions; and to establish direct pathways toward active citizenship at all ages.

*Chapter 2: The Cultural Cage, by Bette Ann Moskowitz.* "The Cultural Cage" begins as a faux-speculative fiction about an upside-down planet (X) on which young people suffer the kind of prejudicial treatment that old people suffer here on Earth. The metaphor, first used in Moskowitz's book, *FINISHING UP: On Aging and Ageism,*[52] refers to the strong history of certain behaviors and beliefs about ageing that self-perpetuate and lead to both ageism and elder abuse. When we return to Earth, the chapter delves into the stereotypes that fuel ageism (wisdom and wrinkles), how ageism becomes elder abuse, the state of institutional living in America, the powerlessness of mandated whistleblowers, and how the medical community treated older people during the deepest part of the pandemic.

*Chapter 3: Living and Aging with Disability: A Personal Account, by Adolf Ratzka.* Through his personal story, Ratzka suggests that society's prejudices against older persons and persons with disabilities cause their low social status. This has led to segregation and marginalization in institutions and the denial of personal assistance services.

As the number of older persons with impairments rises, many will require assistance with the activities of daily living. Ratzka claims that as the role of the family declines in supporting older and disabled family members, high-quality community-based support services are necessary to enable older persons with disabilities to live independently in the community, away from institutions. The COVID-19 pandemic has shown that institutionalized older persons and persons with disabilities were at the highest risk and in the most vulnerable situations. The right to live independently and be included in the community is required by the Convention on the Rights of Persons with Disabilities. But personal assistance services, where they exist, are limited to younger persons.

*Chapter 4: LGBTI Elders Advancing, by Michael Adams.* This chapter reviews available research and testimonies by LGBTI older adults from different parts of the world highlighting the severe challenges they face because of their sexual orientation and/or gender identity that provide barriers to healthy ageing and a dignified life. Challenges vary by region and other factors, but include social isolation, discrimination and abuse, poverty, morbidity, and lack of access to support. Structural ageism, particularly in the lack of culturally competent or accessible healthcare, discriminatory employment practices, and misrepresentation in the media, commerce, and entertainment, exacerbate the challenges. While attitudes and resources may vary with countries and levels of development, LGBTI older adults have less-positive outcomes than their heterosexual peers, no matter where they live. This chapter presents potential solutions including partnering with existing LGBTI elder advocates to ensure their specific needs are addressed, advocating for public policies that provide protection and enhance access to resources, creating specific programs that support sub-communities within the broader LGBTI community, and conducting enhanced research and data collection to better reflect specific issues and shape strategies for change.

*Chapter 5: The Intersection Between Old Age and Disability, by María Soledad Cisternas Reyes.* This chapter analyzes to what extent the United Nations Convention on the Rights of Persons with Disabilities applies to older persons and what are its limitations. The population of older persons is heterogeneous and only a certain percentage may have a disability. It is necessary to discern which is the applicable legal standard, paying special attention to cases of older persons with disabilities in a situation of dependency. Cisternas Reyes cites the Inter-American Convention for the protection of the human rights of older persons that, while being a regional instrument, could provide important normative references guiding the work at the global level toward a UN Convention. The chapter also raises with concern the medicalized approach to old age by the World Health Organization classification of diseases (WHO ICD-11) that threatens to strengthen prejudices and stereotypes, undermining the model of human rights for older people, in clear contradiction with WHO's own Decade of Healthy Ageing 2020–2030.

*Chapter 6: About Us Without Us: The Elephants in the Room, by Kate Swaffer.* This chapter describes and analyzes the oppression of people diagnosed with dementia and of self-advocates. It introduces several unique challenges, about the "elephants still in the room" that most do not talk about publicly, because it may be uncomfortable or embarrassing. Refusing to stay silent, Swaffer tells the story, from her personal experience, of a vulnerable cohort whose global voice is growing, but decisions are still determined by very few, without considering the voice of those directly concerned. Swaffer's experience stems from having been a nurse working in aged and dementia care, a legal guardian and family care partner to three people with dementia who were abused and neglected and died in residential care, and then being diagnosed with dementia herself. She became an "accidental activist" for herself, which led her to advocate for others diagnosed with dementia. She refuses the harmful Prescribed Disengagement®,[53] to go home and prepare to die, which she believes is likely the reason for her being not just still alive, but functional, despite increasing disabilities. She describes several theories about how and why the oppression of people with dementia is evident, having more questions than answers. Although many things appear to have changed, oppression seems to be still palpable but dressed up in a more glamorous outfit.

*Chapter 7: Mental Health, Physical Health, Older Age, and Oppression by Liat Ayalon.* This chapter adopts a life course approach by discussing the impact of varied types of "isms," including mentalism, ableism, and ageism. It highlights the need to move forward and change the way we think, feel, and act toward people because of their age, mental health conditions, and/or disabilities. Such a change is needed to live in an inclusive society that accepts people, regardless of their age, and or functional level. It also brings to the fore the dehumanization experienced in care institutions. Ayalon claims that a UN Convention on the rights of older persons would set clear guidelines as to what constitutes age discrimination, guide governments to adopt anti-discrimination legislation, and form public norms and sway public attitudes and behaviors.

*Chapter 8: Human Rights of Older Persons, Wishful Thinking or Reality? by Claudia Mahler.* After telling us how she got interested in the field, Claudia Mahler, current UN Independent Expert on the enjoyment of all human rights by older persons, gives us a short historical account of the work at the UN around the normative gaps and the need for a Convention within the framework of the UN Open-Ended Working Group on Ageing that has been meeting for over a decade without much progress. She questions why there is no political will and why we need better protection for the human rights of older persons. She discusses who an older person is and describes particular challenges that need attention, such as invisibility, combatting ageism and age-based discrimination, lack of data, older persons in situations of armed conflicts, climate change, and digitalization.

*Chapter 9: "Viva La Nannalution!" Overcoming Ageist Sexism in Environmental Activism: The Australian Knitting Nannas Against Gas and Greed, by Larraine J. Larri.* This chapter tells the story of Australia's Knitting Nannas Against Gas and Greed (a.k.a. KNAG, the Knitting Nannas, or simply the Nannas), an older women's anti-coal seam gas and fossil fuel movement. The Nannas began in 2012 and have captured the engagement of other regional and city-based women around Australia with offshoots in the United Kingdom and the United States.

Larri draws on data from active KNAGs (2016 to 2021). Called "Nannagogy," the research shows older women who have broken through oppressions based on ageist sexism, by utilizing collaborative and transformative social movement learning and contributing their educative energy in these most critical of climate change times. They did this by adopting a creative oppositional discourse, strategically subverting an essentializing of the grandmotherly persona. They challenged the view of older persons as frail, inconsequential, and digitally disengaged. Instead, they became expert in presenting a clearly articulated media profile using digital online tools to complement their offline environmental activism. They shredded the invisibility cloak of ageism to claim space on and offline.

*Chapter 10: The Silver Tsunami, the Ticking Time Bomb and Other Demographic Imaginaries: Moving from Demographic Threat to Demographic Resilience, by Alanna Armitage.* This concluding chapter provides a critical assessment of the demographic imaginaries regarding population ageing. It highlights that the framing of population ageing in apocalyptic terms leads to bias in data collection, intergeneration conflict, ageist attitudes, and an environment which endangers the lives of older persons and society. Armitage introduces the concept of "demographic resilience" calling for a change in narratives and a shift away from the alarmist "demographic threat." She shows the impact that language and imageries at the macro level of the discourse can have at all levels of policy and permeate each one of us.

# Notes

1  Freire, Paulo. *Pedagogy of the Oppressed*. New York: Continuum, 1970. https://envs.ucsc.edu/internships/internship-readings/freire-pedagogy-of-the-oppressed.pdf.
2  Freire, Paulo. *Pedagogy of the Oppressed, 50th Anniversary Edition*. New York: Bloomsbury Publishing, Kindle Edition, 2018.
3  Boal, Augusto. *Theatre of the Oppressed*. London: Pluto Press, 2019. Originally published in 1974 as *Teatro del Oprimido*.
4  La Masacre de Fátima. "Memoria, Verdad y Justicia [Memory, Truth, and Justice]." Accessed January 2, 2023. https://www.masacredefatima.com.ar.

5  Canal Encuentro. "El Future es Nuestro [The Future is Ours]." Accessed January 2, 2023. https://encuentro.gob.ar/programas/serie/8555/6306.
6  Boal, *Theatre of the Oppressed*.
7  Boal, *Theatre of the Oppressed*.
8  Boal, Augusto. *The Rainbow of Desire: The Boal Method of Theater and Therapy.* London: Routledge, 1995.
9  Office of The High Commissioner for Human Rights (OHCHR). "What are Human Rights?" Accessed January 2, 2023. https://www.ohchr.org/en/what-are-human-rights.
10  OHCHR. "International Bill of Human Rights." Accessed January 2, 2023. https://www.ohchr.org/en/what-are-human-rights/international-bill-human-rights.
11  OHCHR. "Treaty Bodies." Accessed January 3, 2023. https://www.ohchr.org/en/treaty-bodies.
12  OHCHR. "Normative Standards and Obligations Under International Law in Relation to the Promotion and Protection of the Human Rights of Older Persons." Report A/HRC/49/70. Accessed January 3, 2023. https://www.ohchr.org/en/documents/thematic-reports/ahrc4970-normative-standards-and-obligations-under-international-law.
13  United Nations. "Universal Declaration of Human Rights." Accessed January 6, 2023. https://www.un.org/en/about-us/universal-declaration-of-human-rights.
14  May, Virginia. *Pursuing Intersectionality, Unsettling Dominant Imaginaries.* London: Routledge, 2015. https://doi.org/10.4324/9780203141991.
15  Truscan, Ivona and Joanna Bourke-Martignoni. "International Human Rights Law and Intersectional Discrimination." *The Equal Rights Review* 16 (2016). https://www.equalrightstrust.org/ertdocumentbank/International%20Human%20Rights%20Law%20and%20Intersectional%20Discrimination.pdf.
16  Butler, Robert N. "Age-Ism: Another Form of Bigotry." *The Gerontologist* 9, no. 4(1) (1969): 243–246. https://doi.org/10.1093/geront/9.4_Part_1.243.
17  Human Rights Council. "Human Rights for Older Persons." Resolution A/HRC/RES/48/3. October 14, 2021. https://undocs.org/Home/Mobile?FinalSymbol=A%2FHRC%2FRES%2F48%2F3&Language=E&DeviceType=Desktop&LangRequested=False.
18  Age Platform Europe. "AGE Platform Europe Position on Structural Ageism." Accessed January 3, 2023. https://www.age-platform.eu/sites/default/files/AGE_IntergenerationalSolidarity_Position_on_Structural_Ageism2016.pdf.
19  Human Rights Council. "Report of the UN Independent Expert on the Enjoyment of All Human Rights by Older Persons." A/HRC/48/53, para 55, page 12. Accessed January 6, 2023. https://www.ohchr.org/en/documents/thematic-reports/ahrc4853-report-ageism-and-age-discrimination.
20  Human Rights Council. "Report of the UN," para 56.
21  World Health Organization. *Global Report on Ageism.* Geneva: WHO, 2021, 36.
22  Human Rights Council. "Report of the Working Group on the Issue of Discrimination Against Women in Law and in Practice." A/HRC/26/39. https://ap.ohchr.org/documents/dpage_e.aspx?si=A/HRC/26/39.
23  Calasanti, Toni, Kathleen Slevin, and Neal King. "Ageism and Feminism: From 'Et Cetera' to Center." *NWSA Journal* 18, no. 1 (2006): 13–30. http://www.jstor.org/stable/4317183.

24  Crockett Cailin, Bonnie Brandl, and Firoza C. Dabby. "Survivors in the Margins: The Invisibility of Violence Against Older Women." *Journal of Elder Abuse & Neglect* 27, no.4–5 (2015): 291–302.

25  World Health Organization, *Global Report*, 11, 36.

26  Calasanti, Slevin, and King, *Ageism*.

27  Cerruti, Gabriela. *La Revolución de las Viejas* [*The Revolution of the Old Women*]. Ciudad Autónoma de Buenos Aires: Planeta, 2020 Archivo Digital. ISBN 978-950-49-7260-0.

28  Red Mayor La Plata. "Estamos Para Ayudarte a Defender tus Derechos. [We Are Here to Help You Stand Up For Your Rights]." Accessed January 2, 2023. http://www.redmayorlaplata.com.

29  Human Rights Council, "Report of the UN," para 21, p. 6.

30  World Health Organization, *Global Report*, 8.

31  Freire, *Pedagogy of the Oppressed*, 87.

32  Human Rights Council. "Report of the UN Independent Expert on the Enjoyment of All Human Rights by Older Persons." A/HRC/42/43. Accessed January 1, 2023. https://ap.ohchr.org/documents/dpage_e.aspx?si=A/HRC/42/43.

33  Human Rights Watch. "Leave No One Behind People with Disabilities and Older People in Climate-Related Disasters." Accessed December 31, 2022. https://www.hrw.org/news/2022/11/07/leave-no-one-behind.

34  Amnesty International. "I Used To Have A Home, Older People's Experience of War, Displacement, and Access to Housing in Ukraine." December 6, 2021. https://www.amnesty.org/en/documents/eur50/6250/2022/en/.

35  Calasanti, Slevin, and King, *Ageism*.

36  Freire, *Pedagogy of the Oppressed*, 55.

37  Walsh, Kieran, Thomas Scharf, Sofie Van Regenmortel, and Anna Wanka. "The Intersection of Ageing and Social Exclusion." In *Social Exclusion in Later Life: International Perspectives on Aging*, edited by Kieran Walsh, Thomas Scharf, Sofie Van Regenmortel, and Anna Wanka. Berlin/Heidelberg: Springer, 2021. https://doi.org/10.1007/978-3-030-51406-8_1.

38  Walsh et al., "The Intersection," 74.

39  Estes, Carroll. *Social Policy and Aging. A Critical Perspective*. Thousand Oaks, CA: Sage Publications, 2001.

40  Gray Panthers. "Our Founder, Maggie Kuhn." Accessed January 6, 2023. https://www.graypanthersnyc.org/maggie-kuhn.

41  Estes, Carroll and Elena Portacolone. "Maggie Kuhn: Social Theorist of Radical Gerontology." *International Journal of Sociology & Social Policy* 29, no. 1&2 (2009): 15–25. https://doi.org/10.1108/01443330910934682.

42  Allen, Laura D. and Liat Ayalon. "It's Pure Panic: The Portrayal of Residential Care in American Newspapers During COVID-19." *The Gerontologist* 61, no. 1 (2021): 86–97. https://doi.org/10.1093/geront/gnaa162.

43  Ayalon, Liat, Anna Zisberg, Ella Cohn-Schwartz, Jiska Cohen-Mansfield, Silvia Perel-Levin, and Siegal Bar-Asher. "Long-Term Care Settings in the Times of COVID-19: Challenges and Future Directions." *International Psychogeriatrics* 32, no. 10 (2020): 1239–1243. https://doi.org/10.1017/S1041610220001416.

44  Beaulieu, Marie, Julien Cadieux Genesse, and Kevin St-Martin. "COVID-19 and Residential Care Facilities: Issues and Concerns Identified by the International

Network Prevention of Elder Abuse (INPEA)." *The Journal of Adult Protection* 22, no. 6 (2020): 385–389. https://doi.org/10.1108/JAP-08-2020-0034.

45 Jimenez-Sotomayor, Maria Renee, Carolina Gomez-Moreno, and Enrique Soto-Perez-de-Celis. "Coronavirus, Ageism, and Twitter: An Evaluation of Tweets about Older Adults and COVID-19. *Journal of the American Geriatrics Society* 68 (2020): 1661–1665. https://doi.org/10.1111/jgs.16508.

46 Steele, Linda, Ray Carr, Kate Swaffer, Lyn Phillipson, and Richard Fleming. "Human Rights and the Confinement of People Living with Dementia in Care Homes." *Health and Human Rights Journal* 22, no. 1 (2020): 7–21. https://www.hhrjournal.org/2020/06/human-rights-and-the-confinement-of-people-living-with-dementia-in-care-homes/.

47 World Health Organization, *Global Report*.

48 Walsh et al., "Social Exclusion."

49 Levy, Becca. *Breaking the Age Code*. New York: Harper Collins, 2022.

50 Ayalon, Liat and ClemensTesch-Römer. "Taking a Closer Look at Ageism: Self- and Other-Directed Ageist Attitudes and Discrimination. *European Journal of Ageing* 14 (2017): 1–4. https://doi.org/10.1007/s10433-016-0409-9.

51 Macedo, Donald. "Introduction." In *Pedagogy of the Oppressed*. New York: Bloomsbury Publishing, Kindle Edition, 2018, 2.

52 Moskowitz, Bette Ann. *Finishing Up: On Aging and Ageism*. New York: DIO Press, Inc., 2020.

53 Swaffer, Kate. "Dementia and Prescribed Disengagement™." *Dementia* 14, no. 1 (2015): 3–6. https://doi.org/10.1177/1471301214548136.

# 1. *Growing Old Among Inequalities in Brazil*

Alexandre Kalache

When I was born in Rio de Janeiro in 1945, male life expectancy at birth (LEB) in Brazil was about 43 years.[1] I was born into a comfortable middle-class home in the more affluent urban south of the country and therefore had a better chance than most Brazilians of the time to live an extended and healthy life that defied the averages. Nevertheless, the Brazil into which I was born was a country where omnipresent infectious diseases, unforgiving capitalism, and the almost total absence of any social welfare net, meant that everyone's life trajectory was precarious.

Despite a COVID-19 dip, the LEB in Brazil is now in the region of 77 years.[2] A Brazilian newborn today can expect to live an additional 20 years even compared to a baby born in the 1960s.[3] The 60+ age group is the only segment of the Brazilian population that has been on the increase since 2000. There are already some 33 million 60+ Brazilians. By 2050, this number will have more than doubled – to 68 million.[4] At this time, the country will have the same age composition as present-day Germany[5] where there are more citizens over the age of 60 than under the age of 25.[6] There are already more Brazilians over the age of 50 than under the age of 30.[7] Brazil shares this demographic trajectory with most of Latin America, the Caribbean, and large parts of Asia, including China.[8] By 2050, the 60+ age group will constitute at least 30 percent of the population in 64 countries[9] representing a worldwide bloc of more than 2 billion people.[10]

Unlike developed countries, the demographic transition in such countries as Brazil has been extremely rapid. It took France 145 years (from 1845) to double its older population from 10 to 20 percent.[11] Brazil, alongside such countries as China, Thailand, and Chile, is on course to experience the same doubling within just 25 years.[12] It is these less developed countries that will experience the greatest proportional increase in the numbers of older people in the coming decades. By 2050, almost 80 percent of the world's older population will be living in these nations.[13] Even those countries with a still relatively small population of older people today will experience very significant demographic changes. Countries such as Brazil are not only ageing faster but they are doing so in a context of unresolved development. Developed countries got rich before becoming old.

As in developed countries, significant numbers of older adults in these developing countries are experiencing an older age that would be unrecognizable to their antecedents. It is an older age that can span as many as 50 years and consist of multiple stages. More people in higher-income countries are living longer, with more choice, better health and, by and large, a shorter period of disability and decline toward the end of life.[14] This can be witnessed among the privileged in countries such as Brazil as well. Within the rapidly reshaping sociopolitical landscape of older age, new realities, perspectives, and aspirations are emerging in the Global South as they are in the Global North.

In all societies, however, this *new age of old age* is far from embracing everybody. Both a long life and a long life with quality are prizes that are still denied to vast swathes of our populations. Dramatic discrepancies between the life expectancies for all age groups can be seen throughout the world – even within community boundaries in the same locality. For example, in the United Kingdom, big disparities of up to 17 years have been detected within London.[15,16] Similar contrasts have been recorded in Rio de Janeiro a few hundred meters apart. The enormous human triumph that is the longevity revolution does not impact evenly and few countries illustrate this imbalance more dramatically than Brazil. The longevity gains are not shared by Brazilians living in poverty and social exclusion. Ageing is a relational process. Those who have lived a life marked by unmet needs, threatening environments, invisibility, disempowerment, or outright exclusion, manifest very different realities. Brazil's rapid ageing is occurring on top of historic failures to address basic structural inadequacies in health, education, sanitation, housing, transport, and labor participation. Living a long life and surviving a long life is not the same thing.

I was born in the middle-class beachfront neighborhood of Copacabana. Access to it was limited until the 1920s when tunnels were constructed under the granite hills that separated it from the city center. As Copacabana developed in the following decades into one of the more fashionable parts of what was then Brazil's capital city, it attracted affluent incomers such as my parents. Like them, many stayed for the rest of their lives – comfortably ageing in place. (My mother passed away at the age of 103 in 2020—well cared for in the same apartment where she had raised her children.) Demand for such occupations as nannies, maids, cooks, and doormen meant that working-class people were also attracted to Copacabana. Many came directly from radically different cultural realities in the poorer northeast of the country. It was the era in Brazilian history of urbanization on a transformational scale. Away from the beachfront, lower-quality housing was established, and shanty communities (favelas) emerged on the unwanted, near-vertical rock slopes that frame the neighborhood. Many of those inhabitants of Copacabana have also aged in place – albeit much less comfortably.

Today, a very socially mixed Copacabana has one of the oldest demographics in the world. Its proportion of older persons exceeds even that of Japan, still the oldest country. Brazil long ago joined the ranks of the 83 countries (46 percent of humanity) where fertility rates are below the population replacement level.[17] The nannies with babies and infants who promenaded on the Copacabana beachfront in my childhood have now been replaced by carers and their older charges. Then, as now, the contrasting skin colors are apparent. So transformed are the demographics within my lifetime that the hospital in Copacabana where I was born (Sao Lucas), no longer even has a maternity ward and today largely operates as a geriatric facility. I have often considered the possibility that I may end up in life exactly where I started it off. As it is a private institution, however, it is unlikely to be where the Copacabana nannies and carers end their days. Throughout much of the twentieth century, Copacabana has played an outsized role in Brazilian cultural life. Despite its worn decadence today, it continues to enjoy an iconic status. Its age and social profile mark it out as a human laboratory and a harbinger of the Brazil to come.

As the study of health promotion rightly identifies, "health is created and lived by people within the setting of their everyday life; where they learn, work, play and love."[18] We cannot talk about older age without talking about the process of ageing. We cannot talk about the process of ageing without talking about lived experiences. And we cannot talk about lived experiences without talking about discrimination. Many years ago, I was fortunate to have a sabbatical in New Zealand and to spend some time with a community of Māori health professionals in the north of the country. In Te Reo, the Māori language, the word for "the past" is *mua*. But *mua* also means "ahead." It conveys the sense that our past is really in front of us. Immortalized by Shakespeare in *The Tempest*, the "past is prologue."[19] The structural disadvantages that have framed younger selves inevitably produce an amplified effect in later life—a cumulative inequality. Furthermore, in an additional perverse turn, individuals themselves are frequently faulted for their poor health and social outcomes in older age.

Social determinants frame older age as well. Eighty-three percent of older Brazilians rely exclusively on the beleaguered public health system (SUS). The percentage is even higher among those aged 80+ and Afro-Brazilians of all ages.[20] Brazil is the only country with a population of over 100 million to have a free-at-delivery, universal healthcare system. Created after the end of the military dictatorship and modeled on the UK National Health System (NHS), SUS has led to impressive health outcomes in Brazil over the past 30 years. In the years of the Bolsonaro government (2019–2022) however, we saw substantial cuts to its funding. (With a budget of only 3.8 percent of gross domestic product (GDP), SUS was already massively underfunded in comparison to other countries.) SUS has made a huge contribution toward social equity in Brazil but there remain glaring disparities based on regional variations, ethnicity, and skin color. Studies have shown that there is a distinct skin color bias that has led to a hierarchy of access in the relationship between older Brazilians and health and social services. It shows the positioning of white Brazilian men at the top, followed by white women, mixed-race men, and mixed-race women, and then black men and black women at the bottom. Regardless of such socioeconomic factors as occupation, education, and marital status, the darker the skin color, the more barriers there are in place.[21] As a consequence, functional impairments and other outcomes are measurably worse for older black Brazilians.

Ageism arrives on top of our mitigating histories. In both its explicit and implicit forms, it is pervasive in all Brazilian settings. At times it is almost willfully unconsidered and all too often it goes completely unchallenged. If we live long enough, we are *all* vulnerable to ageism. It may take some of us by surprise but for large numbers of us, it simply builds on the legacy of other forms of discrimination. Seemingly oblivious to his own age (67 years at the time of writing), Brazilian President Jair Bolsonaro (2019–2022) was unashamedly dismissive of his 33 million fellow older citizens as they struggled with the COVID-19 pandemic. His administration reneged on its duty to adequately protect them in the face of the coronavirus. The indifference of his government resulted in one of the highest death rates (mostly of older Brazilians) in the world. Whether internalized or externalized, overt or covert, ageism in normal times produces measurable negative health and social outcomes. In crises, the repercussions are even more pronounced.

The Organisation for Economic Co-operation and Development (OECD) has observed that inequality is at a global tipping point.[22] The empirical correlation between inequality and negative physical/mental health and a vast range of social dysfunction is well established. Even in countries with robust universal health systems and well-established traditions of primary health care, health and social policies have failed to narrow the gap. In fact, income inequality is increasing in nearly all countries.[23] It is important to note, however, that these increases are occurring at different rates and speeds, revealing that the shaping of that inequality has less to do with national wealth and more do to with policies, institutions, and social infrastructures. Despite its wealthier economy and very high spending on health (around $10,000 per person), the USA is experiencing a declining life-expectancy[24] as well as higher rates of infant mortality,[25] mental illness,[26] drug deaths,[27] and homicides[28] relative to more equal developed nations.

Brazil has consistently ranked among the most unequal countries in the world since data became widely available in the 1980s.[29] After some improvement in the first 10 years of the century, income inequality has significantly worsened in Brazil. In 2021, the labor income of the poorest half of the Brazilian population fell by 17.1 percent while the income of the richest 1 percent rose by 10.1 percent.[30] This is happening in a context where the 5 percent richest Brazilians already have an income commensurate with the other 95 percent of the population.[31] Shamefully, Brazil increased its income inequality in the second quarter of 2019 for the seventeenth consecutive quarter in the most sustained trend ever recorded.[32] The COVID-19 pandemic has further intensified these already appalling levels of inequity. As Amartya Sen has articulated, "relative inequalities in income relate to absolute inequalities in capabilities."[33]

Even though Brazil is the fourth largest food producer in the world,[34] it has been calculated that 58.7 percent of Brazilians in 2022 live with food insecurity—a significant increase on 2021.[35] (Note: Over 20 percent of US households are also living with food insecurity.[36]) Twenty-eight percent of Brazilians are currently experiencing moderate food insecurity, 15.2 percent are living with severe food insecurity, and 15.5 percent (33.1 million Brazilians) have virtually nothing to eat at all except that which arrives from the benevolence of others.[37] Almost half of the Brazilian population lacks access to an adequate sewerage system and 33 million have an irregular water supply.[38] As the world enters the Fourth Industrial Revolution, tens of millions of Brazilians are yet to feel any real gain from the First Industrial Revolution—an event that shaped much of global society more than 200 years ago. Multigenerational households in cramped, low-quality housing; precarious informal employment; and over-burdened public schools, clinics, and transport are ubiquitous. Low educational levels over generations have compromised health, scientific, and citizenship literacy. Unsurprisingly, the proportion of Brazilians of all ages living with both communicable and non-communicable diseases, as well as disabilities, is high. The iconic, early-twentieth-century Brazilian writer Stefan Zweig once famously proclaimed that "Brazil is the land of the future."[39] For all too many Brazilians, however, it is demonstrably the land of the past.

As elsewhere, the COVID-19 pandemic has exacerbated pre-existing conditions. It has been said that COVID-19 is a health crisis that has morphed into an economic and social crisis. In Brazil, it might be more accurate to say that an economic and social crisis has morphed into a health crisis. Still reeling from a 2015–16 recession and further contractions in 2019, the Brazilian economy was struggling even before the pandemic. Many of the nation's states were insolvent, and several municipalities were financially unsustainable. Health and education budgets had been slashed and incredibly, neoliberal federal legislation in 2017 froze all social expenditure for 20 years. In the meantime, the number of Brazilian billionaires has increased, as has their wealth.

Although Brazilians comprise only 3 percent of the global population, we have suffered around 11 percent of the worldwide COVID deaths—over 70 percent of them aged 60 years and over.[40] While this tragic anomaly does not have a single cause, Brazilian congressional hearings in 2022 decried the Bolsonaro administration for its dismissal of the seriousness of the pandemic, its undermining of science, and its willful inactions. Revealing his age prejudices during the pandemic, President Bolsonaro cynically that only the weak will die: "With my history as an athlete, if I were infected by the virus I would not have to worry. I would feel nothing, or, at most, it would be a little flu or a little cold."[41] To this day, he refuses to reveal whether he has been vaccinated. In common with some other countries, two false and particularly virulent dichotomies have emerged out of coronavirus-ravaged Brazil. The first is that there is a choice to be made between health and the economy. The second is that there is a choice to be made between the young and the old. Despite the obfuscations of some of our political leaders, health, and the economy are not divisible silos. Nor are youth and older age. We do not become a different person as we age. We become more of the same person.

It is political actions and inactions—both historic and current—that have brought us to this point. A notorious Brazilian culture of individualism proliferates when the only possible solutions are collective. The widening social disparities are not only contaminating our present, but they are also defining our fast-ageing future. *Our* future ageing depends upon the future ageing of those around us. When we deny others full citizenship, we do so at our peril. The evidence is clear that inequality hurts most of the population. Insecurity and status anxiety, both powerful sources of stress with resulting health consequences, are higher at all levels of income in more unequal countries. Even the most privileged Brazilians cannot build their walls high enough to completely isolate themselves from their own unease, let alone disease, crime, and the hopelessness of others. International research shows that improved equality creates significant gains even for the richest or best-educated third of the population.[42]

A long life in poor health is an empty prize. Years have been added to life, but the best life has yet to be added to all lives. Globally, healthy life expectancy (HALE) at birth has increased at a slower rate than LEB. In 2015, HALE at birth for men and women combined was 63.1 years–8.3 years lower than the total LEB. In other words, poor health resulted in an average global loss of nearly eight years of healthy life.[43] Poor adults in their 50s and 60s consistently have lower functional capacity than more privileged adults 20 or 30 years older. Multi-morbidity onset in deprived populations can be up to 15 years earlier.[44] Notwithstanding wide regional variations, HALE in Brazil in 2019 was 65.4, a drop of almost a full percentage point since 2016, the first recorded decline in at least a decade.[45]

The Brazilian health system is facing a double burden: growing rates of non-communicable and chronic diseases (such as cardiovascular, respiratory, musculoskeletal, and neurological diseases, cancers, and diabetes) alongside the continued presence of the communicable diseases that have long been part of the Brazilian narrative. Our current health system was designed prior to the demographic and epidemiological transitions. It tends to treat chronic illnesses in the same way as acute conditions. Without a major paradigm shift, our healthcare system is going to grow increasingly ineffective, expensive, and rationed as the incidence of chronic conditions rises even further. It is not population ageing per se that is creating unsustainable financial burdens. The societal costs associated with ageing are largely driven by low investment in health promotion; poor disease prevention; over-medicalization (especially in relation to dying) alongside increased public expectation for sophisticated treatments; the absence of a generalized culture of care; and the human resource losses to the formal labor market caused by exclusion, disincentive, debilitation, or retirement.

By almost every measure, Brazil is a brutal society. According to a study carried out by the Brazilian Institute of Geography and Statistics (*Instituto Brasileiro de Geografia e Estatística* – IBGE), based on the National Survey of Health in 2019, a total of 29 million Brazilians experienced physical, psychological, or sexual violence, affecting 19.4 percent of women and 17 percent of men.[46] Although aggressions show significantly higher absolute numbers for men, Brazil has domestic abuse and femicide rates among the highest in the world, behind only El Salvador, Colombia, Guatemala, and the Russian Federation.[47] Data from the Institute for Applied Economic Research (IAER) suggests a worsening situation, although changes in reporting and policing methodology may account for some of this.[48] As in other countries, there is evidence that COVID-19 confinements in Brazil increased household violence, including elder abuse. According to official data from the state security secretariats, Brazil experienced an epidemic of femicides during the coronavirus pandemic.[49] In its four-year term in office, the Bolsonaro government added fuel to the flames by facilitating public access to firearms and waging a high-profile war on so-called gender ideology which has made confrontation of an entrenched Brazilian culture of toxic masculinity and gender violence even more difficult.

Brazil is built on many denials. Our racial apartheid may not have had the same structures as South Africa or the United States but that does not make us any less racist. Large numbers of Brazilians are quick to take pride in our seemingly impressive miscegenation (more than half the Brazilian population has some degree of Afro-descendancy) without acknowledging that it is largely derived from our long history of sexual violence by light-skinned Brazilian men against dark-skinned Brazilian women. That Brazil is a racial democracy is a persistent national myth. How far are we from electing a President Mandela or a President Obama? We still talk disparagingly about those *with a foot in the kitchen.*

Ironically, on national Black Consciousness Day (November 20, 2020), Brazilian Vice-President Hamilton Mourao declared that "there is no racism in Brazil."[50] The uncomfortable truth, however, is that the "structural racism, discrimination and violence that people of African descent face in Brazil is documented by official data."[51] Black Brazilians are "excluded and almost invisible from [most] decision-making structures and institutions."[52] Despite more mainstream media and academic attention to issues of race in very recent years, there is still widespread resistance among the Brazilian political classes even to acknowledge, let alone address endemic and structural racism. In addition, as a visit to most museums of history in Brazil will attest, there exists a comprehensive airbrushing of our past that is sometimes by default and at other times, willful.

Slavery was the engine of the Brazilian economy for more than 350 years. At least four million Africans (40 percent of the transatlantic slave trade) were forcibly transported to Brazil.[53] The German educator, Ina von Binzer, who lived in Brazil in the late 1800s, observed: "Black Brazilians are responsible for all the labour and produce all the wealth in this land. The white Brazilian just doesn't work."[54] Brazil was the last nation in the western world to formally abolish slavery as a legal institution (1888). In its aftermath, there were "no policies to promote integration, or plans to help former slaves become full citizens through providing access to education, land or employment."[55] On the contrary, the post-slavery policy of *branqueamento* was a state-sponsored eugenic attempt to whiten the national bloodline through the targeted immigration of lighter-skinned peoples and it served to further devalue darker-skinned Brazilians and to diminish their opportunities. When my own father stepped off the boat in the port of Rio de Janeiro as a 16-year-old *white* immigrant who spoke no Portuguese, he had almost immediate access to citizenship that was denied to most black Brazilians. To paraphrase the academic Ibram X Kendi, rather than racist ideas leading to racist policies, it tends to be more a case of racist policies leading to racist ideas.[56]

The impacts of transgenerational trauma (psychological and social trauma passed from one generation to the next) in the context of Brazilian enslavement is very under-researched. It is clear, however, that the racial wealth gap has its origins early in Brazilian history. The opportunities for black Brazilians to accumulate assets, particularly property, have been severely circumscribed over the nation's history. It is also clear that the disparities continue today. White Brazilian workers have an average income 74 percent higher than black and brown Brazilian workers.[57] At current rates, black Brazilians will not achieve wage parity with white Brazilians before the year 2089.[58] The empirical correlation between inequality and negative physical/mental health and a vast range of social dysfunction is well established.

In 2018, black Brazilians made up 75.7 percent of the nation's murder victims and black women represented 68 percent of the victims of `1.[59] In 2021, 6,100 people were killed by police.[60] Historically always high, police killings in Brazil have risen sharply and are in the order of six times greater than comparable figures for the United States.[61] Nearly 80 percent of the Brazilians killed by the police are black.[62] Young black Brazilians between the ages of 19 and 24 die at the hands of the police at a rate of more than 200 for every 100,000, in contrast to 28 per 100,000 in the overall population.[63] In 2019, ultra-right-wing President Jair Bolsonaro legislated a euphemistically labelled *crime bill* that has granted the police such wide-ranging immunity from prosecution that it has legitimized something akin to licensed execution squads and a type of state-sanctioned genocide. According to a report to the Human Rights Council by the UN Working Group of Experts on People of African Descent, "Killings of unarmed African Americans by the police is only the tip of the iceberg in what is a pervasive racial bias in the justice system."[64]

As in such countries as the USA and the UK, black people have been disproportionately impacted by COVID-19. During the pandemic, black Brazilians of all ages not only lost their jobs at a higher rate but also died at a higher rate. Data from the municipal government of Sao Paulo shows that the risk of death from COVID-19 is 62 percent higher for black Brazilians than white Brazilians.[65] As Pope Francis articulated, however, "The Coronavirus is special only in how visible it is. There are a thousand other crises that are just as dire, but they are just far enough from [most of] us that we can act as if they don`t exist."[66] Nearly half of the older Brazilian population (48 percent of 33 million adults over the age of 60) are of African descent and are survivors of multiple pandemics. The darker their skin color, the more disadvantages they have likely endured. Older black Brazilians may not be dying in the streets through acts of violence in the same shockingly high numbers as younger black Brazilians, but they too are struggling to breathe. Older Black Lives Matter, too.

The Pan-American Health Organization (PAHO) has recommended that Brazil, along with other member states, promote public policies that address "ethnicity as a social determinant of health."[67] Studies show that "racial discrimination contributes to accelerated physiologic weathering and health declines through its impact on biological systems, including via its effects on telomere attrition."[68] In essence, being on the receiving end of racism leads to higher stress levels, which in turn encourages cells to age more rapidly. Black Brazilians not only experience significantly lower life expectancy than their white compatriots but also higher rates of multiple morbidities including diabetes, high blood pressure, and respiratory and kidney disease. More frequent in the black Brazilian population are maternal deaths (including deaths from septic abortions), leprosy, tuberculosis, Chagas, and sexually transmitted diseases including AIDS.[69]

For Brazilians of African descent, particularly those with darker skin color, older age arrives with an accumulation of race-related stressors frequently accompanied by negative physical and mental health consequences. Older Afro-Brazilians have endured a layering of racism and colorism throughout their lives that is relived with every new discriminatory experience. As in other countries, racism in Brazil intersects with such other forms of discrimination as classism, capacitism, sexism, and LGBTphobia to form a toxic, cross-generational brew. Explicit and implicit ageism adds to this legacy, arriving on top of life histories indelibly marked by such factors as social exclusion, limited educational opportunity, inadequate housing, precarious employment, insecurity, and low self-esteem.

When I moved to England in the 1970s for post-graduation studies, I was amazed to learn that the de-criminalization of male homosexuality had occurred there only a few years earlier. Brazil did not have a specific law that made homosexuality illegal. That fact, however, did not make us any less intolerant toward it. It could even be argued that it was easier to move forward in other societies where prejudices and practices were more formalized because the markers of inequality were more tangible. Some of those societies have since appointed out gay heads of government. Brazil cannot even guarantee the safety of the few openly LGBTI+ elected officials that we have. Assassination and political exile have been the fate of some. Brazil has one of the worst rates of violence and discrimination against LGBTI+ people in the world.

The ascendancy of far-right ideologies and religious fundamentalism in Brazil has been accompanied by a legitimization of hate from the highest levels. President Bolsonaro made no secret of his disdain for the LGBTI+ communities and during his term, crusaded against so-called gender ideology, even though clearly, desire obeys no ideology. Transgender murders in Brazil increased by 41 percent in 2020, further consolidating our position as the country with the highest rate in the world.[70] 2021 data from the National Association of Trans and Queer People (ANTRA) reveal that one trans Brazilian dies every 48 hours and that 82 percent of the trans victims are black. Transgender identity, despite being a risk factor for violent death, does not exist in national Brazilian health statistics and many state public security systems do not even allow for disaggregation of the data.[71]

The current generations of older LGBTI+ Brazilians grew up in an unapologetically prejudiced society where derision, bullying, and acts of violence were commonplace. Their very existence was an act of rebellion because it "confirmed uncertainty, opened a space for difference and constituted a symbol of contradiction."[72] Intrepid iconoclasts and activists bravely, and sometimes extravagantly, broke barriers. Particularly in the more sophisticated urban centers, there existed meeting places of relative safety, such as bars and clubs. For a portion of my childhood in Copacabana, my family lived above one of them—a veritable *La Cage aux Folles*, the glamorously named *La Gondola*. For most young Brazilians of the time whose sexual or gender orientation diverted, however, there were few role models and easy pathways to age in a state of full well-being. Isolation, insecurity, and self-doubt were common, and not infrequently accompanied by self-destructive behaviors. Lesbians were largely invisibilized and transgenderism was ridiculed. When relationships were established, they were often furtive and frequently subjected to intolerable social strains.

The Stonewall Riots in New York City in 1969 marked a turning point for the assertion of LGBTI+ rights across the western world. For the LGBTI+ Brazilians who are today over the age of 60, however, this modern gay age arrived during a military dictatorship that was suppressive of difference, aggressively homophobic, and punitive in instinct. Sadly, even among many of those who rejected the dictatorship, there was a reflexive distaste for sexual and gender nonconformism. And more was yet to come. As in other parts of the world, the HIV/AIDS pandemic demonized sexual freedoms in general (and male same-sex relations in particular) and licensed a new wave of discrimination in Brazil. Nevertheless, there has been significant socio-political progress in relation to LGBTI+ issues in Brazil over the past few decades. We have made some onward movement toward the "world where it is less difficult to love" that was envisaged by Paulo Freire.[73] Recent conservatism and religious fundamentalism, however, are attempting to delegitimize these advances and compromise the principle of state secularism. LGBTI+ Brazilians of all ages continue to be subject to specific stressors and to endure a higher prevalence of particular chronic illnesses as a result. In addition, the heteronormativity of Brazilian health and social services remains a challenge.

Societies such as Brazil are experiencing many of the same cultural and technological shocks as richer nations. With weaker public institutions and infrastructures, however, they are left with much less agility to adapt. Brazil`s capacity to prepare itself for the digital future has actually declined in global rankings.[74] In many cases, new technologies are reinforcing inequalities because they tend to impact disproportionately. According to the OECD, 40 percent of workers with a lower secondary degree are in jobs with a high risk of displacement, whereas less than 5 percent of workers with a tertiary degree are vulnerable.[75] Clearly, education is key. Less education makes individuals, households, and communities more vulnerable. Those Brazilians with lower educational attainment are more likely to be part of the 41 percent of the country`s workforce that is employed informally and who have poverty levels four times higher than the national average.[76]

Although fast ageing, Brazil has still been benefiting from the high fertility rates of its not-too-distant past. As the cohort of Brazilian women born in the 1980s approach menopause, however, this formidable resource of youth is revealing its time-limitedness. By 2038, Brazil will have reached its population peak and its overall population decline will have begun. The youth bulge of today will pass through the Brazilian demographic schemata like a sheep being slowly digested by an anaconda. Since early in my career, I have warned that Brazil only had a brief window of opportunity. Our nation was gifted a period of perhaps two decades to invest in its young people to ready them and Brazilian society at large for their older age—an older age that will be numerically larger and even more heterogeneous. This opportunity has largely been squandered. Although education in Brazil is considered a constitutional right, is mandatory between the ages of four and fourteen, and is technically free in public institutions at all levels, there are serious disparities in access, resources, and quality. The World Bank has calculated that it will take over 260 years at current trends for Brazil to reach the OECD average for reading and 75 years for mathematics.[77] According to the 2020 school census, only 60 percent of Brazilian public schools (considerably less in the north and northeast) have internet connectivity. The government of Jair Bolsonaro slashed funding for the federal higher education institutes to such an extent that many may not survive, a move that was seen by some as an attempt to block the path of the non-white poor into elite spaces.

Of the 22.3 million Brazilians in the age group 15–21, 2.72 million (12.2 percent) have not finished and are not attending high school.[78] Black, brown, and indigenous Brazilians make up 70 percent of the out-of-school numbers with the most excluded living in rural areas.[79] Mário Volpi, head of Adolescent Development and Participation of the United Nations Children's Fund (UNICEF) in Brazil, noted the "very serious situation of school exclusion, which will lead to the worsening of social indicators." He added: "It is a waste of dreams and opportunities."[80] In addition, 12.3 million Brazilians (36 percent) in the 18–24 age group are neither in work nor study, the so-called nem-nems (*nao trabalham, nem estudam*).[81] The questions must be asked: What quality of life will these younger Brazilians have? How will they be able to support or care for their ageing parents? What sort of older age will they themselves experience?

Education deficits can be seen across all age groups in Brazil. More of us are living longer but the relevance of many of our skill sets is expiring earlier. At each stage of life, Brazilians are failing to acquire the necessary intellectual and emotional tools for a rapidly evolving present and an unclear future. Indeed, so unclear is that future that it has been predicted that more than half of the jobs that will be performed by the next generation do not yet even exist.[82] More than ever, contemporary life is a perpetual interplay between risk and protection. Tens of millions of Brazilians are left to contend with the precariousness of employment; the uneven ownership of new technologies; and increasingly, an imposed mobility; a requirement to inhabit multiple identities; and a *family insufficiency* in relation to care provision.

The imperative must be to build a comprehensive national architecture of continuous or lifelong learning. In so far as it currently exists in Brazil, it tends to favor the already advantaged. Brazil is missing opportunities to address the causes of vulnerability, to reinforce preparedness and capacity in all groups, to incorporate such components as cultural safety into policy actions, and to establish direct pathways toward active citizenship at all ages. Despite the promises of the technological age, human capital remains our most valuable asset/renewable resource. We must learn to mine the rich veins of capacity in all Brazilians.

## Notes

1  O'Neill, Aaron. "Life Expectancy (from birth) in Brazil, from 1870 to 2020." *Statista*. June 21, 2020. https://www.statista.com/statistics/1071010/life-expectancy-brazil/.
2  MacroTrends. "Brazil Life Expectancy 1950–2022." Accessed January 1, 2023. www.macrotrends.net/countries/BTA/brazil/life-expectancy.
3  Instituto Brasileiro de Geografia e Estatística (IBGE). "Population." Accessed January 3, 2023. https://www.ibge.gov.br/en/statistics/social/population.html.
4  IBGE. "Population Projections for Brazil and Federation Units by Sex and Age: 2010–2060." Accessed January 3, 2023. https://www.ibge.gov.br/en/statistics/social/population/18176-population-projection.html?=&t=resultados.
5  United Nations Department of Economic and Social Affairs, Population Division. "World Population Prospects: The 2012 Revision. Highlights and Advance Tables." Working Paper No. ESA/P/WP. 228. UNDESA. 2013.
6  United Nations Department of Economic and Social Affairs, Population Division. "World Population Prospects: The 2015 Revision." UNDESA. 2015.
7  Cabral, Umberlandia. "Population Increases, but Number of Persons under 30 Falls by 5.4 % from 2012 to 2021." *Agência IBGE, Social Statistics.* July 22, 2022. https://agenciadenoticias.ibge.gov.br/en/agencia-news/2184-news-agency/news/34449-population-increases-but-number-of-persons-under-30-falls-by-5-4-from-2012-to-2021.
8  UNFPA/HelpAge International. "Ageing in the 21st Century: A Celebration and a Challenge." 2012.
9  UNFPA/HelpAge International, "Ageing in the 21st Century."
10  United Nations Department of Economic and Social Affairs, Population Division. "World Population Ageing 2013." UNDESA. 2013. ST/ESA/SER.A/348.
11  World Health Organization (WHO). *World Report on Ageing and Health.* Geneva: WHO, 2015. https://apps.who.int/iris/handle/10665/186463.
12  WHO, *World Report,* 43.
13  United Nations Department of Economic and Social Affairs, Population Division. "World Population Ageing 2013." UNDESA. 2013. ST/ESA/SER.A/348.
14  Chatterji, Somnath, Julie Byles, David Cutler, Teresa Seeman, and Emese Verdes. "Health, Functioning and Disability in Older Adults: Present Status and Future Implications." *The Lancet* 7, no. 385(9967) (2015): 563–575. https://doi.org/10.1016/S0140-6736(14)61462-8. 5
15  Trust for London. "Life Expectancy by London Borough." Accessed January 6, 2023. https://www.trustforlondon.org.uk/data/life-expectancy-borough/.

16 Keane, Daniel. "Life Expectancy Gap in London as High as 17 Years." *Evening Standard*. November 10, 2022. https://www.standard.co.uk/news/health/life-exp ectancy-gap-in-london-high-years-b1039015.html#.

17 World Population Review. "Total Fertility Rate 2023." Accessed January 6, 2023. https://worldpopulationreview.com/country-rankings/total-fertility-rate.

18 World Health Organization. "Ottawa Charter on Health Promotion." WHO, 1986, https://www.who.int/teams/health-promotion/enhanced-wellbeing/first-global-conference/actions.

19 e notes. "Shakespeare Quotes, The Tempest act 2, scene 1, 245-254." Accessed January 5, 2023. https://www.enotes.com/shakespeare-quotes/whats-past-prologue.

20 Kalache, Alexandre, Alexandre da Silva, Karla Cristina Giacomin, Kenio Costa de Lima, Luiz Roberto Ramos, Marilia Louvison, and Renato Veras. "Ageing and Inequalities: Social Protection Policies for Older Adults Resulting from the COVID-19 Pandemic in Brazil." Editorial. Revista Brasileira de Geriatria e Gerontologia. *Brazilian Journal of Geriatrics and Gerontology* 23, no. 6 (2020): e200122. https://www.scielo.br/j/rbgg/a/pQvWz8j4JZx8B7PL984MHrQ/?lang=en&format=pdf.

21 Da Silva, Alexandre. "Determinants of the Functional Incapacity of Older Persons in the City of Sao Paulo from the Ethno-racial Perspective." Doctoral Thesis, Faculty of Public Health, University of Sao Paulo, 2017. https://doi.org/10.11606/T.6.2017. tde-05072017-100217.

22 Organization for Economic Co-operation and Development, Centre for Opportunity and Equality. "In It Together – Why Less Inequality Benefits All." May 21, 2015. https://www.oecd.org/social/in-it-together-why-less-inequality-benefits-all-9789264235120-en.htm.

23 Alvaredo, Facundo, Lucas Chancel, Thomas Piketty, Emmanuel Saez, and Gabriel Zucman. "World Inequality Report 2018." World Inequality Lab. 2018. https://wir2018.wid.world/files/download/wir2018-summary-english.pdf.

24 Woolf, Stephen H. and Heidi Schoomaker. "Life Expectancy and Mortality Rates in the United States." *JAMA,* 322, 20 (2019): 1996–2016, doi:10.1001/jama.2019.16932.

25 Organization for Economic Co-operation and Development. "Life Expectancy at 65 (indicator). OECD. Accessed December 15, 2019. https://doi.org/10.1787/0E9a3 f00-en.

26 Pan-American Health Organization. "The Burden of Mental Disorders in the Region of the Americas." PAHO. 2018. https://iris.paho.org/handle/10665.2/49578.

27 Ho, Jessica Y. "The Contemporary American Drug Overdose Epidemic in International Perspective." *Population and Development Review* 45, no. 1 (2019): 7–40. https://doi.org/10.1111/padr.12228.

28 World Health Organization. "Homicide Estimates by Country, Global Health Observatory Data Repository." Accessed January 2, 2023. https://apps.who.int/gho/data/view.main.VIOLENCEHOMICIDEv.

29 Alvaredo et al., "World Inequality Report 2018."

30 Neri, Marcelo. "The Escalation of Inequality: How did the Brazilian Crisis Impact Income Distribution and Poverty?" *FGV Social, Centro de Políticas Sociais*. September 2019. https://cps.fgv.br/en/inequality.

31 OXFAM International, Brazil. "Extreme Inequality in Numbers Report." 2017. https://www.oxfam.org/en/brazil-extreme-inequality-numbers.

32  Neri, "The Escalation of Inequality."

33  Sen, Amartya K. "From Income Inequality to Economic Inequality." *Southern Economic Journal* 64, no. 2 (1997): 384–401. https://doi.org/10.2307/1060857.

34  Ross, Sean. "4 Countries That Produce the Most Food." *Investopedia Macroeconomics.* Accessed January 3, 2023. https://www.investopedia.com/articles/investing/100615/4-countries-produce-most-food.asp.

35  PENSSAN. "Food Insecurity and Covid-19 in Brazil." Accessed January 6, 2023. https://olheparaafome.com.br/wp-content/uploads/2022/09/OLHESumExecutivoINGLES-Diagramacao-v2-R01-02-09-20224212.pdf.

36  U.S. Department of Agriculture, Economic Research Service. "Household Food Security in the United States in 2021." USDA. 2022.

37  PENSSAN. "Food Insecurity."

38  Rodrigues, Alex. "More than 50 % Brazilians do not Have Access to Sewage Networks." *AgenciaBrasil.* December 18, 2021. https://agenciabrasil.ebc.com.br/en/geral/noticia/2021-12/more-50-brazilians-do-not-have-access-sewage-networks-says-mdr.

39  Zweig, Stefan. *Brazil: A Land of the Future.* Translated by Lowell A. Bangerter. Riverside: Ariadne Press, 2000.

40  Castro, Marcia, Sun Kim, Lorena Barberia, Ana Freitas Riberio, Susie Gurzenda, Erin Abbott, Jeffrey Blossom, Beatriz Rache, and Burton H. Singer. "Spatiotemporal pattern of COVID-19 spread in Brazil." *Science* 372, 6544 (2021): 821–826. https://www.science.org/doi/10.1126/science.abh1558.

41  Reuters Staff. "Factbox: Brazil's Bolsonaro, Now COVID-19 Positive, has Downplayed Risks." *Reuters*, July 7, 2020. https://www.reuters.com/article/us-health-coronavirus-brazil-quotes-fact-idUSKBN2482QK.

42  Wilkinson, Richard and Kate Pickett. *The Spirit Level – Why Equality is Better for Everyone.* London: Penguin Group Publishers, 2009. ISBN 978-0-241-95429-4.

43  World Health Organization. "Global Health Observatory (GHO)." Accessed January 6, 2023. http://apps.who.int/gho/data/node.main.HALE?lang=en.

44  Barnett, Karen, Stewart W. Mercer, Michael Norbury, Graham Watt, Sally Wyke, and Bruce Guthrie. "Epidemiology of Multimorbidity and Implications for Healthcare, Research and Medical Education – A Cross-sectional Study." *The Lancet* 380, 9836 (2012): 37–43. https://pubmed.ncbi.nlm.nih.gov/22579043/.

45  Knoema DataHub. "World Data Atlas, Brazil – Healthy Life Expectancy, 2019." *Knoema.* https://knoema.com/atlas/Brazil/topics/Health/Health-Status/Healthy-life-expectancy.

46  Mascarenhas, Márcio Dênis Medeiros, Ariel de Sousa Melo, Malvina Thais Pacheco Rodrigues, Camila Alves Bahia, Rafael Bello Corassa, Fabiana Martins Dias de Andrade, Cheila Marina Lima, and Deborah Carvalho Malta. "Prevalence of Exposure to Violence among Adults – Brazil, 2019." *Revista brasileira de epidemiologia, Brazilian Journal of Epidemiology* 24, 2 (2021): e210019. https://doi.org/10.1590/1980-549720210019.supl.2.

47  Yagoub, Mimi. "Why Does Latin America Have the World's Highest Female Murder Rates?" *InSight.* February 11, 2016. https://insightcrime.org/news/analysis/why-does-latin-america-have-the-world-s-highest-female-murder-rates/.

48  The Brazilian Public Security Forum (FBSP). "Atlas da Violencia-2021". Accessed January 6, 2023. https://forumseguranca.org.br/atlas-da-violencia/.

49  FBSP. "Violencia domestica durante a pandemia de COVID-19, 2nd ed." Accessed January 6, 2023. https://forumseguranca.org.br/wp-content/uploads/2020/06/violencia-domestica-covid-19-ed02-v5.pdf.

50  Travae, Marques. "The Myth Continues: For Brazil's President and Vice-President, Racism Doesn't Exist in Brazil." *Black Brazil Today*, November 26, 2020. https://blackbraziltoday.com/the-myth-continues-for-brazils-president-and-vice-president-racism-doesnt-exist-in-brazil/.

51  Shamdasani, Ravina. Spokesperson for the UN Office of the High Commissioner for Human Rights (OHCHR). "Press Briefing on Brazil." November 24, 2020. https://www.ohchr.org/en/press-briefing-notes/2020/11/press-briefing-note-brazil.

52  Shamdasani, "Press Briefing."

53  Viotti da Costa, Emilia. *The Brazilian Empire – Myths and Histories*. Chapel Hill: UNC Press, 2020. ISBN: 978-0 -8078-4840-1.

54  The Brazilian Report. "Slavery in Brazil." *The Brazilian Report*, May 13, 2020. https://www.wilsoncenter.org/blog-post/slavery-brazil.

55  The Brazilian Report, "Slavery in Brazil."

56  Kendi, Ibram X. *How To Be an Antiracist*. London: The Bodley Head, Penguin Random House, 2019.

57  Vieceli, Leonardo. "Whites Earn 74 % More than Blacks and Browns per Hour of Work in Brazil." *Folha de S.Paulo*. November 14, 2021. https://www1.folha.uol.com.br/internacional/en/business/2022/11/whites-earn-74-more-than-blacks-and-browns-per-hour-of-work.shtml.

58  OXFAM International, Brazil, "Extreme Inequality."

59  IPEA, *Atlas de la Violencia 2020*. Brazilian Public Security Forum/Institute of Applied Economic Research. 2020. 47. https://repositorio.ipea.gov.br/bitstream/11058/10214/1/AtlasViolencia2020.pdf.

60  Emici Thug. "Brazil: Nearly 7,500 Fall Victim to Femicide and Police Killings." *Unicorn Riot*. August 24, 2022. https://unicornriot.ninja/2022/brazil-nearly-7500-fall-victim-to-femicides-and-police-killings/.

61  Nugent, Ciara and Regina Thais. "How Black Brazilians are Looking to a Slavery-Era Form of Resistance to Fight Racial Injustice Today." *Time Magazine*. December 16, 2020. https://time.com/5915902/brazil-racism-quilombos/.

62  Human Rights Watch. "Brazil: Invite Experts on Racial Justice." April 18, 2022. https://www.hrw.org/news/2022/04/18/brazil-invite-un-experts-racial-justice.

63  FBSP, "Atlas."

64  Office of the High Commissioner for Human Rights (OHCHR). "Report of the Working Group of Experts on People of African Descent on its mission to the United States of America A/HRC/33/61/Add.2 2016," August 2016. https://ap.ohchr.org/documents/dpage_e.aspx?si=A/HRC/33/61/Add.2.

65  Amnesty International. "Brazil: In Response to COVID-19, Authorities Must Ensure Adequate Healthcare for Marginalised Groups." May 14, 2020. https://www.amnesty.org/en/latest/news/2020/05/brazil-covid19-authorities-must-ensure-access-healthcare/.

66  Pope Francis. "A Crisis Reveals What is in our Hearts." *New York Times*. November 26, 2020. https://www.nytimes.com/2020/11/26/opinion/pope-francis-covid.html.

67  Pan-American Health Organization. "The 160th Session of the Executive Committee, 2017 Resolution Ce160.R11 Policy on Ethnicity and Health." PAHO. 2017. https://iris.paho.org/bitstream/handle/10665.2/34242/CE160-rl1-e.pdf?sequence=1&isAllowed=y.

68  Chae, David H., Yijie Wang, Connor D. Martz, Natalie Slopen, Tiffany Yip, Nancy E. Adler, Thomas E. Fuller- Rowell, Jue Lin, Karen A. Matthews, Gene H. Brody, Erica C. Spears, Eli Puterman, and Elissa S. Epel. "Racial Discrimination and Telomere Shortening Among African Americans: The Coronary Artery Risk Development in Young Adults (CARDIA) Study." American Psychological Association. 2020. https://psycnet.apa.org/manuscript/2020-00718-001.pdf.

69  UN Office on Drugs and Crime, Liaison and Partnership Office (LPO) in Brazil. "Black Lives: Policies to Reduce Health Vulnerabilities need Better Quality Data." UNODC. 2018. https://www.unodc.org/lpo-brazil/en/frontpage/2018/01/experts-point-to-the-need-for-information-that-combines-variables-such-as-race--gender-and-age-to-overcome-inequalities-between-blacks-and-whites-in-the-area.html.

70  Sudré, Lu. "Brazil: Transgender Murders Increased 41 % in 2020." *Brasil de Fato*. January 29, 2021. https://www.brasildefato.com.br/2021/01/29/brazil-transgender-murders-increased-41-in-2020.

71  Pinheiro, Ester. "Brazil Continues to be the Country with the Largest Number of Trans People Killed." *Brasil de Fato*. January 23, 2022. https://www.brasildefato.com.br/2022/01/23/brazil-continues-to-be-the-country-with-the-largest-number-of-trans-people-killed.

72  Trevisan, Joao S. *Perverts in Paradise*. Schopfheim: GMP Publishers, 1986. ISBN: 0-907040-78-0.

73  Freire, Paulo. *Pedagogy of the Oppressed*. London/New York: Continuum, 1970.

74  IMD. *Ranking of World Digital Competitiveness*, 6th ed. Lausanne: IMD World Competitiveness Centre, 2022. https://www.imd.org/centers/world-competitiveness-center/rankings/world-digital-competitiveness/.

75  Organisation for Economic Co-operation and Development (OECD). "Policy Brief on the Future of Work, Automation and Independent Work in a Digital Economy." 2016.

76  OECD. "Economic Surveys: Brazil," December 8, 2020. https://www.oecd.org/economy/surveys/Brazil-2020-OECD-economic-survey-overview.pdf.

77  World Bank. "World Development Report, Learning to Realise Education`s Promise." 2018. https://openknowledge.worldbank.org/handle/10986/28340.

78  Carneiro, Lucianne."Brazil has 2.7m Young People Out of School." *Valor International*. May 29, 2022. https://valorinternational.globo.com/economy/news/2022/05/29/brazil-has-27m-young-people-out-of-school.ghtml.

79  UNICEF. *Out of School Children in Brazil* (New York: UNICEF, 2021), https://www.unicef.org/brazil/media/14881/file/out-of-school-children-in-brazil_a-warning-about-the-impacts-of-the-covid-19-pandemic-on-education.pdf.

80  Carneiro, "Young People Out of School."

81 Desoti, Carol. "IDADOS no Estadão: 12 milhões de jovens no Brasil não estudam nem trabalham [12 Million Young People in Brazil Neither Study Nor Work]." *IDADOS.* January 12, 2022. https://blog.idados.id/idados-no-estadao-12-milh oes-de-jovens-no-brasil-nao-estudam-nem-trabalham/.

82 IMD. "IMD Professor Arturo Bris wraps up OWP with Creative Schemes." World Competitive Centre IMD Business School. 2016. https://www.imd.org/news/ updates/imd-professor-arturo-bris-wraps-up-owp-with-creative-schemes/.

# 2. The Cultural Cage

Bette Ann Moskowitz

On Planet X, the median age is 88. Many people live well beyond their centenaries, so having babies is not considered a big deal, and, though not quite discouraged, the idea that it is a blessing to have a child is foreign on Planet X. In their culture, pregnancy is an annoying side effect of coitus, which, like eating a good meal or dancing, is practiced for the pleasure. Birth control is a welcome and accepted part of life. And since aged people do not need replacing, and are able to function well into their hundreds, on Planet X youth is slightly looked down on, and considered a lower time of existence; therefore, it is a common practice for young people on Planet X, to try their best to look and act old.

The best people on Planet X are both wise and wrinkled. The most charismatic males are gray-haired or balding. They wear white socks rolled down over their spindly ankles, and their ears, from which tufts of hair spring, stick out from their heads. They often cup a hand behind one of those big ears or lean forward with a kind of horn stuck in one ear and say things like, "Eh? Heh? What was that? Come again?" for they are famously hard of hearing. It is said that the ears grow longer as the hearing lessens, and since this is a sign of virility and power, it is a common practice to pull at one's lobes to enhance their droopiness. The most handsome males on Planet X wear bowties and thick spectacles and lean on canes or walkers. The most beautiful Planet X females wear stockings rolled below their dresses, and the most admired of these have breasts that sag so low they reach their knees. Their wrinkles have wrinkles. On Planet X, the more wrinkles the better. And since what we see is always linked to what we believe about people, there is never any doubt that the more attractive citizens are those with the most worth in Planet X's society. They know all there is to know. They have the key jobs, take the key roles, wield all the power, and matter the most. Diseases that affect them get the most funding to stamp them out. Prejudice—because where would a world be without its prejudices? —is, alas, against youth. When someone on Planet X says a person is "so young," the subtext of that phrase contains the words *callow, shallow, unformed, lacking both conviction and sex appeal.* The people on Planet X believe this is the only way to live. Their beliefs are enclosed by how long people have believed them: No one on Planet X has ever known them to be different. You could say they live in a *cultural cage,* where what they know is bound by what they have always known: They don't know what they don't know.

We don't live on Planet X, but we, too, live in a cultural cage. In our world, too, what we see governs how we feel, and what we feel is always ruled by what we have *always* felt and have been told to feel. In our world—an upside-down version of Planet X—youth is revered and being young forever is a common ambition. And because it has always been that way, it always *will* be. Or, so we believe in our cultural cage. Picture those tall, wide bars—the *givens* we were born with—holding us in.

Those beliefs and practices that have been in place since we were born, and are still here as we grow and age, the large cultural givens (once, that women were not equal to men and black people were not equal to white) as well as the small cultural givens (whether we are breastfed or bottle fed, spanked or spoiled, whether divorce is a bane or a boon) are part of what we call our culture. And it takes much dissatisfaction and great imagination to bring about change.

When it comes to aging, the bars of the cultural cage are strong, going back to ancient practices and reinforced by generation after generation. As long as we live penned in by these beliefs, ageism will be the result. Ageism—a word first coined by gerontologist Robert Butler—describes discrimination against people because of their age. In the cultural cage, stereotypical beliefs (for example, that older people are wise, or slow, or technologically challenged, or conservative, or uninterested in sex) and prejudices (such as older people don't belong in the workplace, older people should not be driving, older people drive up medical costs for the rest of us) affect people's lives every day, in large and small ways.

Take, for example, the notion that older people are wise. Are they? Always? Never? Sometimes?

This positive trait leans on an old societal model when elders were the ones the rest of society turned to for advice because they had lived the longest and thus had the most experience. But this was long ago, in a world which remained fairly static from generation to generation. Nowadays, the advances in technology and transportation which have made this a global world, mean this societal model no longer applies. As progeny felt free to unhook from their first families, they lost the strong intergenerational connections that had come with proximity and reliance on their grandparents and great-grandparents. Now, those children may come home to visit but are strangers to the youth-to-age flow and familiarity that was once family life.

The advance of technology has rendered many older people either resistant or frightened (or both) of a world which largely happens in cyberspace and on social media. Email has replaced phone calls. Texting has replaced emails. Grandma is left wondering not only how it works, but what's so good about it. And the grandchildren are impatient and don't think there is anything wise about being old-fashioned. Because of this, many older people find themselves on the margins of modern society, no longer considered wise, maybe even considered vestigial.

And as respect for the experiences and opinions of our older citizens has taken a hit, it has been replaced by another stereotype: that older people are dull, their brains slowing down, along with their eyesight and hearing, so they cannot navigate the complicated methods of communication in our brave new world.

Is this any truer than the previous belief that all older people were wise? Not always, not never.

It is the stereotype itself that causes the trouble. In the cultural cage of ageism, everyone who ages is lumped together, a monolith. Everyone is the same as everyone else when it comes to how they age. A whole segment of society is made to feel unequal to the workings of the modern world. The result of this stereotype is the isolation of older people from the rest of society. This deprivation of human interaction often leads to depression, illness, and even death. Old people are disparaged casually and mocked by the media. It has become a trope of aging that old people can't cope. The idea that everyone over 65 is similarly challenged by the digital world compromises whatever truth there is that in their resistance to those new ways of communicating, there might be some truth, deflecting from the wise notion that there may be value in some of the old ways of communicating.

Older people, themselves, believe these stereotypes, too, ironically. After all, *they* were born into the cultural cage and have lived in it through their own youth and adulthood. They have held stereotypical ideas about their own mothers and grandmothers, and now that they have arrived, they are willing to accept their place behind the bars of this cultural cage.

They acquiesce to the idea, for example, that you should not get behind an older driver on the road. Actually, though auto accidents caused by older people may indeed be a result of slowed reflexes or poor eyesight, it is also true, according to the American Automobile Association, that drivers in their 60s are the safest drivers on the road and are involved in the fewest crashes.[1] Yet, the stereotype persists.

The bars of the cultural cage have the patina of paternalism. Children treat their beloved parents like beloved-but-problematic children. They want to keep them safe and often anticipate a decline that has not yet happened. Can you imagine what terror "She had to take her father's car keys from him" engenders in aging fathers, what self-righteous guilt it engenders in their daughters? Depriving an old person of the ability to drive in many communities is a prison sentence. In anything but a big city, the ability to get around, to go to a doctor, go to the market, go to meet friends, go to the mall to buy a gift—ordinary things that people like to do —are frequently out of the question for someone accustomed to relying on driving themselves. It is the ultimate loss of self-determination and control, and for many old people, it means having to re-think life, succumbing to assisted living, or senior housing, giving up a house or apartment that was home, if the choice includes access to their needs, within the bounds and governed by the rules of that particular senior community. In other words, a trade of freedom for access. Because of the cultural cage, we, old and young, accept this as a rite of passage and put little thought and less money into finding solutions to the loss of mobility that old age brings to some people.

In the cultural cage, it is common to medicalize old age, to look upon all those years from 65 to death as a *condition* that we either need to cure or endure.

In the cultural cage, you should not hire an older person because they are taking a job that a younger person could be hired to do. This drives a wedge between the young and the old. The notion is held that older workers are greedy for wanting to keep their jobs past "appropriate" retirement age, that they do things the old way, and that they are all used up and out of the requisite energy to do the job. (At the same time, early retirement is said, in the United States, to be stressing the Social Security and Medicare system.[2,3]) In the cultural cage of ageism, you can't win.

In the cultural cage, perceived problems of aging are routinely underfunded. Measures that are routinely taken to make life easier and safer for others in the culture are ignored when it comes to older people. (Think of the tamper-proof medicine bottle, created to protect our young. Then think about the tiny print on those medicine bottles which a lot of older people with failing eyesight can't read. An easy fix, but one no one is moved to fix.). Lack of services, lack of reliable transportation options, and diseases of aging, such as Alzheimer's, all may be known to us, but we don't do much about them.

In the cultural cage, older people are no longer interested in sex. (And if they are, the less said about it, the better. Turn your head. It isn't a pretty sight.) Sex among the old is a favorite topic of jokes. (Though it is not a joke that in institutional settings, complicated rules and arrangements must be made in order for people to have sex. Many LGBTQ older people go back into the closet if they are institutionalized.)

Let's talk for a moment about the world of long-term care, because, in many ways and many cases, it represents the intersection of ageism and actual abuse. How does one slide into the other? How does something that purports to care for the older population instead perpetuate the lack of care reflected in the cultural cage?

Long-term care, which includes assisted living and nursing facilities, has long been criticized for its failings, which include, at their most extreme, physical and psychological abuse and neglect—for which people pay an ever-increasing amount of money. I spent almost 10 years in the New York State Long-Term Care Ombudsman Program (part of a Federal mandate), as a volunteer and then as assistant coordinator of the program in two upstate counties. I observed and tried to ameliorate cases of abuse and neglect, working through a cumbersome system which gave (minimally trained) volunteer observers deep access but little power to effect change. In other words, a volunteer could go anywhere in the facility, ask any questions, and see records and reports, but their ability to do anything about what they observed was restricted to reporting to the Department of Health. This agency was in a battle with its own mandate, because of the volume of complaints and their understaffed, overworked ability to address them all, immediately and effectively. And, of course, serious complaints came first, so that less serious ones, such as those having to do with human dignity, were, out of pure need, put on the back burner. I remember complaining about a so-called trivial issue concerning a resident's desire to be taken to the bathroom rather than diapered overnight. A *dignity issue* it is called in nursing home speak. I remember the official I was speaking to being disinclined to cite the nursing home for an infraction. I remember saying to this official, "What if it were your mother? What if it were you?"

It was those dignity issues that were the most ignored, and the most difficult to change because in many cases the residents themselves felt that the loss of dignity came with the territory and was something they had to endure because they were old. They had lived in the cultural cage, and what the cultural cage had built in was an institution that *included* loss of dignity, loss of importance, and loss of power and control. In the end, for me, it was not a matter of one good nursing home versus one bad one. It was the structure itself: long-term care living and institutional life is the real-life version of my metaphorical cage. It may not have bars—though some dementia units have locked doors—but it is prisonlike. Its rules and regulations are established for the smooth running of staff. Its business model is no different from any other profit-making enterprise. Its demands are no different from any congregant living model: food, cheap enough and bland enough to meet the wide requirements of its older population. Systems, such as mealtimes and bedtimes and medicine passes regimented enough to accommodate shift changes and ease of administration—in the cultural cage, institutions that can maintain such efficiency and avoid such gross offenses as physical abuse or neglect, are considered good. Because in the cultural cage, residents themselves cannot be counted on to complain. In a good nursing home, the efficiency and kindness of their jailers make it easy for residents to get used to being put in diapers so that the facility does not have to worry about providing an aide every time someone has to be helped to the bathroom. They enter the institution already understanding that they are giving up a big chunk of their lives. They think, and often say, "It comes with the territory." Their children, relieved to be relieved of the responsibility for their parents' safety, are also mindful not to complain, either because they deem their parents' complaints trivial, or are embarrassed by them, or they fear that complaints will result in retaliation by the staff later on. Remember that resident who wants to be taken to the bathroom rather than being diapered? Multiply them by hundreds of older people with similar desires. Situate yourself outside their rooms, and watch them as they press the call bell for help, and wait, and wait, and wait, beyond what their bladders can do. Imagine the embarrassment and shame when they have accidents because no one came to help them to the bathroom in time. Part of living in the cultural cage means looking at physical changes, such as incontinence, with shame, rather than as a somatic function of the bladder or kidney that no one needs to feel either pride in or shame about. (A good dishwasher or washing machine is only expected to last ten years or so. The human body, by age 80, does pretty well, in comparison.). But in the cultural cage, all of us, young and old, feel secretive and embarrassed by the way our bodies do or don't hold up. We assume blame when they don't hold up, and pride when they do. The occasional resident who tries to live as they did on the outside is often considered a pest. (*Non-compliant* is the nursing home phrase.) And so, in the actual cage of the cultural cage, many residents comply.

Institutional living in the cultural cage means that needs (such as someone to help you to the bathroom), are denied or delayed, while desires and choices are mostly non-existent. Whether you were a morning person or a night owl all your life, now your routine is the routine of the facility. You will get up and go to bed when it is convenient for the running of the whole house. The food you eat is chosen to do no harm, not to give pleasure. It may be salt-free, sugar-free, cholesterol-free, gluten-free—all to keep older people safe from the harmful effects of their various diseases and conditions, like arthritis, hypertension, heart disease, and diabetes—but it is also, often, flavor-free. And, since dining is a powerful physiological and social pleasure, this institutional way with food is a significant deprivation. Food is one of the most common complaints that residents of long-term care make, and yet it is not considered crucial. In the cultural cage, the experts in the field of long-term care address it by acknowledging and understanding it, but not doing much about it.

In recent years, there have been experiments in new models of long-term living, such as smaller, cottage-type living arrangements, and larger institutions that have tried to switch to resident-centered scheduling, but the former are not prevalent and often expensive, and the latter are hard to establish and maintain because they require staff who need to be trained and willing to put the residents first.

Speaking of staffing in the institutional cultural cage, the people who have the most hands-on responsibility for the care of older people are Certified Nursing Assistants (CNA). They are minimally trained, overworked, badly paid, and disrespected. As of 2020, the average yearly wage for a Certified Nursing Assistant in a nursing facility in New York State, according to the U.S. Department of Labor Statistics was about $30,000, while the average yearly wage for a supermarket cashier was about $29,000.[4,5] Consider the disparity between those two jobs, in terms of responsibility, skill, and need. Why would someone do such an arduous and sometimes heartbreaking job of caring for old people in a nursing facility that does not respect them or their charges, when they can work behind a counter and go home at night? No surprise then, that having and keeping CNAs in the institution is a challenge and understaffing is a common complaint. During the COVID-19 pandemic quarantine of 2020, the extent and severity of the shortage of nursing and nursing assistant staff were revealed, when the family members who had been routinely there to pick up the slack in hands-on care were no longer allowed in the facility. People were neglected and suffered the kinds of fates that come with elder isolation, pressure sores, ignored decline, and illness.

In the cultural cage, the slotting of older people's needs beneath those of others gives rise to the idea that those needs are specific only to the people who embody them, and to the rest of us may be negligible, negotiable, perhaps even non-existent.

During COVID, talk about vaccination inevitably included talk about older people as a group: vulnerable and frail. When the media framed the disease as one which strikes mainly older people, the world bought it. Many governments categorized at-risk people by their ages first, before their vulnerabilities. Public policy in many countries followed this with lockdowns of nursing and assisted living facilities, with the results already mentioned. Medical ethics panels discussed rationing medical care using age as a criterion; in Italy and Spain, it is legal to use age to ration medical care. In trying to persuade people to isolate, "Do it for your elders" eventually got the backlash it deserved, when people started to say things like, "They lived their lives, now why should I limit mine for them?" Phrases such as "Boomer Doomer" and "Boomer Remover" were tossed around. And *that* is how ageism becomes elder abuse, fortified by the cultural cage, and all its givens.

Change comes hard to most of us. But recognition of where we are when it comes to our treatment of our mothers, grandmothers, and even ourselves, may lead to dissatisfaction, and therein lies the hope that eventually we can change. That's why I want you to picture it: that tall, wide structure, its strong, paternalistic, restrictive, cruel, isolating bars reaching everywhere into our culture. Picture the cultural cage as if it were a real thing. Because it is.

## Notes

1 Aging and Disability Services. "Older Adults and Driving: Challenging Stereotypes." ADS, September 22, 2022. https://www.agingkingcounty.org/2022/09/22/older-adults-and-driving-challenging-stereotypes/.

2 Dor, Kate. "The Pandemic Drove These Americans into Early Retirement. What to Know before Making the Leap," CNBC. May 9, 2021. https://www.cnbc.com/2021/05/09/the-pandemic-drove-these-americans-into-early-retirement.html.

3 Waggoner, John. "10 Things No One Tells You about Early Retirement." AARP. Updated June 17, 2022. https://www.aarp.org/retirement/planning-for-retirement/info-2021/pre-early-retirement-reality-check.html.

4 U.S. Bureau of Labor Statistics. "Occupational Employment and Wage Statistics." BLS. Accessed January 3, 2022. https://www.bls.gov/oes/current/oes311131.htm.

5 Moore Gerety, Rowan. "Pandemic Exposes Low Pay and Scant Protections for Nursing Assistants and Home-Care Aides." *Los Angeles Times*. April 4, 2020. https://www.latimes.com/business/story/2020-04-04/coronavirus-nursing-assistants-home-health-care-aides.

# 3. *Living and Aging with Disability: A Personal Account*

ADOLF RATZKA

The world's population is getting older. The older individuals get, the more likely they will acquire an impairment. This way, the number of persons with impairments is growing and will continue to grow. According to the UN, "More than 46 % of persons aged 60 and over have disabilities" … This group is projected to grow in numbers between 2015 and 2030 by 56 %.[1] The consequences of physical impairments can be alleviated by assistive technology, such as canes, walkers, and wheelchairs. Cognitive impairments, such as dementia, are more difficult to compensate for. Some will require assistance with the activities of daily living (ADL), for example, bathing or getting dressed, or they will need someone to accompany them to prevent accidents.

How well are our societies prepared for the rapid increase in the number of persons with impairments? Do we, for example, have a built environment and an infrastructure designed for all citizens, including older and disabled persons? That would require mandatory Universal Design[2] standards in new construction, particularly in housing, and state grants for retrofitting existing buildings with accessibility features. For our societies to welcome and include citizens who require assistance from others in their daily lives, community-based support services, such as personal assistance services, have to be in place. The list of required societal changes is summarized in the United Nations Convention on the Rights of Persons with Disabilities (CRPD).[3] The CRPD signposts the road to a world where we all, regardless of disability and age, can feel welcome and enjoy the same conditions. Adjusting to a life-changing disability will always be difficult for individuals and their families. Together we can lessen the impact on the person's quality of life and social status, and challenge society's preconceived notions about persons with disabilities by doing our best in implementing the CRPD.

Today, we are many decades away from this vision. We are reminded of this each time we are struck by natural disasters, wars, or other catastrophes when the older and disabled are hit the worst. Yet, their requirements in emergencies are soon forgotten from one crisis to the next.

A few months after the Covid pandemic outbreak, Swedish media discussed the use of triage when not enough respirators are available. As one of the persons at risk of serious illness, I felt threatened by the discussion and wrote an op-ed letter in the Swedish daily newspaper *Sydsvenskan*.[4] What follows is my translation of the original Swedish text:

"I am 78. For over 60 years, I have lived with a ventilator and nasal mask, used an electric wheelchair, and needed help from my personal assistants with most things. In 1961, at 17, I contracted polio, became paralyzed, could not breathe, and was put into an Iron Lung, a type of ventilator where I lay in a large tube with only my head outside. I saw life ahead of me as a hopeless and prolonged dying. I wanted to die.

Before deciding not to start or not to continue life-sustaining treatment, the doctor in charge must, according to the Swedish National Board of Health and Welfare's Statutory Instrument 2011:7, Chapter 3, consult at least one other authorized professional and document in the patient's record, among other things, their attitude to life-sustaining treatment and that of the patient and their relatives. But is the opposite equally reassuringly regulated when a patient wants to live and needs life-sustaining treatment?

On January 6, 2022, a woman with extensive disabilities and Covid was admitted to the Southern Hospital (Södersjukhuset) in Stockholm with severe breathing difficulties. The doctor in charge was unsure whether she would survive life-sustaining treatment and refused her oxygen or intubation despite the family's pleas. The woman died two days later.

Healthcare providers don't have to respect the wishes of patients and their families when they request life-sustaining treatment. At the beginning of the Covid pandemic, hundreds, if not thousands, of older persons were summarily given palliative care without oxygen or intubation, without being asked, and without seeing a doctor! For older and disabled people, the risk of losing one's life in this way seems far greater than the risk of having to live longer than one would like.

Many people with extensive disabilities, in particular, older persons with disabilities, fear for their lives if they end up in a hospital with Covid or other conditions that might prevent them from expressing their wishes. How does the doctor judge someone's quality of life? Who is completely free of preconceptions? How many doctors who don't know me would think my life is worth living? That's why I've written a letter of intent that my wife and daughter and a few close friends also signed. The following text is attached to my medical record in case I end up in a hospital:

If someone doesn't know me closely and only sees my body, my need for a ventilator around the clock and my extensive need for personal assistance, it is easy to conclude that my life offered no quality of life already before I became ill and will not offer it after any life-sustaining treatment. But I feel that I have had and still have what I consider to be a full, rich, and exciting life together with my wife and daughter, with friends, studies and work abroad as a researcher, project manager, founder of several organizations, a leader in the disability movement also internationally, lecturer in many countries, with many trips, and long stays abroad.

The 60 years with my disability have helped me understand what constitutes quality of life for me: relationships, mainly with my family and friends, meeting new people, feelings of happiness I can experience in nature, contemplating art and listening to chamber music, my work in disability policy, interest in literature and several scientific fields, my daily meditation practice and much more – small things that, together, bring me joy many times a day and make life interesting and worth living. Reaching this realization, and becoming aware of my own preconceived notions about disability and aging has taken me many years, much thought, and many psychotherapy sessions.

I love my life and want to keep living as long as I can. Therefore, I ask the responsible healthcare providers to discuss my expressed wishes with my family and friends. If there is a chance to sustain my life with, for example, medication, oxygen, intubation, tracheostomy, I want to take that chance.

All of us with extensive disabilities, above all older persons, should write similar texts to clarify our own view of our quality of life. To us, life is just as valuable as it is to other people. But with the current fixation on youth and health and the hardening social climate, it has become too easy for others to condemn our lives as lives not worth living."

The pandemic highlighted the vulnerability of disabled persons, older persons, and in particular those who are both old and disabled. According to a Swedish government report, old and disabled persons in institutions formed the group that was least protected from infection and, when infected, received the least medical treatment which led to the group's highest mortality in the Swedish population. The report, referring to the pandemic's effect on institutionalized older persons with disabilities concludes: "The OECD states that 'the pandemic has highlighted a part of society that is undervalued and under-resourced."[5]

What does this tell us about the importance and value of older and disabled citizens in society? Are the lives of these persons less valuable? For an answer to that question, we only need to look at ourselves.

## *I Grew Up with Prejudices against Older Persons*

I was 10 years old when an older couple moved into the tiny apartment upstairs in the tenement house in the small town of Bavaria, Germany, where my family lived. The couple had an ugly, small, ill-tempered mixed-breed dog. With the cruel eyes of a 10-year-old, I saw their blueish lips that reminded me of the earthworms I used for fishing. Both had dark blotches on their faces and the backs of their hands. Their eyes were tiny, their backs crooked, and they walked with canes. I never saw them having visitors. At that age, I hadn't fully grasped that life is a process of accumulating many small changes as we move through time. It didn't occur to me that they had not always had blueish lips and blotches, that they, too, had been young once, had gone to school, fallen in love, had a profession, started a family, and carried with them a treasure of memories, both happy and sad. All I could see were their lips, backs, and canes. I didn't want to get old.

### I Grew Up with Prejudices against Disabled Persons

An aunt of a grammar schoolmate had multiple sclerosis. I only saw her face because she stayed in bed all day in a tiny dark room doing nothing, not even reading. As the adults would explain to me, her suffering was a special gift from God. How could her frightful existence be a gift? The other image of a disabled person from my childhood is an ageless woman sitting in an antique-looking wooden wheelchair with a plaid rug over her lap and legs. A volunteer community sister in a black gown with an equally solemn and saintly demeanor pushed her wheelchair. The stern expression of the woman in the wheelchair reminded me of a female saint in the village church. Wouldn't it be better if she could die?

Most of us grow up with similar prejudices. Unless we become aware and rid ourselves of them, they can harm others—especially when we are in positions of power over society's resources. Our prejudices can also harm us. Due to my prejudices, I was ill-prepared when life took a decisive turn at age 17. When I gradually understood that I'd never again compete in the high jump, dance, or play the violin, I wanted to kill myself. But how, when you can move only a few fingers? Collecting sleeping pills in my cheeks like a hamster didn't work. How lucky for me that no one offered me assisted suicide! Looking back, I feel compassion for the traumatized teenager who lost control over his body in two days and could not know the future opportunities that life would offer.

### I Had No Positive Role Models

The first years after I contracted polio, I saw no future for myself. In the 1950s and 1960s—and still today—society was not ready to include people like me who can't walk or dress, or need much other practical help. These persons have always existed but were invisible to the public. I had not grown up with positive images and role models of such persons at school or in the neighborhood, persons who had impairments and interesting lives with work, family, and friends.

Many years later, when I studied the prerequisites for deinstitutionalization, I understood that the issue has a powerful class dimension. In countries with inexpensive domestic labor, I often observe silver-haired ladies sitting in wheelchairs pushed in parks by Filipino nurses in white uniforms. Wealthy families with generous housing space have always had this option. But for me, in the 1960s, there were only two equally terrifying options to keep me alive.

## Dependence on the Family

The family as a caregiver was—and still is today—the most common solution for people who can't live alone. In my case, our house was too small and inaccessible, and my mother was frail. Building an accessible house was beyond our means.

Today, most societies still expect the family, mainly the women, to be the first in line to care for old and disabled members. In the absence of accessible housing and accessible infrastructure, with the family as the caregiver, a person often can end up in an out-of-view backroom existence. Also, relying on the family is a ticking time bomb. Parents, as they get older, will not always be able to do the physical work involved and someday might need assistance themselves. Siblings who can assist will move out and start families of their own. The same goes for children. Non-disabled spouses often sacrifice their careers and interests and are tied to their disabled partners in mutual dependence like Siamese twins without a life of their own. Today, the role of families in the care of old or disabled members is declining as social and geographical mobility, and women's labor force participation are rising.

## Warehoused in Institutions

The other alternative for people like me, at the time, was spending the rest of my life in a residential institution. As it turned out, I had to stay five years in hospitals. Not because I was medically unstable but because of the lack of accessible housing and community-based support services. Today, 60 years later, this situation is still common in many countries. I spent most of the five years in a ward for children who needed mechanical ventilation. It was not an acute ward; it had the character of a warehousing facility. The treatment we got—for example, weekly physiotherapy—could have been provided on an outpatient basis elsewhere.

It was the worst period of my life. I no longer had use of my body, became dependent on others, and had to swallow my pride and ask for help for just about everything. I lost most of the means for self-determination. As a patient, I was at the bottom of the hierarchy that controlled my body and daily life. Above all of us ruled an anonymous power over which not even the chief physician had much influence: the requirements for the smooth functioning of the ward dictated what everybody, staff and patients alike, had to do, and where and when they had to do it. The plan's implementation demanded precise timing, and strict adherence to orders, leaving no room for individual circumstances. We all were interlocking parts of an intricate mechanism, like the huge clockwork in Charlie Chaplin's movie *Modern Times* that swallows up the powerless individual passing it through its cogs.

Once, I was scheduled to have an X-ray taken and needed to empty my bowels the evening before, which I did. But at 3 am, the night nurse woke me up and, without asking, shoved a suppository up my rectum. "I'm just following the orders in your journal," she countered my protests. After half a century, I still remember the humiliation.

The staff on the ward was always busy. Without assistance from them, there wasn't much I could do on my own except read, study with tutors to finish high school, listen to music, or watch TV. Above all, I could not leave the ward and the hospital compound alone. Somebody needed to push my wheelchair and help me with my jacket in wintertime. I would have loved to go to the movies but needed somebody to accompany me. I hardly knew anyone in Munich and could not meet people unless they came to me in the ward. I felt very isolated.

Worse yet, the few times I did leave the hospital compound, I felt self-conscious, shy, and uncomfortable, and I imagined that everybody stared at me. The longstanding adverse effects of institutionalization are well-known:

> The institutional environment has, in itself, been shown to create additional disabilities that can stay with a person for the rest of their life. The lack of a personal life, lack of autonomy and a lack of respect for one's personal integrity can hamper an individual's emotional and social development.... "social deprivation" and "taught helplessness" ...describe the psychological effects of living in an institution. Language and intellectual development are...affected and institutionalization can lead to various mental health problems, including aggressiveness and depression.[6]

## Who Are Residential Institutions Good For?

Institutions, such as hospitals, daycare centers, prisons, nursing homes, etc., are not designed to promote self-determination. One reason for their existence is the expected labor cost savings when individuals with similar needs share staff in one location. Self-determination is neither intended nor possible when staff is shared. I suggest sharing staff is the most important criterion that constitutes institutions. It has far-reaching implications.

Depending on the staff's size and rate of turnover, residents can't often expect assistance from employees who are familiar with their requirements. In a larger institution, that degree of specialization would be unmanageable. The staff has to be interchangeable for the whole to function smoothly. In the ward in the Munich hospital, every nurse had to work with every patient. What counted was their generic formal training and their rank as denoted by their uniform. As a result, the patients also became interchangeable and were given the one-size-fits-all treatment in everything that was not strictly medical, such as medications. For example, when moving, lifting, or dressing us, the nurses on our ward manhandled everybody much the same way whether or not we had, for instance, contracted joints with restricted movements, which caused pain.

Another consequence of sharing staff is that they, by necessity, make decisions that infringe on the individual resident's self-determination. For example, when several patients need something simultaneously and there are not enough workers, the nurses must decide whose current requirements are most urgent. If you drop your book and need somebody to pick it up, you might have to wait for the attendant on duty who, at this moment, helps somebody next door on the toilet. There's hardly ever enough staff to accompany individual residents to leave the institution for a few hours, not to speak of days or weeks. That means residents are under house arrest if they need much assistance during the day, such as putting on a coat or going to the toilet.

The loss of personal autonomy, the isolation, and the lack of experiences like dating girls, working part-time, or traveling during these teenage years left marks on me that took years to repair. I still feel bitter about these lost years. The only positive outcome of my experience of living in institutions and eventually getting out was my later research and community organizing interest in the prerequisites for deinstitutionalization.

My interest has been lifelong. It is fueled by the fear in the back of my mind that, someday, I might end up in an institution again—even though I have lived, studied, worked, and flourished in the community throughout my adult life. Given my five years of first-hand experience with institutional living, I can't understand how anybody would choose to live the rest of their life in such a place unless acceptable alternatives in the community were lacking. I felt that way when I was 17, and I still feel that way at 78. Although my requirements, preferences, and interests might have changed, my need for the freedom to make my own choices is still the same. I enjoy spending time with my family; working part-time; visiting friends; going to concerts, art exhibitions, and lectures; taking nature walks; and traveling. I need these for my intellectual stimulation and physical and emotional well-being. Living in a residential institution, could I keep up such activities when I want to and not only when staff happen to be around?

In the international Independent Living movement,[7] we work for dein-stitutionalization. "Liberate our brothers and sisters from institutions!" has been one of our slogans. The movement focuses on children with disabilities who are often separated from their families and on younger adults who are to be saved from nursing homes and places where older adults have to spend their remaining years. We have been less vocal about saving older people from being marginalized, segregated, and under-stimulated there. But working for the deinstitutionalization of persons of *all* ages might be more successful. In this way, we can multiply our constituency for the cause, and build alliances with the organizations of older persons for a greater impact. Also, many in the Independent Living and Disability Rights Movement might manage to live by themselves in the community today. But their impairments can change, and they may require assistance from others in the future. It is in their own interest to work for housing and support alternatives outside institutions for all ages. Someday, they might need such alternatives themselves. Once we are old, need much help, and are already in a nursing home, we may not be in the best condition to fight for self-determination in the community and may not manage to leave the nursing home anymore. Now is the best time to mobilize efforts to build acceptable alternatives to institutions in the community.

The work of the Independent Living and Disability Rights Movement for the rights of persons with disabilities received important support in 2006 when the CRPD was adopted. In Art. 19, the Convention declares "living independently and being included in the community with choices equal to others" as a human right.[8] The Convention, whose language was widely influenced by the Movement, particularly in Art. 19, is a great achievement at the normative level. Yet, in most countries, the everyday reality for persons who can't live alone due to cognitive, psycho-social, or physical impairments is essentially unchanged. In Europe, for example, roughly 3 million persons with disabilities of all ages still live in institutions, amounting to 0.8 percent of the total population.[9]

Most likely, these figures are underestimates. What is an institution? In the absence of a standard definition, some countries reserve the term for facilities of 100 or more residents and don't consider group homes with fewer residents as institutions. The definition in General Comment No. 5 uses not size but the residents' degree of self-determination as the criterion which results in a larger number of institutionalized persons:

> Neither large-scale institutions with more than a hundred residents nor smaller group homes with five to eight individuals, nor even individual homes can be called independent living arrangements if they have other defining elements of institutions or institutionalization. Although institutionalized settings can differ in size, name and setup, there are certain defining elements, such as: obligatory sharing of assistants with others and no or limited influence over by whom one has to accept assistance, isolation and segregation from independent life within the community, lack of control over day-to-day decisions, lack of choice over whom to live with, rigidity of routine irrespective of personal will and preferences . . .[10]

By this definition, well over 3 million individuals in Europe are segregated in institutions and excluded from family, friends, and mainstream society. Despite the European Union's responsibility to support Member States in their CRPD implementation, the number of institutionalized persons is increasing, as pointed out in a Council of Europe report.[11]

Older persons are particularly exposed to institutionalization. Although research shows that they prefer staying at home and aging in place, as it is called,[12,13] the institutionalization of older persons who can't manage to live alone has almost become the cultural norm. In Europe, for example, 2.6 percent of the age group 65 and over are institutionalized compared to 0.8 percent of all age groups.[14]

Older persons move into a residential setting as the result of a lack of support from the family or community-based services and, more rarely, by their preference, as already noted. A degree of persuasion or coercion can't be excluded. A study from Argentina suggests that 30 percent of the residents of gerontological centers claimed to be there against their will.[15] In the context of institutionalization, the UN Independent Expert on the enjoyment of all human rights by older persons recently observed:

> While the reasons vary from one context to another, it appears that in most situations where older persons are deprived of liberty, ageism and age discrimination play underlying roles. Ageist attitudes remain persistent worldwide and lead to discriminatory laws, policies and practices that hinder the right of older persons to personal liberty.[16]

## Traditional Community-Based Support Services Are Limited

Article 19 of the CRPD prescribes community-based support services to enable persons with disabilities to live independently and be included in the community. They exist in many countries. Due to their limitations, they are more suitable for persons with less extensive impairments. According to my experience of using such services in Sweden, they offer only a limited number of assistance hours to the client. They are commonly known as "in-home support services" or "home help" and their equivalent in other languages. The terms indicate that support is not intended outside the home for study, work, social activities, or travel–in short, not for life on terms equal to others.

Users typically can't choose workers and must be prepared to admit strangers into their homes. Women often must accept assistance with intimate hygiene from male staff. High staff turnover and absenteeism confront clients with new workers unfamiliar with their requirements who first need to learn how to assist them. Most commonly, community-based services assist with physical personal requirements only and don't enable clients to take their share of family responsibilities for household chores and childcare. Assistance is limited to the basics: help with hygiene, dressing, warming frozen meals, and a shower twice a month. Often, clients can't get the services at times they need and have to adapt their lives to the service.

Community-based services were unavailable in Bavaria in the 1960s, and, as mentioned already, my mother could not physically assist me. How did I manage to leave the hospital?

## *De-institutionalization through Personal Assistance*

In the hospital in Munich, in a U.S. newsletter called *Toomey J Gazette*, edited by Gini Laurie, St. Louis, Missouri,[17] I read about young adults in the United States who required mechanical ventilation and went to college. There, I got the idea of attending university with the help of "roommate attendants," as they were referred to in the articles.

After finishing high school with the help of tutors who came to the hospital, I left for the University of California, Los Angeles (UCLA) in 1966. UCLA was one of the few universities in the world at the time that admitted persons with extensive disabilities. The Bavarian government agreed to pay my expenses, including the costs of what we today call "personal assistance." Compared to the hospital ward, they probably saved money by supporting my move to the United States. More importantly, they saved my life and gave me a future.

Living in a dormitory on campus, I hired fellow students to work for me. I estimated how many hours of daily assistance I would require for needs such as bathing, toileting, getting dressed, etc. Each month, I received a check from the German Consulate in Los Angeles with an amount that covered my number of assistance hours multiplied by the hourly wage, which was slightly above what students would earn for work in the campus libraries or cafeterias. I had what we today call "direct payments" for personal assistance with control over who was to work for me, at what times, where, with what tasks, and how the work was to be done. As the boss, I hired, trained, supervised, and paid them. When things did not work out, I could only blame myself. And things did go wrong, giving me more than enough opportunities to learn from my mistakes!

None of my family could come along and stay with me. The transition from the hospital ward to the student dormitory was scary, mind-boggling, and just wonderful! I was catapulted from the vegetable existence in the hospital to the hotbed of flower-power activism, anti-Vietnam war protests, and student life in California, for the first time living by myself. In the hospital, I had been a patient at the bottom of the hierarchy, forced to adapt every detail of my life to the requirements of the ward. In the dormitory, as the employer of my assistants, I was at the top of the hierarchy and expected to direct them. At age 22 and, more importantly, after five hospital years, it was at first difficult for me to become aware of my needs, not to speak of expressing them and having them realized.

## Personal Assistance Has Given Me a Life

Since 1966, I have supported myself in the community with personal assistants. First in Los Angeles on a scholarship, after 1973 in Stockholm on a research grant, and as a university researcher and, later, as director of the non-governmental organization (NGO) I founded. My assistants—several hundred people over the years—have enabled me to work; get involved in disability politics internationally; and travel widely for lectures, work, and pleasure.

My assistants also played a decisive role when I got married. My wife and I wanted to live together in a relationship where we, independently from each other, could develop and grow as *persons*. We believed this was possible with personal assistance. With the help of my assistants, I'd continue to care for myself and do my part of the household chores. It hasn't always worked out as intended, I'm ashamed to admit.

Our decision to have a child we also based on personal assistance. I would do my share of the physical work in child-raising with the help of my assistants. For example, I took our daughter Katharina to kindergarten in the morning; my wife picked her up after work. I also wanted to be alone with my daughter and do things together – only she and I. Every Saturday, Katharina and I did the grocery shopping, visited museums, or went fishing. I instructed my assistants to stay behind us and only interfere when I'd ask them or to step in to prevent an accident.

I have been able to live in the community, study, or work throughout my adult life, and have a family of my own. I am very satisfied with my life. I am proud of what I have achieved and what has become of me. It has been—and still is—a full, rich life thanks to personal assistance.

## *Personal Assistance Is Not a Cure for All*

Personal assistance can't compensate for the countless obstacles and injustices that the physical environment, peoples' attitudes, and society's structure present. Architectural barriers prevent my friends from inviting me home. Steps at the door force me to wait outside shops while my assistant does the errand inside. If I do get in, the staff often ignore me, addressing the assistant only. Some people choose restaurants by the number of stars in *Guide Michelin;* I go by the number of steps at the entrance. Cities, for me, consist of accessible islands in an inaccessible ocean. Sweden passed accessibility building standards—without tangible sanctions. Sweden ratified the CRPD—without making it legally binding. Technical and administrative solutions for inclusion and commitment to equal opportunities are less developed than politically correct language in Sweden and elsewhere. There were periods when I'd write letters to government agencies, private companies, and the media every day, pointing out violations of my rights. To keep frustration and bitterness over being excluded at bay, I learned, with time, to downplay my interest in what I was missing. That didn't work anymore after we got our child, and I got to feel the pain over and over again. How do you explain to a two-year-old that you can't ride on the mini-train with her with your big powerchair?

Violations of our rights can have far-reaching consequences for us. In the 1980s, I studied psychology in Stockholm but had to quit after my Bachelor's when the department moved to an inaccessible structure. I got the morning paper *Dagens Nyheter* to report about it. When the department, three years later, installed an elevator, I was busy with other things and no longer interested. Once, I could have applied for a position at a research institute based in a historic building with staircases. I didn't take up the fight. They would have hired somebody who'd start working immediately. All I could have done was sue for damages which would have taken years in court, and awarded me perhaps the equivalent of $5,000. But when the City of Stockholm denied my wife and me permission to adopt a child on the grounds of my disability, we went to court and the media. The City claimed I couldn't give a child physical closeness and warmth because of my disability. What an insult! We won. The City appealed and lost several times up to the highest competent court, which took four years.[18]

## Personal Assistance, a Key to Independent Living Regardless of Age?

I consider myself an ordinary person without special gifts or talents. The only thing special about me is that I've lived my entire adult life with personal assistance. That is, sadly, very special. Many persons with similar disabilities could live equally full and rich lives with personal assistance services. Yet, in most countries, these services don't exist. Where they do exist, the law limits them to younger persons. In Sweden, for example, the LSS Act that regulates direct payments for personal assistance services restricts eligibility to persons not older than 65.[19] If you are fortunate and get disabled before that age, you might be entitled to the payments and receive them after you turn 65. I am one of these lucky people.

Persons of my age with requirements similar to mine who got their impairment after 65 can't live in the community without massive family support. Ineligible for direct payments under the LSS Act, they can count on only a few daily hours of the previously described limited community-based in-home services (*hemtjänst*). It's not enough to keep them out of a residential institution.

A few years ago, a government commission charged with finding ways to cap the costs of direct payments under the LSS Act contemplated discontinuing eligibility after 65. People in my situation and my age who receive direct payments were horrified. We have built our lives around personal assistance, as I described earlier, using myself as an illustration. So far, the government has not taken the step, but we fear it might do so in the future. In that case, instead of being entitled to direct payments to pay for 18 assistance hours a day as today, I might receive five hours of the local government's in-home support services a day in kind. As a result, I could not continue my current lifestyle without my wife working for me 13 hours every day of the year for the rest of my life. I can't imagine the pressure under which she'd be living, knowing that I'd have to move into a nursing home the day she could no longer work. Many older people with disabilities in Sweden—and certainly elsewhere, too—live under such pressure. For fear of institutionalization, they limit their activities and their quality of life and try to do things by themselves as much as possible, even at the risk of accidents.

### *Why Don't More Older Persons with Disabilities Qualify for Personal Assistance?*

Why is personal assistance in most countries non-existent or limited to younger persons? There might be regulatory reasons. In some countries, Sweden for example, personal assistance is a social security benefit and, as such, aimed at the working-age population, which automatically limits its eligibility to persons under 65.

A similar regulatory obstacle could be the division in social policy into persons with disabilities under 65 and senior citizens 65 and over. When I turned 65, I was taken aback when I realized that I was no longer a client of the local government's Social Services Department for Disabled Persons but of the Department of Older Persons. Staff, offices, telephone hours, and legislation had changed. The division does not promote the understanding of problems shared by both groups and their common solution.

Also, political motives might limit personal assistance. If older persons were also eligible, the number of applicants would multiply and taxes would need to be raised. Traditionally, the family has cared for old and disabled relatives for free. Any costs in the form of severely restricted quality of life, limited personal growth, and missed life opportunities were borne by the individuals involved and their families–mainly the women. In some countries, governments honor filial duties and strong family bonds with medals to such selfless, unpaid relatives–a low-cost policy appreciated by conservative taxpayers.[20]

Commonly voiced arguments are that older persons are not able or willing to administer, train, and supervise personal assistants, might feel lonely living alone, and prefer the companionship of peers in congregational settings. Such claims seem to be based on stereotypes. We differ in our physical and intellectual conditions in our older years as a function of our genetic makeup, the society we live in, our education, work careers, interests, and habits. One trend seems common: In Western societies, today's 70-year-olds, on average, have the physical and cognitive capacities of 50-year-olds of a couple of decades ago, as some researchers claim.[21] Several persons older than 65 with physical impairments might benefit from living in the community among family and friends with personal assistance and be able to direct their assistants, and recruit, train, and supervise them. Persons unable to do so due to cognitive, sociopsychological impairments, or dementia, don't necessarily need to miss the benefits of personal assistance. About half of the approximately 14,000 Swedish personal assistance users are either under 19 or belong to one of these groups.[22] Their direct payments contain funds for hiring a person who complements—not substitutes—their ability to make the relevant decisions, i.e., Supported Decision Making.[23] The person can be a relative, friend, or trusted assistant who understands the disabled person's situation, needs, and capacities.

Regarding loneliness, personal assistance, combined with housing adaptation to remove physical barriers, enables older persons to age in place, and continue living in their familiar physical and social environment where they visit friends with the help of their assistants.

## *What Does It Take to Accept One's Situation?*

In many countries, the organizations of old and retired persons have not actively joined forces with organizations of disabled persons in working for deinstitutionalization and personal assistance. A large part of their membership have impairments–or are expected to have them in the future. But is this fact openly acknowledged and accepted? In my limited experience with these organizations, older persons have difficulties calling their mobility restrictions a disability. Few visibly disabled members are elected to the board. Is disability a stigma for them?

The organizations of persons with disabilities I know, especially the large established ones, have many older members yet few of them serve on the board. The interest in collaborating with the organizations of older persons is modest. Are ableism and ageism preventing the two groups from addressing their common difficulties in society?

In Western culture, from childhood on, parents, rehabilitation professionals, and the media encourage us to keep up an image of "normality" and "independence." We are supposed to "overcome" our disabilities. For many, exchanging our crutches for a walker, our walker for a wheelchair—not to speak of using personal assistance—is proof of an unacceptable defeat. We, therefore, force ourselves to do things by ourselves at the risk of accidents, overexertion, and ruining our health. We are our worst enemies.

It has taken me many years to, more or less, come to terms with my disability. Would a 70-year-old today who undergoes a similar life-changing transition have enough time to accept and adjust to the new situation? Would it have helped me at age 17 to meet me at age 78? All I would have seen is an old man in a wheelchair with a ventilator facemask who is obviously unable to do a high jump and, therefore, unacceptable as a role model. The fact that I live in the community with personal assistance and not in an institution? At 17, I would not have been impressed. Both situations were equally terrifying, enough to despair and give up. Nor would I have been able to appreciate the self-determination that personal assistance makes possible. Most older persons today with or without the need for ADL assistance can't understand the advantages of personal assistance either—they have not experienced the alternatives. What we can do, as a society, to facilitate acceptance of impairment is to seriously work on implementing the CRPD. In this way, we enable our societies to include everybody. In this way, we can live together with people of all ages, and all types of impairments, in our families, as next-door neighbors, in pre-school, and at work. That will help us to break down our armor of fear and prejudice, for our mutual benefit.

## *Notes*

1  United Nations. "Disabilities and Ageing" UNDESA. Accessed November 4, 2022. http://www.un.org/development/desa/disabilities/disability-and-ageing.html.
2  Universal Design Institute. "Universal Design Principles." 1977. https://www.udin stitute.org/principles.
3  United Nations. "Full Text of the Convention on the Rights of Persons with Disabilities" UNDESA. Accessed November 4, 2022. https://www.un.org/deve lopment/desa/disabilities/convention-on-the-rights-of-persons-with-disabilities. html#Fulltext.
4  Ratzka, Adolf. "Låt livshjälp gå före dödshjälp [Let Life Support Come Before Death Support]." *Sydsvenskan,* February 6, 2022. https://www.sydsvenskan. se/2022-02-06/lat-livshjalp-ga-fore-dodshjalp-jag-kunde-enbart-rora-nagra-fing rar-jag-funderade-pa-hur-jag-skulle-kunna-ta-livet-av-mig.
5  Government of Sweden. *Summary of SOU 2020:80 Elderly Care During the Pandemic.* Stockholm: Government of Sweden, 2020. https://www.government.se/legal-documents/2020/12/summary-of-sou-202 080-elderly-care-during-the-pandemic/.
6  European Expert Group on the Transition from Institutional to Community-based Care. *Common European Guidelines on the Transition from Institutional to Community-based Care.* Brussels: EEG, 2012, 49. https://deinstitutionalisationdot com.files.wordpress.com/2017/07/guidelines-final-english.pdf.
7  In Europe, the umbrella organization is ENIL, the European Network on Independent Living (https://enil.eu/).
8  United Nations Department of Economic and Social Affairs, Disability. "Article 19: Living Independently and Being Included in the Community." UNDESA. Accessed January 3, 2023. https://www.un.org/development/desa/disabilities/ convention-on-the-rights-of-persons-with-disabilities/article-19-living-independen tly-and-being-included-in-the-community.html.
9  Grammenos, Stefanos. *European Comparative Data on Europe 2020 and Persons With Disabilities: Labour Market, Education, Poverty and Health Analysis and Trends.* Brussels: Publications Office of the European Union, 2021, 24. https:// data.europa.eu/doi/10.2767/745317.
10 Office of the High Commissioner for Human Rights (OHCHR). "General Comment No. 5 on Article 19 – The Right to Live Independently and be Included

in the Community." 2017. CRPD/C/GC/5 II A 16. (c). https://www.ohchr.org/en/documents/general-comments-and-recommendations/general-comment-no5-article-19-right-live.

11  Council of Europe Committee on Social Affairs, Health and Sustainable Development. "Deinstitutionalisation of Persons with Disabilities." 2021. AS/Soc (2021) 46, 5. https://assembly.coe.int/LifeRay/SOC/Pdf/DocsAndDecs/2021/AS-SOC-2021-46-EN.pdf.

12  Hellström, Ylva and Ingalill Rahm Hallberg. "Perspectives of Elderly People Receiving Home Help on Health, Care and Quality of Life." *Health & Social Care in the Community* 9 (2001): 61–71.

13  Zank, Susanne and Claudia Schacke. "Evaluation of Geriatric Day Care Units: Effects on Patients and Caregivers." *The Journals of Geronology, Series B: Psychological Sciences and Social Sciences* 57 (2002): 348–357.

14  Grammenos, *European Comparative Data*, 24.

15  Kléver, Parades. "Privados de su libertad o asilados por su voluntad [Deprived of their Liberty or Isolated by their Will]." *Red Latinoamericana de Gerontología*, December 1, 2016. https://www.gerontologia.org/portal/information/showInformation.php?idinfo=3622.

16  United Nations General Assembly Human Rights Council. *Older Persons Deprived of Liberty, Report of the Independent Expert on the Enjoyment of All Human Rights by Older Persons, Claudia Mahler* (Geneva: UNHRC, 2022), A/HRC/51/27.

17  "Quads on Quadrangles: Higher Education by the Totally Disabled." *Toomey J Gazette*, 5, No. 1 Spring-Summer (1962), http://www.polioplace.org/GINI.

18  Ratzka, Adolf. "Four Years of Struggle to Adopt." Paper presented at The Right to Parenthood Conference, Sweden, October 4, 1995. https://www.ratzka.se/wp-content/uploads/2022/05/Four-years-fight-to-adopt-1995.pdf.

19  See the translation of the original Act of 1993 at www.independentliving.org/docs3/englss.html. About the origins of the Act see www.independentliving.org/docs7/Independent-Living-movement-paved-way.html.

20  N-Land. "Pflegemedaille für Anna Pesel [Nursing Medal for Anna Pesel]." September 21, 2020. https://n-land.de/lokales/neuhaus/pflegemedaille-fuer-anna-pesel. Here, an example from Germany, where the mother of a son with a developmental disability was honored with a medal by the regional government for 65 years of "selfless," "exemplary," and "unpaid" care of her son.

21  Skoog, Ingmar. "70 is the New 50." December 22, 2021. https://www.youtube.com/watch?v=7bG05Pr9LHw.

22  Swedish Social Insurance Agency. "Vilka får assistansersättning? [Who Receives Assistance Compensation?]." Försäkringskassan. Accessed January 3, 2023. https://www.forsakringskassan.se/statistik-och-analys/funktionsnedsattning/statistik-om-assistansersattning/vilka-far-assistansersattning.

23  National Resource Center for Supported Decision-Making. "Supported Decision-Making in Your State." Accessed January 3, 2023. http://www.supporteddecisionmaking.org.

# 4. LGBTI Elders Advancing

Michael Adams

## Introduction

After lifetimes of invisibility and silence, LGBTI elders across the globe are emerging to demand that they be respected and that their needs be addressed as part of broader movements toward equity and inclusion for LGBTI people and older adults. Their stories are the essential starting point for any discussion of LGBTI elders advancing.

As an older transgender woman in Nepal recounts, when she began to dress according to her gender identity, not her assigned gender, villagers verbally abused her until she was forced to flee. She moved to a nearby town but now has no way to support herself because discrimination prevented her from obtaining enough education to become literate and transphobic employers refuse to hire her. Having been expelled from her village, she has no access to land for farming. Because her identity differs from that on her birth certificate, she does not have the protections of citizenship and will not benefit from the usual social security/national insurance programs. Her life expectancy as a transgender woman in Nepal is only 50–60 years.[1]

Lisa Oakley was a transgender woman who lived in the southwestern United States.[2] In 2020, battling severe diabetes and limited mobility, she recognized that she could no longer live on her own. Like many elders in her country, this meant moving to an elder care facility. However, for Lisa, it was much more complicated. Astonishingly, Lisa was rejected by 60 long-term care facilities because of her gender identity. One facility that did agree to admit Lisa would only house her with a male roommate. Eventually, shortly before her death, Lisa found a home at a welcoming facility, though it was many miles away from the community where she lived.

According to the UN Department of Economic and Social Affairs, there were over 771 million people aged 65 and older in 2022, or about 10 percent of the world's population, and this number is projected to double by 2050, reaching 16 percent.[3] LGBTI people have been systemically excluded from population studies across the globe, making it impossible to generate highly specific numbers for this sub-population. In the United States, research data indicates that approximately 5 percent of the overall population identifies as LGBTI; it is estimated that the LGBTI older adult population will reach at least 7 million by 2040. In most parts of the world, discrimination, ostracism, and fears of abuse and violence prevent many LGBTI older adults from revealing their identities. Nonetheless, assuming that the U.S. population trends are representative, it is reasonable to estimate that the worldwide population of LGBTI older adults will reach at least 33 million by 2040.

This group of elders represents one of the most marginalized and neglected populations of older adults. "They often experience severe human rights violations based on their sexual orientation and/or gender identity (SOGI) status combined with stigma and discrimination on the basis of age."[4] These violations intersect also with other factors, such as race and ethnicity. They combat social isolation, invisibility, discrimination, and abuse. The cumulative impact of these struggles over lifetimes results in high levels of poverty and increased morbidity. Thanks to the brave struggles of pioneering LGBTI aging activists, this panorama is slowly changing. To date, however, progress has been limited and unevenly distributed by geography, class, race, and gender, among other distinguishing factors.

In my work with the growing number of LGBTI aging advocates and with LGBTI elders themselves across the globe, I have learned that there are both similarities and differences in the aging experiences they navigate in their countries. Among the significant similarities are high levels of invisibility, isolation, and marginalization of LGBTI elders by society at large, as well as disregard for older people within LGBTI communities and movements themselves. The structures of elder care and services, as well as differences in religious traditions and cultures, are among the prominent differences.

Herein, I outline some of the key challenges faced by LGBTI older adults around the globe. In addition to the factors that are specific to sexual orientation and gender identity, I shine a spotlight on how the experiences of LGBTI older people are shaped (in the negative) by the intersections of their LGBTI identities with other powerful forces like systemic racism and structural ageism. At the same time, our communities' elders demonstrate tremendous resiliencies, and advocates working with and on behalf of LGBTI elders have advanced solutions that are improving lives. The wisdom and spirit behind this elder resiliency and advocacy are generating the outlines of a powerful equity agenda for LGBTI older adults that is starting to build momentum across the globe.

## Challenges

*Social Isolation.* Throughout the world, a common problem voiced by LGBTI elders is social isolation. While this is true to a significant degree for elders in general, data and experience demonstrate that the problem is more severe for LGBTI older adults who navigate lifetimes of discrimination, social marginalization, and family rejection. As a result, LGBTI elders often age alone and with very thin support networks.

Among LGBTI older adults surveyed in the United States, "76 percent report that they have no one they can rely on for care as they age",[5] and almost 33 percent fear aging alone.[6] They are twice as likely to age without a partner and four times less likely to have children. "In the United Kingdom, 50 percent report feeling that they do not belong in their neighborhood and 25 percent report loneliness."[7] Experiences of LGBTI elders in Bolivia and Central America suggest similar dynamics around social isolation, as does anecdotal evidence from other parts of the globe.[8,9]

The isolation of LGBTI older adults is compounded by negative social attitudes among age peers. In surveys conducted around the globe, older respondents are less likely to know LGBTI people and, as a result, have more negative attitudes. For example, in South and Central America, only 34 percent of those over 55 report being comfortable socializing with someone who is LGBTI.[10]

In addition, elder isolation is often exacerbated by ageism within organized LGBTI communities. There is substantial evidence that, at least in the Global North, these communities are often marked by elder invisibility and highly youth-oriented cultures. For example, LGBTI older adults in focus groups in Canada and Sweden report that "safe spaces and communities tend to be youth-focused and that they feel within the LGBT community that they are excluded and discriminated against because of their age."[11] In Bolivia, many LGBTI older adults report that they do not visit the few LGBTI social centers that exist because they do not feel included.[12]

Rejection by birth families because of their identity means that many LGBTI elders lack the kinship support that can shield elders from some of the challenges of aging. Instead, many of these elders have endured lifetimes of poverty and danger as a result of being rejected by their families of origin. An older LGBTI woman in Costa Rica explains:

> I left home at a very young age—like at 12 years old—because of the discrimination I experienced in my family and home, especially from my father. I had to leave my home, my house, and head out to the streets of San José.[13]

Family rejection is not the only reason for thin support networks. The loss of so many LGBTI community members to hate-based violence and

AIDS makes isolation that much more difficult. Elizabeth Coffey-Williams, an older transgender woman living in an LGBTI elder housing development in Philadelphia, shares:

> Most of our peers, most of the. . .people who live in my building, have another level of isolation, . . . [b]ecause an extraordinarily large percentage of their peers, their friends, their chosen family, they died at a young age. So, when you put all of that together, the numbers of available connections are very low.[14]

Closely related to social isolation is the stark problem of invisibility. LGBTI elders are largely ignored in societies across the globe. And they are equally ignored in research studies, statistics, and public policy.

Invisibility often results from an active or passive reluctance to recognize the existence of LGBTI elders. For just one example, elder care workers in El Salvador and other countries report that they are unaware of the *existence* of LGBTI older adults.[15] In most countries, there are no visible signs of LGBTI older adults in social or care settings for elders. Similarly, in many countries where there are organized LGBTI communities, there is little to no visible evidence of the existence of elder community members. This is particularly poignant given that those elders rendered invisible are the pioneers who paved the way for the emergence of the very communities that now erase them.

*Discrimination and Abuse.* Discrimination, harassment, and abuse remain severe problems for LGBTI older adults everywhere, despite improvements in legal protections in some countries. The problem is universal:

- In Costa Rica and El Salvador, LGBTI older adults report "high levels of discrimination and negative attitudes from both residents and staff of long-term care facilities."[16]
- "In Portugal, 51 percent" of LGBTI elders report having experienced "discrimination or harassment within the last 12 months."[17]
- "In Russia, 17 percent" of LGBTI older people report having "experienced violence in the last 12 months and 32 percent had experienced workplace discrimination and/or harassment."[18]
- "In the United States, 63 percent" of LGBTI elders report "experiencing verbal harassment and 30 percent were threatened with violence at some point in their lives.[19] Among older transgender older adults, 75 percent fear that discrimination will reduce their access to health care or housing."[20]

Rates of "discrimination and abuse are even higher" for those at the "intersections" of LGBTI and racial "minority" identities. For example, in a U.S.-based survey of LGBTI older adults "conducted by the American

Association of Retired Persons (AARP), 37 percent of respondents who were black and 25 % who were Latinx responded that they were very concerned about abuse and discrimination in long-term care facilities, as opposed to 19 percent who were white."[21]

"It is worth noting that LGBT research subjects tend to under-report their experiences of discrimination and abuse due to internalized stigma and generational conditioning."[22] As a result, the available statistics in all likelihood severely underestimate the problem.

A significant amount of the discriminatory animus targeting LGBTI elders (and LGBTI people in general) around the world is framed as religious belief. Unfortunately, these attitudes are encouraged by numerous religious institutions and traditions across the globe. While this is changing in some denominations and some religious leaders are more inclusive, anti-LGBTI religious views continue to be widespread and have tremendous force.

*Poverty.* "One result of a lifetime of discrimination and abuse is that" LGBTI older adults often are "in a more precarious financial position" than older adults in general.[23] "For example, in the United Kingdom, there is a negative lifetime pay gap of 16 percent" for LGBTI older people, with 44 percent having less than £10,000 in savings (about $12,000); transgender older adults are even "more likely to be low income or unemployed."[24] "In Bolivia, 43 percent" of LGBTI elders "report an annual income less than or equal to the minimum wage, which already is considered inadequate."[25]

"As a result, around the globe, LGBT people report expecting to work well past the standard retirement age. In Bolivia, the average life expectancy is 69. However, 71 percent of LGBT people interviewed" in a report by the non-profit *Manodiversa* said they expected "to work well into their 60s out of financial necessity."[26] For transgender elders, access to employment, and other social structures, is even more difficult because their appearance and name may contradict those on legal documents. A transgender immigrant to Costa Rica describes her difficulties finding employment, saying, "I decided to look for work again, but I had. . .made my transition. . .and my appearance is totally female, nothing [like my]. . .residence card."[27]

Mitini Nepal, an advocacy and services organization for LBTI women, reports that most of the residents of their temporary housing shelters are LGBTI elders with no savings or social support.[28] Meanwhile, my organization, SAGE, provides services at two innovative residences for low-income LGBTI elders in New York City.[29] Many of the elders who live in SAGE's residences are driven there not only by the desire for a welcoming place to live but also by acute financial need. They have spent their lives struggling to earn a living, often hiding their true selves from coworkers and supervisors. They have little or no savings and often no family to turn to. Deidra Nottingham, an older black lesbian, recounts her experience at the various low-income residences she lived in during the 12 years before she came to SAGE's Stonewall House.

> They did not want gay people there. They always made remarks and cursed at me when I came outside. So, I just couldn't take it, I was afraid that they were going to set my door on fire or something.[30]

*Morbidity.* LGBTI elders also struggle with increased levels of illness. Research in the United Kingdom found that LGBTI elders are 50 percent more likely to report poor health than the general older population in that country.[31] In the United States, LGBTI older adults "report significantly higher levels of illness associated with poverty and age,"[32] such as diabetes, obesity, and asthma. This is particularly true for women and members of racial and ethnic "minorities," who suffer higher rates of these conditions.[33]

At the same time, as we have seen, LGBTI elders face significant barriers to access to healthcare. In many countries, LGBTI older people "report that they must conceal" their sexual orientation and/or gender identity from their healthcare provider or "delay needed health care due to fears of discrimination or poor treatment."[34] In many countries, access to healthcare has become more complicated for LGBTI elders during the COVID-19 pandemic. Shila Gurung is an LGBTI Nepalese man in his 1950s with high blood pressure and other medical concerns. He has trouble managing his health conditions because of the difficulty he has encountered finding welcoming medical providers. When he fell ill, he was unable to find a doctor willing to examine him. When he tried to fill prescriptions, he faced abusive questioning by pharmacists and police because of his appearance.[35]

LGBTI elders in all regions also have more mental health issues, including "high levels of depression and suicidal ideation."[36] "A study of LGBT people in Chile demonstrates that a lifetime of verbal 'wounds' from discrimination, harassment, and verbal abuse leads to a greater incidence of psychiatric disorders, psychological stress, and low self-esteem."[37] "Similarly, in Israel, 38 percent of LGBT people queried reported that a physician had diagnosed them with depression or anxiety; this number is twice as high for older LGBT people."[38]

The barriers to mental health services are high. When Jack Winston's partner died suddenly, he was overwhelmed with grief. He joined a local grief support group for surviving spouses but was the only gay man there. There were no support services available where his particular issues would be understood.

I wish I could be in a group with other gay men. I feel like an outsider in the group I am in because I am the only gay man—I wasn't someone's wife. But I also didn't lose a wife. We just need our own queer supports.[39]

*Lack of Access to Elder Support.* Support systems for elders vary greatly in different parts of the world. In the Global South, these systems often are based on family or religious structures, while in the Global North there tend to be more public and private services and care programs. Regardless of the structure of elder care available, LGBTI elders across the globe often have no access to this support, leaving them vulnerable and isolated, without the care they need.

For example, LGBTI elders face severe challenges in finding welcoming housing as they age—both in countries with established elder housing options and those without. Where elder housing is not an option, the usual recourse of moving in with a family member often is not possible for LGBTI older people, who are rejected by and estranged from their families.

One example illustrates both the opportunities for progress as well as the obstacles. The Home for Golden Gays in the Philippines was established in 1975 by Pasay city councilor Panfilo C. Justo to provide housing and services for poor LGBTI elders. Upon the death of councilor Justo in 2012, his family evicted the residents, many of whom have remained homeless since then.[40]

While many elders worry about being forced to leave their homes, for LGBTI elders this is compounded by fears of moving to a hostile environment where they might well face harassment or even violence. Many LGBTI older adults report that where they feel least safe being openly LGBTI is where they live, because of hostility and harassment from their neighbors. In 2018, Marsha Wetzel sued Glen St. Andrew Living Community for Seniors in suburban Chicago, where she moved after the death of her partner. Wetzel said that soon after she moved in, other tenants began calling her derogatory slurs and physically assaulted her. After she complained to management, they restricted her access to shared spaces.[41]

Lack of access to social services is another barrier to safety, comfort, and independence for LGBTI elders. In much of the world, such services do not exist due to a lack of resources along with cultural beliefs that help should come from family. But even where these services do exist, it is often difficult for LGBTI elders to benefit. In Bolivia, 80 percent of LGBTI elders surveyed stated that they never use elder services.[42] Similarly, in the United States and the United Kingdom, almost three-quarters of LGBTI older adults surveyed report that they do not feel they can use mainstream elder services without concealing their LGBTI identity.[43,44]

## The Role of Structural Ageism

*Roots in Social Structures.* LGBTI older adults live at the intersection of two disadvantaged and marginalized social groups: They are both LGBTI and older. As a result, they battle bias based on their sexual orientation and/or gender identity as well as the scourge of ageism. Ageism is not a problem of attitudes alone, but also of structures that are embedded in society, arguably even more so in highly industrialized countries. The process of industrialization involves moving labor into factories and large production centers as opposed to homes. In these contexts, labor becomes valued for its productive capacity and is treated as a commodity, to be acquired or dismissed by employers. Ageist attitudes create ageist structures when youth and endurance are judged as essential to high productive capacity. Elders are mistakenly seen as a drain on profits, and employers use these misguided considerations to structure their employment decisions and arrangements.

This deep-seated thinking becomes embedded in social and institutional structures. LGBTI older adults are among those who are particularly impacted by these dynamics since they often are seen as less valued or expendable for additional reasons—because of bias based on sexual orientation and/ or gender identity, notions that they don't "fit" in the social environment of the workplace, perceptions that they may cost more to insure or be less reliable as they age because of health disparities, and the like.

In addition, because LGBTI older adults are more likely than older adults in general to be caregivers and to need care, they are more likely to be negatively impacted by structural workplace barriers like the lack of healthcare insurance and paid family and medical leave. Facing the likelihood of discrimination and abuse in elder care facilities, and often lacking family support, LGBTI elders are more likely to rely on friends as caregivers when they need help.[45] Lack of paid leave for caregiving is an example of how structural ageism disparately impacts LGBTI elders. These challenges tend to be even greater for those LGBTI older people who live at the intersections of other identities that are marginalized and disfavored in their home countries—for example, older lesbians; transgender and gender non-binary (TGNB) older adults; and LGBTI older adults from historically marginalized racial, ethnic, and indigenous communities.

*Healthcare.* We also see structural ageism in LGBTI elders' struggles to access culturally competent healthcare. In the Global South, where medical resources are often limited, vaccines, medication, and treatment are often reserved for younger patients, as is the case for COVID-19 treatment and vaccination in India.[46] This presents a greater level of risk to LGBTI older adults, who have higher rates of disease and chronic illness, and often have difficulty obtaining medical care in any event due to negative attitudes and discrimination.

In the Global North, where resources are more plentiful (though often distributed in deeply inequitable ways), it remains the case that elders are often denied treatment. In a landmark study of 9,000 hospitalized patients in the United States, healthcare professionals were significantly more likely to withhold life-sustaining treatments for older people, even after controlling for prognosis and patient preferences.[47] Here again, sexual orientation and gender identity add another level of challenges. Many LGBTI older adults in both the Global North and the Global South are at risk of poor health outcomes due to their inability to find welcoming care. In many countries, most elder care workers are not even aware that they have LGBTI elders in their facilities. In the United States, over a third of LGBTI elders report that their primary health-care provider is unaware of their LGBTI identity.[48]

*Employment.* Ageist employment structures also exclude elders, with LGBTI older adults among those most impacted. In the Global South, there are often no legal protections against age discrimination in employment. At the same time, the pressures of poverty often mean that elders are forced to continue demanding physical labor long after they want to. Here again, LGBTI older adults are disproportionately impacted due to higher rates of poverty and lower financial security. Mandatory retirement rules are another serious structural underpinning of ageism. In many industries, like finance and law, it is common practice for employees to be required to sign contracts stating that they will leave the business once they reach a certain age. In Brazil, job retraining programs are reserved for those deemed of "employable age."[49] Here again, LGBTI older adults and other subpopulations who often are forced for financial reasons to work later in their careers, are particularly impacted by these early retirement requirements.

And ageism pervades hiring practices themselves, where the emphasis on younger workers is well documented. Screening algorithms for online job applications automatically detect and reject older applicants. Older workers often are excluded from training opportunities, challenging assignments, and client meetings. Where they exist, employment advice sites sometimes dedicate whole sections to ways to disguise one's age on a résumé or when talking about previous work experience.

In the Global North, many countries have adopted laws banning age discrimination in employment, but they are uneven in their reach and often go unenforced. Ageist employment structures place a terrible burden on many LGBTI older adults. Forced to work longer in life and at lower wages than the general population, these elders often find that as they age, they are forced into less skilled work, with fewer hours and lower pay. At the end of a lifetime of struggling against discrimination in employment due to their sexual orientation and/or gender identity, they find that their financial survival is compromised further by their age.

*Media, Commerce, and Entertainment.* Structural ageism is apparent in media, commerce, and entertainment. In 112 episodes of U.S. television shows aired between 2004 and 2018, only 6.6 percent included an older adult, an underrepresentation by almost a factor of three. And most of these were "young-old," male, white, able-bodied, and straight.[50] The limited images of LGBTI people in media, including in telenovelas in Mexico, Brazil, and Argentina, are almost always of young people. LGBTI older people are almost completely absent from media images, reinforcing the myth that they don't exist.

Elders who do appear in media too often are stereotypes: the shrew, the wise-cracking but ineffectual grandparent, the "golden oldie," etc. When older people are portrayed in advertising, they are seven times more likely than younger people to be portrayed in denigrating ways.[51] Moreover, in entertainment, the structures of ageism frequently are gendered, as illustrated by the often-discussed plight of older actresses and models.[52] Women often are portrayed with negative stereotypes: angry and withholding or foolish and naïve. Far too often, portrayals of elders in commercials rely on gender stereotypes, with women and men engaging in gendered activities like gardening and cooking for women and carpentry for men. This stereotyping is particularly marginalizing for LGBTI older adults and others who often defy traditional gender norms.

## Driving Toward Solutions

*LGBTI Elder Leadership.* Across the globe, there is growing evidence of a budding movement *with* and on behalf of LGBTI elders. As we note regularly in our work at SAGE, the "with" is key because elders' voices must be in the lead in this struggle. Good work is being done in this area. Organizations like Older Lesbians Organizing for Change (OLOC) in the United States,[53] Alice's Garage in Australia,[54] and *Manodiversa* in Bolivia offer LGBTI elders *themselves* the opportunity to set the agenda and drive their own destiny. In 2021, SAGE and colleagues from Costa Rica, El Salvador, the Philippines, and Nepal launched *LGBTI Elders Advancing*, a multi-year initiative with older adult leadership as a central component. It seeks to expand human rights protections and social and economic inclusion for LGBTI older adults in countries in Latin America and Asia.

Initiatives to lift the leadership of LGBTI elders, and to support elder-instigated skills-building, are of critical importance to building a global movement for change in LGBTI aging in the Global South and Global North. Across the globe, organizations that work with and on behalf of LGBTI elders must constantly interrogate their practices to ensure that they are not elevating the perspectives of young activists and staff members over the vision of elders themselves, and similarly must ensure that professionalized efforts to advance advocacy and other work on behalf of LGBTI elders do not have the ironic effect of marginalizing LGBTI elder activism and leadership.

But there are obstacles to centering LGBTI elder leadership, including high levels of stigma and discrimination resulting in widespread closeting, lack of support for elders within local LGBTI communities, hostility to LGBTI people and elders among older adults in general, and the repression of LGBTI activists of all ages by authoritarian governments and many religious institutions.

In particular, it is critical to support elder leadership from deeply marginalized communities. Marginalized subgroups differ by region and country but generally speaking include ethnic, indigenous, and racial minorities; cultural and religious subgroups; women and gender variant people; and persons with disabilities, among others. While there is still far too little support for the leadership of particularly marginalized LGBTI elders in the Global North, the work of New York City's GRIOT Circle with black and brown elders stands out.[55] In the Global South, interesting movements like the reclaiming of the history of *la China Morena* in Bolivia are emerging. It is urgent to elevate the voices of LGBTI elders living at the margins who battle bias and exclusion on multiple fronts and often are the most disadvantaged, suffer the most violence, and have the fewest resources.

*Public Policy Advocacy.* Lifting the voices and experiences of LGBTI elders is key to building anti-discrimination policies and protections that can allow these older people to participate in public life and benefit from available resources. But advancing this agenda is a struggle. In many countries in the Global South, there are no LGBTI legal protections, although this is certainly not universal. For example, Costa Rica and El Salvador have ratified the LGBT (but not intersex)-inclusive Inter-American Convention on Protecting the Human Rights of Older Persons.[56] South Africa's constitution was the first in the world to bar sexual orientation discrimination. Other countries have followed suit with constitutional guarantees for LGBTI people, including Nepal. But progress is uneven. The United States, for example, has no federal law prohibiting discrimination against LGBTI people. In too many countries, laws designed to protect older adults ignore the existence of LGBTI elders.

Similarly, inclusive best practices need to be inculcated in public and private institutions. This requires training and education but also the development of frameworks for care homes, social services, and public services, among others, that respect and accommodate LGBTI elders and their needs.

Unfortunately, public policy advocacy by and for LGBTI elders is not practical everywhere. Particularly in authoritarian regimes and in countries where conservative religions hold sway over government, there is little foundation or opportunity for LGBTI rights advocacy. In numerous countries, even talking about LGBTI identity is illegal and subject to severe reprisals. In many other countries, the space for such advocacy is only theoretical while constant repression is the reality.

This is one of the reasons why LGBTI elder advocacy must be front and center for key international and regional bodies like the United Nations, the World Health Organization, and the InterAmerican Commission on Human Rights (IACHR). These are among the international entities that have begun to pay attention to LGBTI elder issues. In 2017, the IACHR held its first-ever official hearing on LGBTI aging issues. More recently, for the first time, the concerns and needs of LGBTI elders were highlighted in two reports by the United Nations Independent Expert on the enjoyment of all human rights by older persons.

*Creating LGBTI-Specific Programs.* LGBTI older adults have specific histories, life experiences, and challenges that result in a greater need for services and care. While their need for support is great, far too often these elders are excluded, marginalized, and ignored by elder programs and providers. Recognizing the acute gaps in support, movements are emerging in some countries to create programs and spaces designed specifically for LGBTI elders. Such programs address multiple needs. For example, social programs and LGBTI cultural celebrations create spaces for LGBTI older adults to build social connections and celebrate their collective histories and identities. Group meal programs provide desperately needed nutrition while reducing isolation. Community centers for LGBTI older adults offer a broad array of programs and support. LGBTI-friendly elder housing communities provide a home and shelter in welcoming and affirming environments. Intergenerational programs bring together older and younger LGBTI people for mutual support.

Recognizing that even within specific countries LGBTI elders are not a homogeneous population, programs designed for subpopulations with like experiences and needs are important. In the United States, for example, SAGE and other organizations offer programs specifically for older lesbian and bisexual women, transgender elders, and LGBTI elder veterans.

Organizations like GRIOT Circle focus specifically on LGBTI elders of color. In Bolivia, *Manodiversa* has organized programs for rural and bisexual elders.

*Training and Capacity Building.* In many parts of the world, services and support for elders are mainly provided by the private realm—families, religious institutions, and in some cases secular organizations and charities. There have been early initiatives in various regions focused on developing LGBTI-inclusive best practices. Notable examples of cultural competency training and best practices include the work of SAGE's National Resource Center on LGBTQ Aging in the United States and similar work undertaken in Costa Rica, Panama, and other countries.

Best practices must be communicated by rigorous staff and volunteer training, as in many parts of the world, cultural competence requires overcoming ingrained attitudes and hostility. This kind of culture-change work can be supported by credentialing programs such as *Rainbow Tick* in Australia and *SAGECare* in the United States for elder care and service providers that commit to LGBTQ cultural competency training and standards.[57,58]

While training is a good start, it is not enough. Agency-wide practices need to be overhauled so that every aspect of the provider's work is LGBTI-inclusive. And special programs and activities can be provided within provider settings to both ensure that LGBTI needs are being met and that a message of inclusion is consistently delivered.

*Partnerships.* Successful advocacy for the interests of LGBTI elders depends on strong partnerships. These can take many forms: from better-resourced groups in the Global North working alongside those with fewer resources in the Global South; to those closer to the seats of power redistributing resources and influence to those who are most marginalized and living at the intersections; to mutually respectful collaborations involving LGBTI elders and allies of different ages; and many other collaborative permutations. An exciting example is the *LGBTI Elders Advancing Project*, an ambitious collaboration and campaign coordinated by SAGE that includes key roles for the Center for Research and Promotion of Human Rights for Central America (CIPAC) of Costa Rica, Outright Action International, *Asociación Aspidh Arcoiris Trans* (the Aspidh Rainbow Trans Association) of El Salvador,[59] Mitini of Nepal,[60] and EnGendeRights of the Philippines.[61] This multi-year effort seeks to catalyze LGBTI elder leadership, advocacy, and capacity-building in Central America and South Asia, with the goal of expanding impact wider and deeper in both regions.

Intergenerational partnerships, bringing youth and elders together, can be particularly valuable for LGBTI communities. Collaborations across generations can reduce isolation at both ends of the LGBTI age spectrum, solve practical problems (e.g., younger people's need for mentorship and older people's need to be connected and contribute), allow mutual sharing and the communication of experience across generations, and so much more. Intergenerational ties can foster positive identity development and reduce latent ageism within LGBTI communities.

*Enhanced Research*. A major obstacle to addressing the structural oppression of LGBTI older adults is the lack of research on LGBTI aging experiences. Without hard information, advocates are left with anecdotal reports which, while compelling and accurate, have less impact on policymakers. In most regions, government and academic institutions are largely responsible for conducting health and aging research. To date, little attention has been given to LGBTI elders in these research efforts. While there has been a slow accumulation of research studies on LGBTI issues in some (predominantly Global North) countries in recent years, older adults are rarely included.

A primary need is to document discrimination and abuse targeting LGBTI elders around the world. In many countries, even violence is unreported, due to fears of retribution or the danger of visibility. But research needs to extend beyond extreme and life-threatening circumstances to include specific information on LGBTI elders' interactions with legal, institutional, and care-delivery structures, including in less-studied parts of the world (recognizing that there is no place in the world where LGBTI elders are properly represented in relevant research). In one positive sign of progress, the Williams Institute at the University of California Los Angeles (UCLA) is joining with SAGE to spur and support LGBTI aging research in Global South countries through a new program of mini-grants and cross-learning among researchers.

Among other things, there needs to be investment in developing and implementing innovative research methods designed to reach LGBTI older adults. Standard social science research methodologies, such as surveys and interviews at public locations, often will not reach LGBTI elders who are not, and do not feel, safe in most settings being open about their experiences. Just as attention is being paid to developing methods to reach people who lack literacy or technological skills, there needs to be funding and attention to reaching LGBTI older people in compromised settings. This innovation in research will only succeed if it is informed by LGBTI elders themselves.

## Conclusion

I have explored the unique challenges LGBTI elders face, the structures that exacerbate those challenges, and the solutions that are emerging.

Recognizing that circumstances are deeply distinctive in different regions and countries, and for different social identities, I nonetheless highlight some of the overarching trends and themes that are apparent. Focusing on challenges like severe isolation, marginalization, discrimination and abuse, and economic and health insecurity illustrates the depths of the challenges. At the same time, LGBTI older people across the globe are resilient and proud. They have overcome personal adversity, fought for equity and equality, and founded movements of self-help and political advocacy. In many contexts and in many surprising ways, LGBTI elders continually declare that "we refuse to be invisible." It is this spirit of resilience and determination that animates the solutions—often driven by LGBTI elders themselves—that are gradually emerging.

The struggle for basic rights and a better life for LGBTI elders is a cross-border struggle. It occurs at the individual and group level, within communities and countries, across national borders, through partnerships and multinational projects—in every way we know change to be possible. It also occurs across intersectional identities and life experiences. This multi-dimensional push for progress by and for LGBTI elders reflects the foundational principle that *all* elders deserve a life of dignity, respect, and support, and that sexual orientation and gender-identity experience should not keep *any* elder from healthy aging. This is the world of aging that we can, and *must*, build together.

## Notes

1 Mitini Nepal. "The Situation of LGBTI Elders in Nepal." 3:47. March 2, 2022. https://www.facebook.com/watch/?v=938678813508030.

2 Cleveland, Claire. "For One Colorado Trans Woman, Long-Term Care Was Her Only Option for Housing – but Getting in was an Eight-Month Struggle." CPR News. October 26, 2021. https://www.cpr.org/2021/10/26/for-one-colorado-lgbtq-woman-long-term-care-was-her-only-option-for-housing-but-getting-in-was-an-eight-month-struggle/.

3 United Nations Department of Economic and Social Affairs, Population Division. "World Population Prospects 2022: Summary of Results." UN DESA/POP/2022/TR/NO. 3.

4 Adams, Michael. "Submission to United Nations Independent Expert on the Human Rights of Older Persons." 2021. https://www.ohchr.org/sites/default/files/Documents/Issues/OlderPersons/AgeismAgeDiscrimination/Submissions/NGOs/SAGE.pdf.

5 Houghton, Angela. "Maintaining Dignity: Understanding and Responding to the Challenges Facing Older LGBT Americans." A.A.R.P. Research. 2018. 32. Cited in Adams, "Submission."

6  Espinoza, Robert. *Out & Visible: The Experiences and Attitudes of Lesbian, Gay, Bisexual and Transgender Older Adults, Ages 45–75.* New York, NY: SAGE, 2014, 8.
7  LGBT Foundation. "Housing, Ageing + Care. 2020. 5. Cited in Adams, "Submission."
8  Manodiversa Asociación Civil. *Conociendo las necesidades y vivencias de las personas adultas mayores de diversa orientación sexual e identitad de género en el Estado Plurinacional de Bolivia [Knowing the Needs and Experiences of Older Adults of Diverse Sexual Orientation and Gender Identity in the Plurinational State of Bolivia].* Santa Cruz de la Sierra, Bolivia: Manodiversa, 2014.
9  Centro De Investigación y Promoción Para América Central de Derechos Humanos (CIPAC). *Situación de población adulta mayor LGBT en Costa Rica, El Salvador y Panamá [Situation of the Older LGBT Population in Costa Rica, El Salvador, and Panama].* San José, Costa Rica: CIPAC, 2015.
10  SAGE. "SAGE Global Report 2018: Public Attitudes Toward Aging Sexual and Gender Minorities Around the World." 2018. 4–7.
11  Siverskog, Anna and Janne Bromseth. "Subcultural Spaces: LGBTQ Aging in a Swedish Context." *The International Journal of Aging and Human Development* 88, no. 4 (2019): 334. https://doi.org/10.1177/0091415019836923. Cited in Adams, "Submission."
12  Manodiversa Asociación Civil, *Conociendo las necesidades*, 52.
13  CIPAC, *Situación de Población Adulta Mayor*, 10.
14  Sosin, Kate. "A Year into the Pandemic, LGBTQ+ Life and Death Remains Largely Invisible." *The 19ᵗʰ.* March 12, 2021. https://19thnews.org/2021/03/a-year-into-the-pandemic-lgbtq-life-and-death-remains-largely-invisible/.
15  CIPAC, *Situación de Población Adulta Mayor*, 59.
16  CIPAC, *Situación de Población Adulta Mayor.* Cited in Adams, "Submission."
17  Pereira, Henrique, Brian de Vries, Antonio Serzedelo, Juan Pedro Serrano, Rosa Marina Afonso, Graça Esgalhado, and Samuel Monteiro. "Growing Older Out of the Closet: A Descriptive Study of Older LGB Persons Living in Lisbon, Portugal." *The International Journal of Aging and Human Development* 88, no. 4 (2019): 423. https:doi.org/10.1177/0091415019836107. Cited in Adams, "Submission."
18  Equal Rights Trust. "Права на Равенство и Дискриминации в России [Rights to Equality and Discrimination in Russia]." 2017. 1. Cited in Adams, "Submission."
19  Choi, Soon Kyu and Ilan H. Meyer. "LGBT Aging: A Review of Research Findings, Needs, and Policy Implications." The William Institute of the UCLA School of Law. 2016. 16.
20  AARP Research. "Caregiving in the U.S." 2014. 10. Cited in Adams, "Submission."
21  Houghton, "Maintaining Dignity," 32. Cited in Adams, "Submission."
22  Adams, "Submission."
23  Choi and Meyer, "LGBT Aging," 9. Cited in Adams, "Submission."
24  LGBT Foundation, "Housing, Ageing + Care," 9. Cited in Adams, "Submission."
25  Manodiversa Asociación Civil, *Conociendo las necesidades*, 61. Cited in Adams, "Submission."
26  Manodiversa Asociación Civil, *Conociendo las necesidades*, 34. Cited in Adams, "Submission."
27  CIPAC, *Situación de Población Adulta*, 17.

28  Outright Action International. "Age and Age Discrimination." Submission to United Nations Independent Expert on the Human Rights of Older Persons. 2021. 7.

29  "Housing". SAGE. Accessed January 7, 2023. https://www.sageusa.org/news_c ategory/housing/

30  Feliciano, Ivette. "LGBTQ Seniors Fear Discrimination When Searching for Housing." *PBS*. October 10, 2021. https://www.pbs.org/newshour/show/lgbtq-seniors-fear-discrimination-when-searching-for-housing.

31  LGBT Foundation, "Housing, Ageing + Care," 5.

32  Adams, "Submission."

33  Choi and Meyer, "LGBT Aging," 24.

34  Adams, "Submission."

35  Mitini Nepal. "Together: Resisting, Supporting, Healing!"2021. 18–19.

36  Adams, "Submission."

37  Barrientos, Jaime and Manuel Cárdenas. "Homofobia y calidad de vida de gays y lesbianas: Una Mirada Psicosocial [Homophobia and Quality of Life of Gays and Lesbians: A Psychosocial Perspective]." *Psykhe (Santiago)* 22, no. 1 (2013): 3–14. https://doi.org/10.7764/psykhe.22.1.553. Cited in Adams, "Submission."

38  Shnoor, Yitschack and Ayelet Berg-Warman., "Needs of the Aging LGBT Community in Israel." *The International Journal of Aging and Human Development* 89, no. 1 (2019): 84. https://doi.org/10.1177/0091415019844452. Cited in Adams, "Submission."

39  Brownworth, Victoria A. "Care Crisis for LGBT Elders." *Philadelphia Gay News* November 15, 2019. https://epgn.com/2019/11/15/care-crisis-for-lgbt-elders/.

40  International Lesbian, Gay, Bisexual, Trans and Intersex Association Women's Steering Committee. "The Human Rights of Lesbian, Bisexual, Trans and Intersex Older Women." ILGA. 2021. 15.

41  "Wetzel v. Glen St. Andrew Living Community." Lambda Legal. Accessed April 29, 2022. https://www.lambdalegal.org/in-court/cases/il_wetzel-v-glen-st-andrew.

42  Manodiversa Asociación Civil, *Conociendo las necesidades*, 53–4.

43  Houghton, "Maintaining Dignity," 12.

44  LGBT Foundation, "Housing, Ageing + Care," 7.

45  AARP, "Caregiving in the U.S."

46  Lloyd-Sherlock, Peter, Gideon Lasco, Martin McKee, Arokiasamy Perianayagam, and Lucan Sempé. "Does Vaccine Ageism Amount to Gerontocide?" *The Lancet* 398, no. 10304 (2021): 952–3. https://doi.org/10.1016/S0140-6736(21)01689-5.

47  Inouye, Sharon K. "Creating an Anti-Ageist Healthcare System to Improve Care for Our Current and Future Selves." *Nature Aging* 1 (2021): 150–152. https://doi.org/10.1038/s43587-020-00004-4.

48  Espinoza, *Out & Visible*, 14.

49  Goldani, Ana Maria. "The Challenges of Ageism in Brazil" *Education Society* 31, no. 111 (2010): 411–434. https://doi.org/10.1590/S0101-73302010000200007.

50  Markov, Čedomir and Youngmin Yoon. "Diversity and Age Stereotypes in Portrayals of Older Adults in Popular American Prime Time Television Series." *Aging and Society* 41 (2020): 12. https://www.cambridge.org/core/journals/ageing-and-society/article/abs/diversity-and-age-stereotypes-in-portrayals-of-older-adults-in-popular-american-primetime-television-series/46F3951791C966A8231E9C605FB48299.

51 Dychtwald, Ken and Robert Morison. "How Ads Do a Terrible Job Portraying Older Adults." *Forbes*, July 15, 2020. https://www.forbes.com/sites/nextave nue/2020/07/15/how-ads-do-a-terrible-job-portraying-older-adults/?sh=5e9f7 6025c13.

52 Garelick, Rhonda. "The Cruel Paradox of Linda Evangelista's Fate." *The New York Times*. October 16, 2021. https://www.nytimes.com/2021/10/16/fashion/ linda-evangelista-cool-sculpting-lawsuit.html.

53 Old Lesbians Organizing for Change (OLOC). "Join Us." Accessed January 7, 2023. https://oloc.org/.

54 Alice's Garage. "Our Projects." Accessed January 7, 2023. https://alicesgarage.net/.

55 GRIOT Circle. "About." Accessed January 7, 2023. https://griotcircle.org.

56 Organization of American States. "Inter-American Convention on Protecting the Human Rights of Older Persons" art. 70. Accessed January 7, 2023. https:// www.oas.org/en/sla/dil/inter_american_treaties_A-70_human_rights_older_pers ons.asp.

57 Rainbow Tick Australia. "What is it?" Accessed January 7, 2023. https://rainbow healthaustralia.org.au/rainbow-tick.

58 SAGE. "What We Do." Accessed January 7, 2023. https://www.sageusa.org/ what-we-do/sagecare/.

59 ASPIDH Arcoiris Trans. "ASPIDH." Accessed January 7, 2023. https://aspid hsv.org/.

60 Mitini Nepal. "Women Led NGO for LBT Rights and Dignity. "Accessed January 7, 2023. https://mitininepal.org.np.

61 EnGendeRights. "About." Accessed January 7, 2023. https://engenderights.wordpr ess.com/about/.

# 5. The Intersection Between Old Age and Disability

MARÍA SOLEDAD CISTERNAS REYES

## Introduction

According to current estimates, there are approximately 1 billion older persons in the world today, the equivalent of 15 percent of the global population, and it is estimated that by 2050 they will make up 22 percent of the total.[1] It is important to note that in these estimates, an *older person* is considered someone aged 60 or over. Not all older persons are disabled. Another 1 billion people are currently living with one or more disabilities. More than 250 million older persons, one-quarter of the total, experience moderate to serious disability.[2]

Old age has been defined as a "social construct of the last stage of the life course."[3] We know that today's society is undergoing an advanced demographic transition toward an increasingly larger population of older persons because life expectancy is being extended.

Some older persons see their physical mobility, or sensory or cognitive acuity, affected over time. Nevertheless, this must be considered on a case-by-case basis. Some older persons continue to enjoy good physical, sensory, intellectual, and mental conditions. *Being an older person does not mean being a person with a disability.* Some older persons may experience disability at some point in their lives, but it is not a correlative or equivalent identification.

Clearly, in some segments of life, there may be a space where the rights holders who are older persons and those who are people with disabilities converge, although this must be observed person by person. The application of scientific or legal rules does not apply here. I observe here this situation, highlighting the applicable legal standards, since the population of older persons is heterogeneous and only a certain percentage of it may have a disability, at which time it is necessary to discern which is the applicable standard, paying special attention to cases of older persons with disabilities in a situation of dependency.

## Stereotypes and Prejudices: Ageism

The role of culture in how ageing is experienced and given meaning is essential to shaping societal identity. If the social experience features stereotypes and prejudices linked to ageing, they will negatively influence how the social environment interacts with this reality, particularly in human beings who reach old age.

Butler describes *ageism* as the set of negative, socially stereotyped attitudes and prejudices held by the population to the detriment of old age, and of older persons simply for being older.[4] How can there be such a wide gap between certain social visions and their counterpart in reality? Butler answers this question by pointing out that these stereotypes, prejudices, and forms of discrimination are related to a rejection of ageing, due to a fear of it.[5]

Since the stereotype and prejudice are to consider the older person as a small child, there is a tendency to discourage their decision-making in a personal and direct manner, losing sight of the essence of what it is to be human and creating a strong basis of discrimination due to limiting the expression of their desires and preferences. In this context, ageism would encourage the use of different therapeutic guidelines with older persons, solely because of their age.[6] A significant number of older persons have social and affective networks and are not depressed[7]; therefore, the correlation between depression and old age is just a myth.[8] Sometimes a medical team's decision to discontinue a treatment is documented as having been taken because the person is older, without consulting their opinion.[9]

As can be seen, older adulthood involves various factors leading to impoverishment, which generates other forms of multiple and intersectional discrimination if they are combined with such conditions as gender, indigenous origin, disability, rurality, and humanitarian emergencies.

Furthermore, sometimes the older person is placed in legal or illegal long-stay nursing homes without consulting their opinion. Many of these nursing homes are not duly regulated, which leads to the serious risk that the older person will not be well-fed or cared for. Cases have been recorded in which the long-term facility becomes *just another business*, without consideration for the ethical conditions of providing care to older persons.

For example, there are cases in which the older person in a situation of dependency is left lying down all day, without any access to sunlight. If the person cannot report this form of abuse, their lack of mobility can cause bedsores and poor living conditions. Possibly no one ever talks to the older person, and they are never taken to an outdoor space. Furthermore, in some of these places, a common or community system is used for clothing and other items, leaving no space for personal property. This is very hard for older persons, especially those in a situation of dependency, when they have been independent in their previous lives. If they complain about any situation, they are labelled as "conflictive." Sometimes, these establishments do not care about maintaining their installations in good condition.[10] There are also cases of lack of training for staff to provide good care for older residents.

Clearly, the contextual factors surrounding an older person have their own specificity. Analytical investigation uncovers situations of discrimination, negligence, violence, and abuse involving older persons at different levels, be they familial, institutional, or of any other kind, which also results in structural violations of older persons' rights. This leads us to ask ourselves whether it is necessary to address these situations from a legal perspective, also considering the necessary awareness-raising on the part of society and state authorities.

Today, it is essential to talk about palliative care for older persons facing situations of pain or a terminal diagnosis. The denial of palliative care is undoubtedly another form of structural abuse.

## *What Is Happening in the Normative Framework?*

At the multilateral level, the United Nations General Assembly, in response to the follow-up to the Second World Assembly on Ageing, established the Open-Ended Working Group on Ageing, with the aim of increasing the protection of the human rights of older persons by examining the current international framework on the issue, determining its possible deficiencies, as well as the best ways to correct them.[11]

The United Nations Human Rights Council recognized the problems related to the exercise of human rights by older persons in such areas as prevention of and protection against violence and mistreatment, social protection, food and housing, employment, legal capacity, access to justice, healthcare, or the need for long-term care and palliative care, for which it urged all States to provide the full exercise and equal conditions of all human rights and fundamental freedoms of older persons.[12]

The General Assembly requested that the Open-Ended Working Group on Ageing initiate, beginning at its fourth session in 2013, the examination of proposals for an international legal instrument to promote and protect the rights and dignity of older persons, presenting as soon as possible a proposal containing, among other things, the main elements that an international legal instrument should include to promote and protect the rights and dignity of older persons, which were not sufficiently contemplated in the then existing mechanisms and therefore they required greater international protection.[13] There have been 12 sessions of the United Nations Open-Ended Working Group on Ageing, where the specific exercise of civil, political, social, economic, and cultural rights has been discussed, but there has not yet been significant progress to develop a global instrument on the rights of older persons.

Currently, the only normative standard at the international level has a regional scope: the Inter-American Convention on Protecting the Human Rights of Older Persons (hereinafter "the Inter-American Convention" or "the Convention"), whose purpose is to promote, protect, and ensure the recognition and full enjoyment and exercise, on an equal basis, of all human rights and fundamental freedoms of older persons, to contribute to their full inclusion, integration, and participation in society.[14] The Convention defines an *older person* as someone aged 60 or older, except where legislation has determined a minimum age that is lower or higher, provided that it is not more than 65 years.[15]

Therefore, the Inter-American Convention is a normative reference that we can bear in mind for analytical purposes, even though it is only valid for the Region of the Americas.

This Convention poses interesting legal challenges, including independence and autonomy,[16] participation and community integration,[17] long-term care services,[18] and palliative care.[19]

*Being an older person does not mean being a person with a disability, and therefore they are not equivalent terms.* The previous statement notwithstanding, because at some point in their lives, they may have a disability, from that point on the United Nations Convention on the Rights of Persons with Disabilities (CRPD) may apply to older persons.

The CRPD is the first international human rights treaty of the twenty-first century. It describes discrimination on the basis of disability as any distinction, exclusion, or restriction which has the purpose or effect of impairing or nullifying the recognition, enjoyment, or exercise, under equal conditions, of all human rights and fundamental freedoms in the political, economic, social, cultural, civil, or other spheres. It includes all forms of discrimination, including the denial of reasonable accommodation.[20]

Based on equality and non-discrimination, the CRPD has addressed in specific articles certain sectors of the population with disabilities that are doubly invisible and underprotected, as is the case of women with disabilities[21] and children with disabilities.[22] However, there is an innovation in mentioning "age" generically in some articles of the CRPD, such as awareness-raising,[23] access to justice,[24] and freedom from exploitation, violence, and abuse.[25]

Although the generic wording on age can apply to older persons with disabilities, this is often unclear, mainly because of the high profile of the Convention on the Rights of the Child and all the work around it means that any reference to age is generally understood to mean this population.

The CRPD is also the first treaty in the international system that mentions two specific aspects regarding older persons with a disability: the *right to health*, in relation to "prevention to avoid the appearance of further disabilities,"[26] and the *right to an adequate standard of living and social protection,* in terms of the application of social protection programmes and poverty reduction strategies.[27] In these provisions, it is clearly recognized that there may be older persons with disabilities, which implies that there is another segment of *older persons without disabilities.*

From another angle, ageing produces new legal challenges that must be incorporated into the laws, such as active ageing, positive ageing, palliative care, and intergenerational culture.

An example of the impact that a treaty has on human rights with respect to their holders is reflected in the CRPD, which has made it possible to make the subject of law visible in all areas, catalyzing the greater enjoyment of human rights and fundamental freedoms for this segment of the population and its clear presence in sustainable development, which includes the segment of older persons with disabilities.

## *The Triple Dimension*

Evidently, many older persons are independent and fully exercise their autonomy, will, and preferences and anonymously carry on with their lives. Each reader can remember family members who, as an older person, performed important tasks in the context of the home and the extended family. At the same time, some older persons have played a prominent role on the world stage, for example, Tu Youyou, a Chinese pharmaceutical scientist and physician, who received the 2015 Nobel Prize in Medicine at age 85; Bilkis Dadi, an Indian activist on issues of religious minorities and freedom of conscience, who at age 83 was recognized by the BBC and by *Time* magazine among the 100 most influential and inspiring people in the world in 2020, and as 'Woman of the Year 2020' by *The Muslim 500*; Betty Reardon, the American founder of the International Institute on Peace Education, who at 92 continues to publish and give interviews and lectures; and Nelson Mandela of South Africa, who was 81 when his presidential term ended and at 89 announced the creation of The Elders, an international non-governmental organization (NGO) formed by a group of well-known global leaders and defenders of peace and human rights. Also noteworthy are religious leaders including the Dalai Lama, an 87-year-old Tibetan, and Pope Francis, an 86-year-old Argentine.

The Inter-American Convention defines *ageing* as "a gradual process that develops over the course of life and entails biological, physiological, psycho-social and functional changes with varying consequences, which are associated with permanent and dynamic interactions between the individual and their environment."[28] It is a natural process in the human life course and does not in itself imply a disability. Furthermore, today we speak of *active and healthy ageing*, which the Convention calls:

> The process of optimizing opportunities for physical, mental and social well-being, participation in social, economic, cultural, spiritual and civic affairs, and protection, security and care in order to extend healthy life expectancy and quality of life for all people as they age, as well as to allow them to remain active contributors to their families, peers, communities and nations.[29]

Even when older persons lead an active life, they are in various situations affected by what the Convention calls "age discrimination in old age", which it conceptualizes as:

> Any distinction, exclusion, or restriction based on age, the purpose or effect of which is to annul or restrict recognition, enjoyment, or exercise, on an equal basis, of human rights and fundamental freedoms in the political, cultural, economic, social, or any other sphere of public and private life.[30]

Hence the innumerable cases of inability to access education or work, among others.

It is very clear to us that older persons are rights holders, and the concept of a person with a disability refers to another subject of law. What can exist and does exist is an area of intersection between older persons and persons with disabilities, in the same way that there can be an intersection between children and disability.

Persons with disabilities, under the CRPD, "include those who have long-term physical, mental, intellectual, or sensory impairments which in interaction with various barriers may hinder their full and effective participation in society on an equal basis with others."[31]

When an older person experiences disability, they undoubtedly have a broad possibility of experiencing *multiple discrimination*, defined in the Inter-American Convention as "any distinction, exclusion, or restriction toward an older person, based on two or more discrimination factors."[32] This is an aspect of "splitting hairs" in human rights since an older person with a disability can also express their desires and preferences autonomously. This was the case with Stephen Hawking, who passed away at the age of 76. He used a voice synthesizer to communicate, despite having quadriplegia and being unable to speak. However, the case of this theoretical physicist is an exception because he had access to the latest technology and a life environment conducive to the empowerment of his knowledge and being.

In general, older persons with disabilities in a situation of dependency will be more exposed to *negligence*, which the Inter-American Convention calls:

> Involuntary error or unintentional fault, including, inter alia, neglect, omission, abandonment and failure to protect, that causes harm or suffering to an older person, in either the public or the private sphere, in which normal necessary precautions proportional to the circumstances have not been taken.[33]

They may even be more exposed to *abuse*, defined under the Convention as:

> A single or repeated act or omission to the detriment of an older person that harms their physical, mental, or moral integrity and infringes the enjoyment or exercise of their human rights and fundamental freedoms, regardless of whether or not it occurs in a relationship of trust.[34]

Similarly, the person is more exposed to *abandonment*, which is a "lack of action, deliberate or not, to comprehensively care for an older person's needs, which may jeopardize their life or physical, psychological, or moral integrity."[35]

This neglect of an older person in a situation of dependency can occur in their own family environment or home, or in long-term nursing homes that are not supervised by the authorities, especially when they are clandestine.

Therefore, when we talk about the *triple dimension*, we are first referring to the universe of older persons who are in a stage when they do not have disabilities and can fully develop their lives. A second stage is that of older persons who, although they have disabilities, are not in a situation of dependency, especially if they can express their desires and preferences as well as have personal mobility. A third stage is that of older persons with disabilities in a situation of dependency. Undoubtedly, these last two categories of older persons can experience multiple discrimination, which can be aggravated in the cases of older persons with disabilities in a situation of dependency.

## *Personal Care and Assistance*

Older persons with disabilities in a situation of dependency need to be provided with personal assistance that always respects their autonomy, will, and preferences, considering their well-being, proper treatment, and physical, economic and social security, strengthening family and community protection.[36]

Addressing the rights of caregivers, with a gender approach, is a contingent issue. For example, the Inter-American Commission of Women (Comisión Interamericana de Mujeres, or CIM) correctly emphasizes this aspect:

> Caregiving is at the centre of daily life and is indispensable for well-being; however, as it has historically and for the most part fallen to women, it is not recognized socially, economically or politically. . . . The lack of caregiving policies or actions by the State, businesses, and the community, and the absence of co-responsibility between men and women, constitute the main obstacles to women's equal participation in all spheres.[37]

In principle, it could appear that there is an antagonism between the rights of the older person with a disability in a situation of dependency, in terms of *personal assistance*, and of the rights of caregivers. However, we are proposing a complementary approach that must give due protection to two different rights holders: the person with a disability in a situation of dependency, and the caregivers. There is a common element between the two, which is personalized support service or personal assistance: one person receives it, and another person gives it. But this common action must always be carried out considering the dignity of the older person with a disability in a situation of dependency, as well as their human rights and fundamental freedoms. Along these same lines, as the CIM points out, "Caregiving should therefore be a right, and its protection and promotion a responsibility of the State."[38]

In the case of older persons with a disability in a situation of dependency, the CRPD becomes fully applicable by noting that persons with disabilities should have access to "a range of in-home, residential and other community support services, including personal assistance necessary to support living and inclusion in the community, and to prevent isolation or segregation from the community."[39] This provision falls within the framework of Member States' obligation to recognize the right of persons with disabilities to an independent life and to be included in the community, adopting all the necessary measures for this purpose.

For its part, the Inter-American Convention on Protecting the Human Rights of Older Persons expressly refers to long-term care services, focusing on the right of the older person to receive that care:

> Older persons have the right to a comprehensive system of care that protects and promotes their health, provides social services coverage, food and nutrition security, water, clothing and housing, and promotes the ability of older persons to stay in their own home and maintain their independence and autonomy, should they so decide.[40]

This regional standard takes the viewpoint of the older person in a situation of dependency.[41]

The Inter-American Convention also places the obligation of personal care on the State, which must design assistance measures for families and caregivers through the introduction of services for those providing care to older persons.[42]

Consequently, under the Convention, the State must develop a comprehensive personalized support service, commonly called a care service, "that takes particular account of a gender perspective and respect for the dignity, physical and mental integrity of older persons."[43] This obligation of the State is further described in the Convention, indicating the basic aspects that must be considered. For example, developing a service with trained staff that always respects the autonomy, will, and preferences of the older person; having a regulatory framework that enables evaluation and supervision; enacting the necessary legislation so that the managers and staff of long-term care services are administratively, civilly, and criminally liable for acts they commit to the detriment of older persons; and adopting appropriate measures so that older persons have access to palliative care services.[44]

For all older persons, and especially for older persons with disabilities, regardless of whether they are in a situation of dependency, there are two factors of great importance for the development of their lives: the recognition of their legal capacity, and universal accessibility.

The State has the obligation to provide older persons with disabilities with decision-making support in the exercise of their legal capacity, applying adequate and effective safeguards to prevent abuse, in accordance with international human rights law. Under the CRPD, such safeguards shall ensure that measures relating to the exercise of legal capacity respect the rights, will and preferences of the person, are free of conflict of interest and undue influence, are proportional and tailored to the person's circumstances, apply for the shortest time possible and are subject to regular review by a competent, independent and impartial authority or judicial body. The safeguards shall be proportional to the degree to which such measures affect the person's rights and interests.[45]

This new paradigm recognized in the CRPD produced a transcendental legal change since the *substitute will* model, which implies a judicial declaration of interdiction and appointment of a guardian, is replaced by the model of *will with support (or supported decision-making)*. This aspect also concerns older persons with certain disabilities, especially cognitive disabilities, which is why the new paradigm is fully reproduced in the Inter-American Convention. All of this presents a major challenge for States, in terms of making legal amendments in accordance with the new model.

Another legal innovation of the CRPD is *accessibility*, which is addressed in general terms by establishing the obligation of States Parties to:

> Take appropriate measures to ensure to persons with disabilities access, on an equal basis with others, to the physical environment, to transportation, to information and communications, including information and communications technologies and systems, and to other facilities and services open or provided to the public, both in urban and in rural areas.[46]

The Inter-American Convention also integrated the concept of accessibility in its provisions, enabling rights holder to demand it.[47]

A pertinent issue here is that when the general conditions of accessibility do not satisfy the needs or requirements of a person with a disability, reasonable accommodation must be applied in the individual case, meaning the:

> Necessary and appropriate modification and adjustments not imposing a disproportionate or undue burden, where needed in a particular case, to ensure to persons with disabilities the enjoyment or exercise on an equal basis with others of all human rights and fundamental freedoms.[48]

It is a right for the person, and its denial implies discrimination.[49] Therefore, legal capacity and accessibility must go hand in hand to ensure that older persons, with and without disabilities, are able to fully exercise their human rights and fundamental freedoms.

## Final Comment on Ageing and ICD-11

The International Classification of Diseases (ICD) is a tool that the World Health Organization (WHO) has maintained since 1948, with a coding system to enable the recording, analysis, interpretation, and comparison of data on mortality and morbidity compiled in different countries and regions around the world.[50] Likewise, ICD has become a diagnostic standard, as well as a way of classifying registered data under such categories as "Cause of Death," "Reason for Admission," "Conditions Treated," and "Reason for Consultation."

The latest revision of this study, called ICD-11, has generated confusion and discontent in the general public, civil society organizations for older persons, and the academic community, as well as rejection at the international level. This is because ICD-11 addresses the ageing process in the "General Symptoms" section, and in the "Initial and Final Geriatric Periods," which implies a medicalized approach to old age.[51]

As mentioned, the ICD is used by health professionals to diagnose and determine diseases, and WHO has stated its intention to include old age in ICD-11, which came into effect in January 2022.

What would be the reason for incorporating old age into ICD-11? This would be related to physicians' role in certifying deaths: In a significant number of cases, they fill in "old age" as the cause of death for older persons. This justification can only cause a negative impression of the actions of these health professionals, who instead of identifying the real reason for an older person's death, simply write down "old age." If the situation continues to occur in some parts of the world, then what must be done is to correct such bad practices.

In view of this, it is pertinent to mention how contradictory it was for WHO to accept the idea of old age as a disease, since its plan for the Decade of Healthy Ageing 2020–2030 states that it "will be based on the human rights approach, which addresses the universality, inalienability and indivisibility of the human rights to which everyone is entitled, without distinction of any kind."[52] In addition, this document, published in 2020, emphasizes its commitment to the guiding principles of the 2030 Agenda for Sustainable Development, as well as those principles that inspire the global strategy to fight age-based discrimination, including those of the Inter-American Convention.

The Inter-American Convention reaffirms in its preamble the importance of eliminating all forms of discrimination based on age, emphasizing that older persons have the same human rights and fundamental freedoms as others. Therefore, it is necessary to understand that, like childhood and adulthood, old age is a vital, natural, and non-pathological stage that is part of the human life course. Everyone ages differently, which ultimately raises the need to recognize that this process cannot be reduced to its purely biological nature and treated as a synonym for disease.

Although it is true that as we age there is a higher risk and probability of contracting diseases or having accidents and disability, it is no less true that part of the population belonging to the older persons group continues to be active, independent and, as defined by WHO itself, healthy. We can clearly see in this regard that ICD-11 marked a setback in the vision and appreciation of older persons; no interpretative effort will be enough to obscure what is already written in that document.

Today, the various international, governmental, and local authorities, among others, must promote the enjoyment of a full, independent, and autonomous life by older persons, with health, safety, inclusion, and active participation; moreover, there is a need to address all matters related to ageing from a human rights perspective.

For these reasons, we consider it a mistake for WHO, through ICD-11, to associate old age with a disease situation or health disorder, or to perceive it as a symptom, sign, or clinical result, since this would constitute another form of discrimination against older persons, attacking the human rights model for this segment of the population.

## Conclusions

The ageing process that every person goes through determines, when they reach old age, the possibility of beginning to experience society's stereotyped and prejudiced image, reducing possibilities of full and effective participation in the community for this segment of the population, in terms of its enjoyment of human rights and fundamental freedoms. Ageism, as a form of prejudice and stereotyping that can lead to harmful and discriminatory practices, is present in healthcare, education, and work, and in decisions regarding the lifestyle of older persons, among other areas.

There are, as noted, three stages in which an older person can be found: an older person without a disability, an older person with a disability, and an older person with a disability in a situation of dependency. Approximately 250 million older persons, one-quarter of the total, experience moderate to severe disability.[53] There are no statistics on how many older persons have a severe disability that places them in a situation of dependency.

The scourge that older persons with disabilities can suffer, regardless of whether they are in a situation of dependency, is multiple discrimination, which often undermines their personal dignity, especially when they are dependent on third parties.

For this reason, it is noteworthy that in the case of an older person with disabilities, their protected status flows from the United Nations Convention on the Rights of Persons with Disabilities, ratified by 184 Member States, which can be considered a level of universal ratification. It is important to note that the person's disability determines the application of this Convention, *not the age of the person.*

According to United Nations statistics, 54 percent of older persons do not have disabilities, which represents the majority of this segment of the population, who may also experience discrimination based on age but do not have a universal instrument that guarantees their rights.[54]

Notwithstanding, it is striking that the only international standard, of regional scope, is the Inter-American Convention, ratified by nine Member States, and therefore in force in those countries. (The tenth ratification by Mexico, in December 2022, is to be deposited at the OAS secretariat). Its vanguard status in the legal field makes it necessary to consider the Convention's provisions as valuable guidelines for the rest of the world, as well as for the States of the Region of the Americas that have yet to ratify it.

We should note that both the CRPD and the Inter-American Convention coincide on two central aspects for the inclusion and the full and effective participation in society of all people: legal capacity and universal accessibility.

To us, it is important to emphasize that *older people with disabilities in a situation of dependency are more exposed to the violation of their rights.* It is crucial for States to assume their responsibility as guarantors of the well-being and respect for the dignity of this segment of the population. For the same reason, in considering the CRPD, special importance should be given to the provision on ensuring:

> Persons with disabilities have access to a range of in-home, residential, and other community support services, including personal assistance necessary to support living and inclusion in the community, and to prevent isolation or segregation from the community.[55]

This provision is two-fold, ensuring that community services and facilities for the general population are available on an equal basis to persons with disabilities and are responsive to their needs.[56]

This issue is so relevant that the Inter-American Convention has expressly advocated "a comprehensive care system that takes particular account of a gender perspective and respect for the dignity, physical and mental integrity of older persons."[57] In this regard, the Convention has mandated that:

> Older persons have the right to a comprehensive system of care that protects and promotes their health, provides social services coverage, food and nutrition security, water, clothing and housing, and promotes the ability of older persons to stay in their own home and maintain their independence and autonomy, should they so decide.[58]

This has its counterpart in the CRPD, which emphasizes that persons with disabilities must "have the opportunity to choose their place of residence and where and with whom they live on an equal basis with others and are not obliged to live in a particular living arrangement."[59]

Undoubtedly, these legal instruments must each be used within the scope of their respective Member States, always taking into account *respect for the autonomy, will, and preferences of people*, which is a right of every human being until the end of their days. This is a basic principle of international human rights law.

Finally, we have considered it important to comment on ICD-11, which provides a medicalized approach to old age that strengthens prejudices and stereotypes, undermining the model of human rights for older people, in clear contradiction with the plan for WHO's own "Decade of Healthy Ageing 2020–2030,"[60]

## *Notes*

1 World Health Organization. "Ageing and Health." October 1, 2022. https://www. who.int/en/news-room/fact-sheets/detail/ageing-and-health/.
2 United Nations Department of Economic and Social Affairs (UNDESA). "Ageing and Disability." Accessed February 10, 2022. https://www.un.org/development/ desa/disabilities/disability-and-ageing.html.
3 Organization of American States (OAS). "Inter-American Convention on Protecting the Human Rights of Older Persons, Article 2." 2015. UN Registration no. 54318.
4 Butler, Robert. "Age-Ism: Another Form of Bigotry." *The Gerontologist*, 9, no. 4 (1969): 243–246.
5 Butler,. "Age-Ism."
6 Baltar, Andres L. "Edadismo: Consecuencias de los estereotipos, del prejuicio y la discriminación en la atención a las personas mayores. Algunas pautas para la intervención [Ageism: Consequences of Stereotypes, Prejudice and Discrimination in Care for the Elderly. Some Guidelines for Intervention]." *Informes Portal Mayores*, No. 14. 2004.
7 Sánchez, Concepción. "Estereotipos negativos hacia la vejez y su relación con variables sociodemográficas, psicosociales y psicológica [Negative Stereotypes Towards Old Age and Their Relationship with Sociodemographic, Psychosocial and Psychological Variables]." Doctoral thesis, Departamento de Psicología Evolutiva y de la Educación, Universidad de Málaga, 2004.
8 Kabanchick, Alicia. Francisco Kadic, María Cristina Shahade and Benzión Winograd. "Duelos y depresiones: Indicaciones, clínica y abordaje en psicoterapia psicoanalítica [Grief and Depression: Indications, Symptoms and Approach in Psychoanalytic Psychotherapy]." Presentation at the XVII Conference of the Argentina Associacion of Psychatrists (APSA), Mar del Plata, 2001. https://www.psicomundo.com/argent ina/apsa2001/depresin.htm.

9 Kornfeld-Matte, Rosa. "Report of the United Nations Independent Expert on the Enjoyment of All Human Rights by Older Persons." UNHRC.2015. A/HRC/30/43.

10 Urquieta, Claudia. "Fiscalía investiga asilo de ancianos: abuelo habría muerto de hambre y viejitos no reciben sus pensiones [Prosecutor's Office Investigates Nursing Home: Grandfather Might Have Died of Hunger and Old People do not Receive their Pensions]." *El Mostrador*, June 7, 2016. http://bit.ly/2EYUR9o.

11 United Nations General Assembly. "Follow-up to the Second World Assembly on Ageing." Resolution 65/182. December 21, 2010.

12 United Nations Human Rights Council. "The Human Rights of Older Persons." Resolution 21/23. September 28, 2012. https://www.right-docs.org/doc/a-hrc-res-21-23/.

13 United Nations General Assembly. "Towards a Comprehensive and Integral International Legal Instrument to Promote and Protect the Rights and Dignity of Older Persons." Resolution 67/139. December 20, 2012.

14 OAS. "Inter-American Convention on Protecting the Human Rights of Older Persons." 2015. art. 1.1. https://www.oas.org/en/sla/dil/docs/inter_american_treaties_A-70_human_rights_older_persons.pdf.

15 OAS, "Inter-American Convention," art. 2.10.

16 OAS, "Inter-American Convention," art. 7.

17 OAS, "Inter-American Convention," art. 8.

18 OAS, "Inter-American Convention," art. 12.

19 OAS, "Inter-American Convention," art. 2, 6, 11, 12, and 19.

20 United Nations (UN). "Convention on the Rights of Persons with Disabilities (CRPD)." December 13, 2006. art. 2.

21 UN, "CRPD," art. 6.

22 UN, "CRPD," art. 7.

23 UN, "CRPD," art. 8.

24 UN, "CRPD," art. 13.

25 UN, "CRPD," art. 16.

26 UN, "CRPD," art. 25b.

27 UN, "CRPD," art. 28b.

28 OAS, "Inter-American Convention," art. 2.6.

29 OAS, "Inter-American Convention," art. 2.7.

30 OAS, "Inter-American Convention," art. 2.5.

31 UN, "CRPD," art. 1.2.

32 OAS, "Inter-American Convention," art. 2.4.

33 OAS, "Inter-American Convention," art. 2.9.

34 OAS, "Inter-American Convention," art. 2.8.

35 OAS, "Inter-American Convention," art. 2.1.

36 OAS, "Inter-American Convention," art. 3.

37 OAS Inter-American Commission of Women. *Decalogue for a Human Rights-based and Feminist State*. Washington, D.C.: OAS, December 14, 2021. Section 5.

38 OAS Inter-American Commission of Women. *Decalogue*.

39 UN, "CRPD," art. 19.b.

40 OAS, "Inter-American Convention," art. 12.

41 OAS, "Inter-American Convention," art. 12.

42  OAS, "Inter-American Convention," art. 12.
43  OAS, "Inter-American Convention," art. 12.
44  OAS, "Inter-American Convention," art. 12.
45  UN, "CRPD," art. 12.4.
46  UN, "CRPD," art. 9.1.
47  OAS, "Inter-American Convention," art. 26.
48  UN, "CRPD," art. 2.
49  UN, "CRPD," art. 2.
50  World Health Organization. "ICD-11 Implementation or Transition Guide." Accessed October 8, 2021. https://icd.who.int/en/docs/ICD-11%20Implementation%20or%20Transition%20Guide_v105.pdf.
51  University Council of the University of Costa Rica. "Pronunciamiento sobre la vejez como una etapa de la vida humana [Declaration on Old Age as a Stage of Human Life]." Final Agreement of Session 6513. August 9, 2021. https://www.cu.ucr.ac.cr/uploads/tx_ucruniversitycouncildatabases/pronouncement/pronun124.pdf.
52  World Health Organization. "UN Decade of Healthy Ageing." Accessed January 7, 2023. https://www.who.int/initiatives/decade-of-healthy-ageing.
53  UNDESA. "Ageing and Disability." Accessed February 19, 2022. https://www.un.org/development/desa/disabilities/disability-and-ageing.html.
54  UNDEAS, "Ageing and Disability."
55  UN, "CRPD," art. 19b.
56  UN, "CRPD," art. 19c.
57  OAS, "Inter-American Convention," art. 12.3.
58  OAS, "Inter-American Convention," art. 12.1.
59  UN, "CRPD," art. 19a.
60  WHO, "Decade of Healthy Ageing."

# 6. *About Us Without All of Us: The Elephants in the Room*

KATE SWAFFER

*Forgive no error you recognize,*
*it will repeat itself.*

Yevgeny Yevtushenko[1]

## *Dementia Prevalence, Ethics, Inclusion, Advocacy, and the Emergence of Self-Advocacy*

I will explore here some of the reasons dementia continues to be "about us, without all of us," and the notion that people with dementia are no less oppressed in 2022 than they were in 1982. It tackles the multiple oppressive structures experienced by people with dementia, such as reduced opportunities to participate equitably, or at all, in everyday activities due to attitudinal, social, and environmental barriers.

The World Health Organization (WHO) states dementia is a major cause of disability and dependence globally, and in 2019, there were an estimated 55 million people with dementia and nearly 10 million new cases annually.[2] The Alzheimer's Disease International (ADI) 2021 World Alzheimer's Report (WAR)[3] estimated 42 million people with dementia do not have a formal diagnosis. The global prevalence includes people living with all forms of dementia including those with Young Onset Dementia (YOD), and people under the age of 65[4] who present with significant cognitive disabilities. While prevalence data varies, the number of people living with cognitive and other disabilities due to dementia is increasing. There is no ambiguity; we are facing a critical point in how we view and treat people of any age with dementia, to ensure a higher quality of life and improve the care and support currently available. This potentially reduces the human and economic costs to individuals and their families, and to governments. Despite the increasing numbers of people with dementia, there continues to be an ageist approach to people with dementia and to older persons, in policy and research,[5,6] which I've experienced personally, as most still view dementia as an older person's condition.

In 1980, the Alzheimer's Association in America was founded by a group of family care partners and other individuals who saw the need for an organization that would unite and support family members and care partners, as well as provide support to those facing dementia and advance research into the disease.[7] Four years later, a small group interested in dementia and experts in the field, discussed the formation of an international organization for Alzheimer's disease and other dementias. Representatives from existing Alzheimer associations in the United States, the United Kingdom, Australia, and Canada joined with observers from Belgium, France, and Germany and ADI was founded.[8] ADI has grown from four members to a worldwide federation of over 100 dementia associations and is the global voice on dementia.

In 2008, I was diagnosed with a rare YOD, the semantic variant of Primary Progressive Aphasia (svPPA). I was at that time a married working mother of two teenage sons, undertaking two degrees at the University of South Australia. Post diagnosis, I was not advised to fight for my life, or that I could live well, nor provided with disability and rehabilitative support; I was advised to prepare for the end. Specifically, I was advised (not my diagnosing neurologist) to "get my end-of-life affairs in order, to give up work, give up study, and start attending aged care day respite once a month, to get used to it." My husband was also told he'd "need to give up work soon, to care for me." We both experienced moral injury, defined by Shay[9] as when there has been or continues to be a betrayal of what is right, by a person, organization, or authority who should not allow it to happen. The post-diagnostic experience was death from the outside. The moral injury was "killing me from the inside out."[10] I continue to experience moral trauma and moral injury, after being betrayed and abandoned by a system meant to care for people who are diagnosed with any critical condition, including dementia. A meaningful, purposeful life doesn't just predict happiness; it increases longevity and well-being. Yet people with dementia have this taken away at diagnosis. People with dementia have human rights.[11] It is wrong to deny them hope and their human rights.[12] It is wrong to segregate them[13] based on disability, yet the dementia and aged care sector including service providers, researchers, and governments, continue to endorse it within nursing homes inside "secure memory units" and now within dementia villages. Having dementia is not a crime. Institutional living and segregation cause further moral injury, and the sense of betrayal is profound. It is constantly being reinforced, pushing people with dementia and their families further toward desperation and the person with dementia to earlier dependence, perhaps even earlier death. There are many other issues at play, causing harm, including "moral exclusion," defined by Opotow as "when individuals or groups are perceived as *outside the boundary in which moral values, rules, and considerations of fairness apply.* People who are morally excluded are perceived as nonentities, expendable, or undeserving; consequently, harming them appears acceptable, appropriate, or just."[14] Opotow explains that a common feature of moral exclusion is that "the perpetrators perceive others as psychologically distant, lack constructive moral obligations toward others, view others as expendable and undeserving, and deny others' rights, dignity, and autonomy."[15] We experience isolation and loneliness, and Stauffer defines "ethical loneliness" as "the experience of having been abandoned by humanity compounded by the experience of not being heard."[16] I feel ethically lonely, as I have "been unjustly treated and dehumanized by human beings and political structures, who emerge from that injustice only to find that the surrounding world will not listen to or cannot properly hear their testimony ... on their terms."[17] Through my witnessing over 14 years and through Dementia Alliance International virtual peer-to-peer support groups and cafés, it is clear that other people with dementia experience this too. Therapeutic nihilism also exists. It is systemic, perhaps because most still believe there is nothing they or we can do, and because there are still no disease-modifying or curative drugs available for dementia. There is a pervasive myth that people suddenly become late-stage soon after diagnosis, with immediate loss of all capacity. Stigma and discrimination are endemic, despite decades of research and costly surveys and reports on those topics.[18,19] People with dementia and their care partners and families experience shame, self-shame, discrimination, stigma, and paternalism, among many other negative attitudes about and toward them after the disclosure of a diagnosis of dementia. Thankfully, my university supported me to continue living my life by providing disability support; it is immoral and unethical that the healthcare sector does not do this.

In the twentieth century, it was uncommon for patients to mix with "experts" such as medical doctors, health care professionals, researchers, and service providers, outside of clinics, hospitals, and nursing homes as patients, or for them to be at the same conferences, meetings, or social events. In 2015, when I made my first invited keynote speech at the WHO First Ministerial Conference on Dementia,[20] this was uncommon for people with health conditions like dementia. We were more commonly represented through member states or international organizations, rather than individuals with lived experience. The lack of inclusion was especially evident to me when considering people with the lived experience of intellectual, psychosocial, or cognitive disabilities; the cognitive capacity of people from these cohorts is still extremely underestimated. Persons with other disabilities have been included for longer, and when the pioneer dementia self-advocates started to seek inclusion by registering to attend events and conferences about dementia, primarily to learn more about their own conditions, it was neither expected nor welcomed. These pioneers self-funded their own registrations, accommodation, and transport. On arrival at the venues, the conference organizers actively attempted to deny access to some. This was the beginning of the dementia community of people who themselves were diagnosed with dementia, taking on the disability community's slogan, "Nothing about us without us." Yet almost four decades on, people with dementia are still too often advocating for that same basic right most others have: equal inclusion.

The oppression of people with dementia remains palpable; it is just dressed up in a more glamorous outfit. The inclusion of people with the lived experience of dementia is now highly sought after by people with and without dementia. Researchers and organizations label their publications as equitable, inclusive, and collaboratively co-designed. Dementia charities regularly nominate advocates for awards, honorary degrees, and so on, hence it has become extremely competitive among self-advocates, and in my experience, many with dementia have moved from the saying "We advocate to make it better for future generations," to "How can I raise my profile as an advocate?" Tokenism abounds, as inclusion is almost exclusively for advocates who agree with the researchers, charities, or other organizations and do not request payment at commercial rates and are exclusive of anyone who advocates against them. Many dementia charities even request advocates to sign an informal contract that they will not say anything negative about the charity they are becoming advocates for. This ensures advocacy in its truest form is silenced and undermines the very essence of advocacy. That the many dementia working groups and advisory committees around the world have not impacted real change, and instead have glamourized advocacy, is a bitter pill to swallow, as someone who has always volunteered, but who campaigned for and founded the Australian Dementia Advisory Committee.

There have been initiatives and medical responses to dementia that have caused further oppression, and even harm. For example, the paradigm known as the Behavioral and Psychological Symptoms of Dementia (BPSD), although well intended, has caused harm, through the persistent medicalization of dementia, leading to neglect and abuse including chemical and physical restraint, incarceration, and segregation.[21,22,23] Hill describes domestic violence as abuse,[24] suggesting people who are violated don't necessarily understand that violence is not always physical and that other forms of abuse are violations of someone's rights. The Royal Commission into Quality and Safety in Aged Care in Australia found there are an estimated 50 sexual assaults per week of people in residential care, most being women with dementia,[25] a difficult statistic to grasp, although it did not include specific recommendations[26] to prevent sexual assault, nor to stop incarceration and segregation. The overuse of chemical and physical restraint of people with dementia remains rife; it is abuse, and relevant to Hill's discussion on abuse, because it happens through ignorance or acceptance of these abuses by those who should prevent them. Our focus must be on preventing harm to people with dementia, for which people without dementia must now bear some accountability.

To be excluded, ignored, insulted, demeaned, disrespected, undervalued, underestimated, and then not to receive adequate post-diagnostic care, despite decades of research focused on improving quality of life, is negligent and shameful. For this, we need a form of moral repair, defined by Walker[27,28,29] as "the ethics and moral psychology of responses to wrongdoing. Explaining the emotional bonds and normative expectations that keep human beings responsive to moral standards and responsible to each other." Everyone must be held accountable if we are to ensure moral repair. We know it is wrong to deny people with dementia their human rights, such as adequate health care including rehabilitation, but we allow it to continue.[30,31] We know it is wrong to incarcerate and segregate people, but we do it to people with dementia. We know it is wrong for people with dementia to experience violence, abuse, and neglect, but we've done little to stop it or to provide reparations for past wrongs.

The difficulties faced by researchers from university ethics committees agreeing to consent to directly involving people diagnosed with dementia as research participants have changed greatly over the last decade, as this cohort was once considered too vulnerable to be included. Instead, family members, care partners, or legal guardians were involved in the research about people with dementia. Although people with dementia are still considered a vulnerable cohort, ethics guidelines are relaxing, but that we are vulnerable appears to have been ignored by the dementia charities. Including people with dementia is usually required for co-design, and for successful research or project funding applications. Ethics committees are increasingly accepting people with dementia as research participants, and researchers are engaging with us as co-designers, and as collaborators and investigators. Today, if they don't include us, research and other funding proposals are less likely to be accepted. However, advocacy organizations and many researchers select people who agree with their hypotheses, research methods, or advocacy goals, rather than anyone who questions them. The lack of any ethics regarding the way persons living with dementia, which is a progressive terminal illness, where cognitive capacity is deteriorating, is currently not being considered by advocacy organizations is of grave concern and needs questioning,[32] as there appear to be no ethics policies in place for the inclusion of dementia advocates. My concerns about the ethics of co-design, co-production, and intellectual property in 2016[33] highlighted the need to consider ownership of creative and intellectual content, photographs, intellectual copyright and Creative Commons belonging to dementia advocates. This issue has been neglected or ignored, but others providing intelligence or creativity to a piece of work receive full credit; they are usually paid a commercial rate for their contribution and are always credited for their work.

When working with First Nations Australians, even in advocacy projects, the ethics criteria and guidelines are more stringent than for non-Aboriginal Australians. Any projects involving human participants discussing all issues, not only highly sensitive and traumatic ones, require ethical approval. Research involving Aboriginal and Torres Strait Islander (ATSI) people requires an additional set of ethical guidelines required to ensure risk mitigation strategies have been provided to prevent any potential harm. Working with older persons of Aboriginal descent, who have been subjected to a history of personal and inter-generational trauma, there is a duty of care not to subject them to anything that may cause further psychological harm. This duty of care is not apparent outside of research, or for people with dementia who are also a highly marginalized and vulnerable cohort with a high potential for harm.

## The Emergence of Self-Advocates with the "Lived Experience of Dementia"

> *Life can only be understood by looking backward;*
> *but it must be lived looking forward.*
>
> Soren Kierkegaard

In contrast to the advocacy charities that were founded by family members or care partners, the Dementia Alliance International (DAI),[34] which is a registered charity, and a support and advocacy group by and for people with dementia, was founded by eight people diagnosed with varying types or causes of dementia from three countries. It was launched on January 1, 2014, and is the peak body globally representing people diagnosed with dementia, the *global voice of people with dementia.* Until September 2022, it operated with no paid staff and minimal funding, providing free membership and free services to its members now in 49 countries, as well as to the wider dementia community. It is the only organization globally that authentically follows the "Nothing about us without us" philosophy, as it is run by, and for people with dementia, and staff or volunteers without dementia work under the direction of people with a dementia diagnosis.

Being diagnosed with YOD taught me firsthand about self-shame, stigma, discrimination, paternalism, unconscious bias, and therapeutic nihilism, and about "difference," "otherness," and exclusion.[35] It helped me understand from the inside out that "sense of nobodiness,"[36] first published in 2016.[37] YOD also added ageism, as most see dementia as an older person's condition. It increased my understanding of racism and the fight for the rights of other marginalized groups such as people from the LGBTIQA+ community. My Aboriginal friends say it is obvious I am being treated as "other" now; it often feels like I'm treated as "no longer human." In Australia, although Aboriginal Australians have lived here for 70 million years, and is the oldest civilization in the world, they were only allowed to vote from 1967, and it wasn't until 1984 that First Nations people were finally treated like other voters and required to enrol and vote at elections. White people have a lot to answer for in my country; people without dementia do too.[38]

My post-diagnostic experiences which led me to dementia advocacy, now lead me to consider how self-advocacy may be having the opposite effect of what self-advocates have campaigned for. If you are articulate and willing to provide your expertise and time without being paid, charities and others in the field of dementia love you. They stop loving you (and including you) if you openly disagree with them, if you request equitable payment for your time and expertise, or if you deteriorate. This silence and exclusion are a form of emotional abuse, and if you dare to become too autonomous, even other self-advocates turn against you as they think you are betraying them or demeaning what they do. I have volunteered my whole life, but this next discussion is not about valuing volunteers; it is about the abuse of people with dementia who become volunteer advocates. A presentation by Gavin et al. titled *From Neglect to Modern Slavery: Specialized Disability Employment Programs in Australia,*[39] depicts precisely what has happened to people with dementia. I've also written about the economic stigma noting the emergence of unpaid work by advocates, resulting in exclusion if you seek to be paid at commercial rates.[40] If we refuse to remain silent, we are proactively denied access to meetings and events on topics they know you disagree with them on, with strategies such as telling you that they "only want voices of new advocates this time," even though all the dementia working groups/advisory committees persist with long-term membership of the same advocates. The charities have their favorites, which feeds into *passive competitive*™,[41] behaviors; like when I attended school, students who did not threaten anyone or who didn't speak up too much became "the teacher's pet," a term that has been in use since 1890.[42] It is difficult to accept that many of the dementia advocates who see themselves as leaders are vying to be the favored ones; to be chosen to speak at special events or in the media. I have heard many with dementia proclaim to be best friends with a top researcher, or the CEO of their local or national dementia charity. There is much to consider since my own diagnosis. Considering the unpaid labor I have provided to multiple local, national, and international organizations, and to individuals including researchers, founders of startup companies, and dementia consultants, it is difficult to reckon with so little change. The significant amount of personal funds I have spent on travel and conference registrations, alongside having to fund my own disability support to ensure inclusion highlights another disparity; you must either concede to others' views or have personal funds to advocate honestly.

In *Otherness*,[43] Brin says, "Otherness has a theme. A loose one, but persistent ... That familiar things may become strange, and we may have to adapt to others who will rock our past assumptions." It is providing meaningful engagement and the ability to reinvest in their own lives,[44] moving people with dementia back to living and away from the harmful *prescribed disengagement*®,[45] that people are still experiencing. It is little wonder people with dementia embrace advocacy, and then, do not want to pass the baton, as being an advocate not only becomes familiar and comforting, but it also gives them a reason to get out of bed, to feel useful and valued again. This creates the potential to be used for fundraising, and other pursuits of dementia charities, to the detriment of the very cohort they proclaim to represent. It is critical to review the assumptions that dementia self-advocacy is worthwhile, as when aligned to and funded by powerful and wealthy charities, is not creating change. It may actually be doing harm. That so little has changed for anyone living with dementia, or their families or care partners,[46,47] proves this and is partly the impetus for this chapter.

Over the last few years, I have felt increasingly used and mistreated, now likening it provocatively to being pimped and prostituted. I view my own experience with a new perspective, and even if unintentional, see it happening to others. It has reached levels that are disturbing and indefensible. Since developing such a large global network of friends with dementia, researchers, and others working in the field, I've felt like, and often been told I am the "dementia dating agency," connecting people without dementia to people with dementia. In a commercial world, people would need to pay for this; in my world, it is expected for free. Beyond that, when people with dementia no longer have the capacity to be the poster boy or girl for an organization, they are thanked, then excluded and forgotten. Those vision and mission statements, with phrases about including and respecting people with dementia, are powerful fundraising tools, but they are misleading.

This type of division among self-advocates is widening, and the exclusion of people who may advocate against organizations or their policies is palpable. For example, responses to the Rally for Access video,[48] a U.S.-based campaign for access to the drug *Aduhelm*, calling on the U.S. Centers for Medicare & Medicaid Services (CMS) to overturn their ruling to stop coverage of Aduhelm, highlighted the divisions among dementia advocates, and the conflicts of interest within organizations. The comments on the Facebook post with the heading, "Not for just SOME but for EVERYONE!," highlighted arguments among dementia self-advocates. Publicly available commentary on Facebook such as: "...this missed the mark by excluding those that didn't completely agree. So much for everyone. I am so sick and tired of professed advocacy groups that make decisions without us and then cherry pick from us to be a puppet," reflected the discontent.

Although it is human not to agree on everything, it is unethical to divide people with cognitive disabilities who may have more difficulties coping with division and stress. It is unfair for people without dementia to cherry-pick people with dementia to sell their viewpoints. Another Facebook post protested: "Advocacy groups should not be cheerleaders for [the] pharmaceutical industry!!! They are supposed to protect us!!" National and international charities, many of whom receive millions in funding from pharmaceutical companies, with significant conflicts of interest, still promote new drugs, even if they are potentially unsafe or costly. I understand why some people with dementia wanted this drug, despite many scientists believing it to be unsafe and unethically approved[49]; for some, any form of hope is better than none.

The emergence of dementia-friendly initiatives (DFIs), such as dementia-friendly communities (DFCs), dementia friends, and dementia villages, keeps otherness alive. The labeling of people with dementia by disease (and therefore disability) is another form of segregation introduced without evidence-based research (EBR). Dementia charities and others have been funding research to build evidence for the DFIs, while not doing enough to reduce the stigma or discrimination in the daily lives of most people with dementia.

While the DFIs and dementia villages are the current popular phenomenon, let's for one moment, imagine a world where we re-introduced leprosy, cancer, schizophrenia, diabetes, and bipolar villages; they would be seen as ghettos. If we funded initiatives such as Indigenous-Friendly Communities, run entirely by and employing only non-indigenous people, or LGBTIQ+ Friendly Communities, run by and employing only heterosexuals as the experts, most would campaign against them. The DFIs have potentially increased stigma, discrimination, paternalism, and ageism, not improved them. We need an assets-based approach,[50] not a deficits and disease-specific labeling approach. The inclusion of people living with dementia globally remains tokenistic, as few if anyone with dementia is employed; only people without dementia are, perhaps with a few unpaid advisors with dementia. Representation remains inequitable, and it is reprehensible when organizations or individuals who represent people with disabilities due to dementia, refuse to embed dementia as a disability in their work. Although a few people with dementia in some countries have been included in decision-making, most have been sweet-talked into believing a small committee or advisory group, often consisting of the same members for years, is acceptable.

The paradigm of the BPSD was introduced with little or no evidence. In any other area of clinical practice or social care, EBR is required. Numerous researchers have spent their careers building evidence for BPSD, after implementation. BPSD was well intended, but many persons living with disabilities disagree with it. It has pathologized and medicalized dementia and caused excessive use of chemical and physical restraints. The medical model of care, which has been the premise for providing care for people with dementia, is part of the problem because it denies access to social and disability rights. Borsay and Shapely[51] embrace the now widely accepted view of medicine as an active force in the exercise of government power, casting medical practitioners as neither villains nor heroes, highlighting how in many individual instances, such as in the development of prosthetic limbs and the treatment of chronic illness, medical interventions improved the lives of disabled people. At the same time, they present medicine as both a witting and an unwitting ally in the economic (and consequently the political and social) exclusion of disabled people in modern Britain. Medical experts, through institutions such as workhouses, schools, and hospitals in the nineteenth century, as well as in the establishment of government health services in the twentieth century, helped define the normative structures that would equate the ability to do paid labor with full qualification for citizenship, thereby further marginalizing disabled people.

## *Pimping, Harlotry, and the Intoxication of Fame*

Starting with my own experience of prescribed disengagement, then a period of emotional recovery from the diagnosis, due entirely to my own resilience and ability to self-fund my own prescription of grief and loss counselling and rehabilitation, I became an accidental author and activist. Initially, advocacy returned meaning and purpose to my life; it seemed I was contributing to a better future for others with dementia. Of course, being wanted and valued again felt brilliant, but I was yet to find out how futile—and challenging—that advocacy would become. I soon noticed I was the only one at the table not being paid for my time or expertise (lived experience of dementia, researcher, retired nurse, business owner, and numerous other roles I have current or past expertise in and experience with), and then expected to represent a national or global population. I was often self-funding my inclusion, to be their tick-box. Most of the time, I still self-fund my disability support when traveling, even when a host organization funds disability travel support for their paid staff.

After advocating to include a person with dementia in the DFC initiatives in Australia, I was employed by Alzheimer's Australia on a 6-month contract. Ironically, once contracted, I was denied attendance at internal DFI meetings by the other paid staff. The experience of being employed again initially re-empowered me, but it soon felt more like I was an experiment. There are continuing examples confirming dementia self-advocates are used primarily for fundraising and research or project grant applications, but the label of being "inspirational" is causing harm, contributing to the intoxication of fame. Many other disabled people, including me, do not want to be labeled as inspiring or labeled by their disease or disability either. The late Australian journalist and comedian Stella Young said, "Some disabled people, including athletes, have been highly outspoken about their desire to be perceived as athletes, not tokens."[52] Like Young, I have "lost count of the number of times that I've been approached by strangers wanting to tell me that they think I'm brave or inspirational."[53] What I really want is change!

In our global quest for equal rights, especially seeking to realize art. 19[54] of the Convention of the Rights of Persons with Disabilities (CRPD), that is the right to live independently in the community, people with dementia are inadvertently being promoted, pimped, and then harloted, as speakers, as advocates, in the media, and in dementia working groups or committees. They do this because they believe their unpaid work is helping others, and they have been able to get back to living. I've not found this expressed in this way before, when discussing dementia self-advocacy, and it is difficult to face that I allowed myself to be treated in this way. That the way people with dementia are encouraged to become advocates is little different to pimping or prostitution, is a bitter pill to swallow and many will be unable or unwilling to even consider it as remotely valid. But actively promoted by dementia charities, based on *equal inclusion*, only a minutia of people living with dementia— usually the same people— will be publicly included. This suits their fundraising campaigns and organizational goals, but not always ours.

In Ashendel's article "Notorious Home of Harlotry: Regulating Prostitution in the Ohio Valley, 1850–1860,"[55] he quoted historian Joel Best who argued, "The study of prostitution can reveal much about the limited choices available to women." This discussion on the "limited choices" relates well to people with dementia, as our economic security as well as a meaningful life disappears when we are prescribed disengagement. Hence, we are enthusiastic when almost anyone wants to involve us, often using the unconsciously biased rationale referred to earlier, that we are making things better for future generations. Advocates from the last century tell me little has changed, except the language is more sophisticated, and we are better able to articulate our right to health and equitable inclusion. While provocative, I suggest there are few differences between dementia self-advocates and pimping or prostitution. A voucher such as a gift card for a specified amount of money for my expertise and time is insulting. Before dementia, my time and expertise were highly valued and commercially remunerated. Accepting a monetary gift card for multiple hours of work as an advocate keeps the stigma and discrimination alive.

In 1989, Brancati[56] defined the term pimping as occurring when an attending physician (the Pimper) poses a series of difficult questions to a resident or medical student (the Pimpee). Detsky[57] claimed that "Pimping is indeed alive and well within academic medicine." I claim that key personnel of dementia organizations have become pimps and that dementia self-advocates have unwittingly become pimps, and the use of self-advocates for fundraising, campaigns, and other activities of the national or international dementia charities has turned into harlotry. LeBlanc used the term harlotry when discussing Anna Karenina, and I find the analogy between Karenina and dementia self-advocates striking. LeBlanc states in his abstract:

> [. . .] some inclined to condemn Tolstoy's heroine categorically as a manipulating female and an immoral adulteress, while others have preferred to see her as a pathetic victim of her society's hypocritical moral code and a noble sacrifice to her own passionate capacity for love.[58]

That statement highlights the imbalance of the scales, between people with dementia, and the persistent labeling of us as sufferers. Human suffering, and martyrdom, perceived or real, is a powerful fundraising tool.[59,60] The grooming of new advocates by exposing them to opportunities to appear on radio, television, and in other forms of media, as well as wining and dining them on trips to speak at Parliament House, and so on, is not dissimilar to the art of pimps, who groom young girls with proclamations of love and gifts and then get them hooked through drugs.[61] Exposure to these types of activities and the celebrity status some start to feel, act like a drug, no differently to heroin or cocaine; it looks to me as if the road to advocacy now provided by the charities is not only addictive but also harmful. There has been little or no consideration of ethics in this movement of inclusion.

In the dementia sector, everyone loves you, if you are willing to work for free. If you request reasonable accommodation for disabilities as provided to paid staff, the love (inclusion) also disappears. When you speak up publicly against any of those discriminations or refuse to go home and accept the prescribed disengagement, you become a problem and are proactively excluded, causing further division among advocates. People with dementia have become a commodity, as without us, most applications for funding or research proposals are not approved. That itself, is another illusion, as in the 14 years since diagnosis, I have not seen a tangible change in the lived experience following and during a diagnosis of dementia. However, I have seen the increasing numbers of people without dementia being employed in the sector, hundreds of new organizations focused on dementia, increased research on dementia, and everyone but those with dementia receiving the kudos for and being paid for our collective knowledge and time.

Radziwill in her 2016 book review[62] of *The End of Protest: A New Playbook for Revolution* by lifelong activist, Micah White, asks us to ponder:

> Why review a book written by the creator of the Occupy movement for an audience of academics and practitioners who care about quality and continuous improvement in organizations, many of which are trying to not only sustain themselves but also (in many cases) to make a profit.[63]

She then says: "The answer is simple: by understanding how modern social movements are catalyzed by decentralized (and often autonomous) interactive media, one will be better able to achieve some goals he or she is very familiar with." This is relevant to the power imbalances between people in places of power without dementia, and the dynamics this power imbalance sets up between them and people diagnosed with dementia. White outlines eight principles of revolution, and that "Understanding the principles behind revolution allows for unending tactical innovation that shifts the paradigms of activism, creates new forms of protest and gives the people a sudden power over their rulers."[64] In an interview, White admits to "a constructive failure .... did not achieve what we had hoped."[65] We need more people to admit to failure. Activism could be seen as a form of professionalization, as a case of *neoliberal governmentality*,[66] but if applying that theory to dementia activism, this has not yet eliminated or reduced the cost of care, deregulated the aged care industry, or reduced the many barriers to receiving a diagnosis and post-diagnostic care. Activism has also not yet influenced the UN or the industry in general. Perhaps only a revolution will change the power imbalances and provide equal inclusion and access and therefore disability support for all people diagnosed with dementia, including those who become advocates, campaigners, or activists. Dementia advocates and activists need to work together; currently, they do not. The other oppressive barrier advocates face is the need for funding, heightened because no one will employ us, and partly why many will advocate for free.

The gross and systemic underestimation of all people with dementia, even in the later stages of the condition, continues to ensure that a large majority of people with dementia are not included, and the tokenistic inclusion of a few people with dementia continues, until they no longer agree with the charities they advocate for, or the persons dementia progresses. Publicly expressed autonomy ensures subtle but definitive exclusion, but also, how can one person with dementia on an international board represent the 55 million people with dementia, or how can seven or eight people with dementia represent a continent, national, or regional cohort, especially when the same people have been providing advice for many years. One challenge organizations and individuals with dementia often share with me is that once an advisory or working group of any kind is formed, most Terms of Reference don't have specified terms for membership, allowing them to become what some describe as "elitist private clubs" that others feel unwelcome at and unable to join. It is an example of disableism, not ableism. That most dementia charities don't employ people with dementia is ableism. There is much work to do.

Individuals' profiles, developed through DAI, have resulted in what can be viewed as the theft of active DAI members, to become advocates in local, national, and international charities. DAI does the work of empowering people with dementia to live, mentoring them to become advocates. Then the advocacy organizations entice them away, often causing significant division among dementia self-advocates themselves. It is not currently financially viable for DAI to compete with a national charity, as they do not have the capacity or money to wine and dine their advocates or fund them to make speeches and attend events in places like Parliament House. It also cannot provide paid staff to do all the behind-the-scenes work for advocates to operate. Hence, DAI is always losing its advocates to national or international charities. The poaching of primary care physicians from low- and middle-income countries (LMICs) is another example of poaching, and some are questioning it as "morally defensive."[67] Jenkins et al. review the negative impact of the importing of doctors from other countries on culture and practice and suggest that "Creative international policy approaches are needed to ensure the individual migration rights of health professionals do not compromise societal population rights to health, and that there are public and fair agreements between countries within an internationally agreed framework."[68] This is important in the context of self-advocacy, and the inclusion of people with any condition who have lived experience, as these are groups of people who have predominantly been excluded, ignored, or used for fundraising with narratives of tragedy. We need to move beyond listening to the discourse of suffering, which negatively impacts people diagnosed with dementia, and keeps the myths, stigma, discrimination, and the underestimation of capacity alive.

Perceived fame is extremely intoxicating, so people with the lived experience of dementia are being embraced as advocates and competing to become advocates. Some privately refer to it as the "shiny-star syndrome." The obvious, albeit subtle and unintentional grooming, pimping, and harlotry of new advocates is flourishing and is not only harmful to the people diagnosed with dementia, but to the change they all want. This is not only relevant to people with dementia. For example, if you have been a keynote speaker at conferences, with applause, media interest, and so on, would you want to give up your place on the podium, radio, or television for someone else? If you were a plumber, or a florist, or a mother, or any other person with no public celebrity profile, and now, due to a diagnosis of dementia, ABC or the BBC wants to make you one by doing a documentary about you, are you likely to say no? Despite three decades of advocacy to change the negative narrative of suffering, media content is rarely balanced and continues to focus on the tragedy, failing to highlight the fun and laughter many still have.

Providing a person with dementia, whose life was thrown in the bin at the time of or soon after diagnosis, with opportunities to be heard via a high-profile media outlet, or through other media and public formats, makes it extremely hard to pass on the baton. While it may not seem harmful to keep people with the lived experience of dementia on the podiums, telling their stories of "bravery" and "courage," it is important to question it. After almost four decades of this, little has changed in terms of diagnosis, stigma and discrimination, and attitudes towards people, as has been repeatedly proven through expensive research and reports.[69,70]

## *Conclusion*

For many years, other people with disabilities, such as athletes have been questioning the use of adjectives such as inspiring, courageous, or special (e.g., the Special Olympics), as having the potential for harm. For over a decade, WHO has listed dementia as a major cause of disability globally. The health sector continues to ignore this fact, which directly allows the care system to continue denying us our rights under the CRPD[71] and other conventions. It is time to stop others using our illness or disability for their gain. In her article, "How the 'Inspiring' Narrative Restricts and Fetishizes Disabled Athletes", Smith says, " ... when the athlete is disabled, a fraught tension emerges: Are abled people celebrating an athlete for their performance or falling into the trap of believing that someone is 'inspiring' simply because they're disabled?"[72] To be "inspiring" is not sufficient reason to become an advocate, without a tangible reduction in the levels of stigma and discrimination, and the provision of post-diagnostic support.[73] I do not want to be labeled *inspiring*, especially when there is no action for real change. But I have also been labeled *militant, outspoken, kind, optimistic, determined, resilient, persistent*, and *too direct*. Labels are just that; they are the opinions of or labels used by others. I believe in the philosophy, "What you think of me, is none of my business."[74,75] Having been bullied on social media twice since campaigning for people with dementia, and publicly defamed by people who once were my family and friends, including proclamations that I was "faking it," I needed a strong belief in myself and in what I advocate for. The vocal group of dementia experts (specialist medical doctors and academics), like Professor Howard, who have become outspoken about doubting the diagnoses of many people with dementia,[76] including on social media, has meant dementia self-advocates need to be more resilient than most others. Professor Hu from the United States responded to Howard, with an article, "No Doubts about Dementia Advocacy," by providing his personal observations to "narrow the gap between the purely medical model of dementia and the lived experience of persons with dementia, likening dementia advocates to Olympians with disabilities."[77] Hu suggests "Dementia advocacy is a form of John Henryism, and the advocates' health can be made worse by the persistent curiosity of dementia professionals into their abilities."[78] My response to Howard and Hu, discussed issues such as the harms that publicly diagnosing people over social media can do.[79] This challenge of one's medical diagnosis may in part be due to many more people with dementia refusing to accept the prescribed disengagement, and instead, demanding disability support and rehabilitation. This has resulted in public accusations of people not having "real dementia," which should be seen and acted on as defamation. If it happened to persons with any other type or cause of more invisible disabilities, it could result in litigation. That medical experts are doing this should result in their deregistration as they have taken the Hippocratic Oath, which includes to do no harm.[80] The pervasive and persistent questioning of the diagnosis of anyone with dementia, done through reading a book, or hearing them give a speech, is a form of oppression and is a "public diagnosis" without merit. A diagnosis of any medical condition, of any person, can only be done with medical investigations done by medical doctors, on and with their patient being present. It cannot be done through public platforms such as social media. In the world of dementia, it has continued, without any action taken by any oversight body.

Finally, just like you, the reader, and the late Dr King, I too have a dream.[81] I have a dream all people with dementia will receive a timely diagnosis. I have a dream all people with dementia will no longer be prescribed disengagement. I have a dream all people with dementia are advised that their symptoms are disabilities. I have a dream all people with dementia are provided with disability assessment and support at the time of diagnosis. I have a dream all people with dementia receive proactive rehabilitation and early nonpharmacological interventions to maintain or improve their quality of life, soon after diagnosis. I have a dream all people with dementia are equally included. I have a dream that environmental design provides equal access for people with invisible disabilities due to dementia,[82] in the same way we provide wheelchair ramps and hearing loops. I have a dream all people with dementia have equal access to the CRPD. I have a dream all dementia professionals stop using the harmful paradigm known as BPSD. I have a dream all people without dementia stop holding people diagnosed with dementia to a much higher account.[83] I have a dream all people with dementia make the pimping and harlotry stop! I have a dream all people with dementia are paid fairly for their time and expertise not only of their lived experience but their professional experience.

That people with dementia, who are the experts with lived experience, but whose pre-diagnosis expertise is most often ignored and who are being used to support everyone else's paid work is unfair. It is not only time for reciprocity, but for the tokenism to stop. I have found, the more I learn, the less I know; the more I understand, the more I am compelled to question things.

## *Notes*

1 Yevtushenko, Yevgeny. "Lies." Poemhunter. Accessed January 7, 2023. https://www.poemhunter.com/poem/lies-69/,

2 World Health Organization. "Dementia." Accessed January 3, 2022. https://www.who.int/health-topics/dementia/.

3 Alzheimer's Disease International. "World Alzheimer's Report 2021." Accessed January 5, 2023. https://www.alzint.org/resource/world-alzheimer-report-2021/.

4 Hendriks, Stevie, Kirsten Peetoom, Christian Bakker, Wiesje M.Van Der Flier, Janne M. Papma, Raymond Koopmans, and Young-Onset Dementia Epidemiology Study Group. "Global Prevalence of Young-Onset Dementia: A Systematic Review and Meta-Analysis." *JAMA Neurology*, 78, no. 9 (2021): 1080–1090. https://doi.org/10.1001/jamaneurol.2021.2161.

5 Barrett, Anne E. and Cherish Michael. "Spotlight on Age: An Overlooked Construct in Medical Sociology." *Journal of Health and Social Behavior* 63, no. 2 (2022): 177–190. https://doi.org/10.1177/00221465221077221.

6 Choudhry, Niteesh K., Robert H. Fletcher and Stephen B. Soumerai. "Systematic Review: The Relationship between Clinical Experience and Quality of Health Care." *Annals of Internal Medicine* 142, no. 4 (2005): 260–273. https://doi.org/10.7326/0003-4819-142-4-200502150-00008.

7 Alzheimer's Association. "About." Accessed January 5, 2023. https://www.alz.org/about.

8 Alzheimer's Disease International. "Our History." Accessed January 5, 2023. https://www.alzint.org/about-us/our-history/.

9 Shay, Jonathan. "Moral Injury." *Psychoanalytic Psychology* 31, no. 2 (2014): 182–191. https://doi.org/10.1037/a0036090.

10 Meagher, Robert E., Stanley Hauerwas, and Jonathan Shay. *Killing from the Inside Out: Moral Injury and Just War*. Eugene, OR: Cascade Books, 2014, 75.

11 Swaffer, Kate. "Human Rights, Disability and Dementia." *Australian Journal of Dementia Care* 7, no. 1 (2018): 25–28.

12 Steele, Linda, Kate Swaffer, Lyn Phillipson, and Richard Fleming. *Human Rights for People Living with Dementia: An Australian Anthology*. Sydney: University of Technology, 2020. ISBN 978-0-464-81571-8.

13 Steele, Linda, Kate Swaffer, Ray Carr, Lyn Phillipson, and Richard Fleming. "Ending Confinement and Segregation: Barriers to Realising Human Rights in the Everyday Lives of People Living with Dementia in Residential Aged Care." *Australian Journal of Human Rights* 26, no. 2 (2020): 308–328. https://doi.org/10.1080/1323238X.2020.1773671.

14 Opotow, Susan. "Moral Exclusion and Injustice: An Introduction." *Journal of Social Issues* 46, no. 1 (1990): 1–20. https://doi.org/10.1111/j.1540-4560.1990.tb00268.x.

15 Opotow, "Moral Exclusion."

16 Stauffer, Jill. *Ethical Loneliness: The Injustice of Not Being Heard*. New York: Columbia University Press, 2015.

17 Stauffer, *Ethical Loneliness*, 9.

18 Alzheimer's Australia. "Report 2017: Dementia and the Impact of Stigma." Accessed January 5. 2023 https://www.dementia.org.au/sites/default/files/documents/Dementia-Social-Stigma-Report-2017.pdf.

19 Alzheimer's Disease International. "World Alzheimer Report 2019: Attitudes to Dementia." https://www.alzint.org/resource/world-alzheimer-report-2019/.

20 Swaffer, Kate and Dementia Alliance International. "WHO First Ministerial Conference on Dementia." Dementia Alliance International. March 3, 2015. https://dementiaallianceinternational.org/blog/who-first-ministerial-conference-on-dementia.

21 Macaulay, Susan. "The Broken Lens of BPSD: Why We Need to Rethink the Way We Label the Behavior of People Who Live With Alzheimer Disease." *Journal of the American Medical Directors Association* 19, no. 2 (2018): 177–180. DOI:https://doi.org/10.1016/j.jamda.2017.11.009.

22 Steele, Linda, Kate Swaffe, Ray Carr, Lyn Phillipson, and Richard Fleming. "Ending Confinement and Segregation." *Australian Journal of Human Rights* 26, no. 2 (2020): 308–328. https://doi.org/10.1080/1323238X.2020.1773671.

23 Steele, Linda, Kate Swaffer, Richard Fleming, and Lyn Phillipson. "Questioning Segregation of People Living with Dementia in Australia: An International Human Rights Approach to Care Homes." *Laws, 8*, no. 3 (2019): 18. https://doi.org/10.3390/laws8030018.

24 Hill. Jess. *See What You Made Me Do: Power, Control and Domestic Violence.* Melbourne: Black Inc., 2019, 8.

25 Branley Alison and Loretta Lohberger. "Aged Care Royal Commission Hears there are around 50 Sexual Assaults a Week of Residents Nationally." *ABC News*, October 22, 2020. https://www.abc.net.au/news/2020-10-22/aged-care-royal-comm-told-of-50-sex-assaults-a-week/12801806.

26 Royal Commission into Aged Care Quality and Safety. "Final Report, List of Recommendations." 2020. https://agedcare.royalcommission.gov.au/publications/final-report-list-recommendations.

27 Walker, Margaret U. *Moral Repair: Reconstructing Moral Relations after Wrongdoing,* New York: Cambridge University Press, 2006.

28 Cohen, Andrew I. *Apologies and Moral Repair: Rights, Duties, and Corrective Justice.* New York: Taylor and Francis, 2020.

29 Lucie-Smith, Alexander. "Moral Repair: Reconstructing Moral Relations after Wrongdoing." *The Heythrop Journal* 53, no. 5 (2012): 845–845.

30 Steele, Linda, Ray Carr, Kate Swaffer, Richard Fleming, and Lyn Phillipson."Human Rights and Confinement of People Living with Dementia in Care Homes." *Health and Human Rights Journal*, 22, 1 (2020): 7–19.

31 McKillop, James. "Dementia and Human Rights: The View from Someone who is Living with Dementia." In *Textbook of Dementia Care, An Integrated Approach,* edited by Graham Jackson and Debbie Tolson, 187–190. New York: Routledge, 2019.

32 Silva, Olivia, M. Ariel Cascio, and Eric Racine. "Person-Oriented Research Ethics and Dementia: The Lack of Consensus." *Anthropology and Aging* 41, no. 1 (2020): 31–51. https://doi.org/10.5195/aa.2020.211.

33 Swaffer, Kate. "Co-Production and Engagement of People with Dementia: The Issue of Ethics and Creative or Intellectual Copyright." *Dementia*, 5, no. 6 (2016): 1319–1325.

34  Dementia Alliance International. "The Global Voice of Dementia." Accessed January 7, 2023. www.dementiaallianceinternational.org.

35  Balibar, Etienne. "Difference, Otherness, Exclusion." *Parallax* 11, no. 1 (2005): 19–34.

36  King, Jr, Martin Luther. "Letter from a Birmingham Jail." April 16, 1963.

37  Swaffer, Kate. *What the Hell Happened to my Brain? Living Beyond Dementia.* London: Jessica Kingsley Publishers, 2016, 190.

38  National Museum Australia. "Right to Vote." Accessed February 1, 2022. https://www.nma.gov.au/defining-moments/resources/indigenous-australians-right-to-vote.

39  Mihajla, Gavin, Linda Steele, Simon Darcy, and Kathryn Johns. "From Neglect to Modern Slavery: Specialised Disability Employment Programs in Australia." Presentation at the Association of Industrial Relations Academics in Australia and New Zealand (AIRAANZ) Conference *Work not as Usual*, University of Sydney, *February 10, 2022.*

40  Swaffer, Kate. "Economic Stigma: They Love You Until They Have To Pay You." *Dementia Connections.* November 10, 2020. https://dementiaconnections.org/2020-11-10-economic-stigma-they-will-love-you-until-they-have-to-pay-you/.

41  Swaffer, Kate. "Passive competitive."™ June 26, 2012, https://kateswaffer.com/2012/06/26/passive-competitive/.

42  Grammarist. "Teachers Pet." Accessed January 3, 2023. https://grammarist.com/idiom/teachers-pet/.

43  Brin, David. *Otherness*, New York: Bantam Books, 1994, 2–3.

44  Swaffer, Kate. "Reinvesting in a Life is the Best Prescription." *Australian Journal of Dementia Care* 3, no, 6 (2014): 31–32.

45  Swaffer, Kate. "Dementia and Prescribed Disengagement." *Dementia* 14, no. 1 (2015): 3–6. https://doi.org/10.1177/1471301214548136.

46  Alzheimer's Disease International & McGill University. "Journey through the Diagnosis of Dementia, Chapter 18: Limited Access to Health Care Resources." Accessed January 7, 2023. https://www.alzint.org/resource/world-alzheimer-report-2021/

47  Alzheimer's Disease International & McGill University. "World Alzheimer's Report: Life after Diagnosis: Navigating Treatment, Care and Support. 2022. https://www.alzint.org/resource/world-alzheimer-report-2022/.

48  Alliance for Aging Research. "Rally for Access." March 15, 2022." https://youtu.be/f_TpcAj7pJ4.

49  Chappel, Bill. "Experts have Resigned from an FDA Committee over Alzheimer's Drug Approval." NPR, June 11, 2021. https://www.npr.org/2021/06/11/1005567149/3-experts-have-resigned-from-an-fda-committee-over-alzheimers-drug-approval.

50  Rahman, Shibley and Kate Swaffer. Assets-Based Approached and Dementia Friendly Communities." *Dementia* 17, no. 2 (2018): 131–137. https://doi.org/10.1177/1471301217751533.

51  Borsay, Anne and Peter Shapely. *Medicine, Charity and Mutual Aid: The Consumption of Health and Welfare in Britain, c.1550-1950.* Aldershot, U.K. Burlington, VT: Ashcroft, 2007.

52  Young, Stella. "I'm Not Your Inspiration." TEDxSydney. Accessed January 7, 2023. https://www.ted.com/talks/stella_young_i_m_not_your_inspiration_thank_you_very_muc.

53  Young, "I'm Not Your Inspiration."

54  Unites Nations. "Convention on the Rights of Persons with Disabilities." Article 19. Accessed January 7, 2023. https://www.un.org/development/desa/disabilities/convention-on-the-rights-of-persons-with-disabilities/article-19-living-independently-and-being-included-in-the-community.html.

55  Ashendel, Anita. "Notorious Home of Harlotry: Regulating Prostitution in the Ohio Valley. 1850-1860." *Ohio Valley History* 3, no. 1 (2003): 17–39. https://www.muse.jhu.edu/article/572698.

56  Brancati, Frederick L. "The Art of Pimping. *JAMA* 262, no. 1 (1989): 89–90. https://doi.org/10.1001/jama.1989.03430010101039.

57  Detsky, Allan S. "The Art of Pimping." *JAMA* 301, no. 13 (2009): 1379–1381. https://doi.org/10.1001/jama.2009.247/.

58  Leblanc, Ronald. "Levin Visits Anna: The Iconology of Harlotry." *Tolstoy Studies Journal* III (1990): 1–20.

59  Olivola, Christopher and Eldar Shafir. "The 'Martyrdom Effect': When the Prospect of Pain and Effort Increases Charitable Giving." In *Advances in Consumer Research,* edited by Ann L. McGill and Sharon Shavitt, 190–194. Duluth, MN: Association for Consumer Research, 2009.

60  Schwöbel-Patel, Christine. "Spectacle in International Criminal Law: The Fundraising Image of Victimhood." *London Review of International Law* 4, no. 2 (2016): 247–274.

61  Lawrence, David T. "American Pimp, and: American Pimp: Raw Outtakes and the Hard Truth (review)." *Journal of American Folklore* 120, no. 475 (2007): 85–87. https://doi.org/10.1353/jaf.2007.0017.

62  Radziwill, Nicole M. "The End of Protest: A New Playbook for Revolution." *Quality Management Journal* 23, no. 4 (2016): 52–52. https://www.tandfonline.com/doi/abs/10.1080/10686967.2016.11918492.

63  Radziwill, "The End of Protest."

64  White, Micah. *The End of Protest.* Toronto: Penguin Random House Knopf Canada, 2016, 124.

65  White, Micah. "Are We Creating the Activists that We Need?" A conversation with Mila Atmos on Future Hindsight (Apple Podcast). https://podcasts.apple.com/us/podcast/future-hindsight/id1334328470?i=1000443110001.

66  Çalışkan, Gul and Alexander J. McGregor. "You Can Change the World. 'We're Just Here to Help": Activist Consultancy Firms as Forms of Neoliberal Governmentality." *Globalizations* 16, no. 5 (2019): 625–643. https://doi.org/10.1080/14747731.2018.1562510.

67  Hagopian, Amy.. "Recruiting Primary Care Physicians From Abroad: Is Poaching From Low-Income Countries Morally Defensible? *The Annals of Family Medicine* 5, no. 6 (2007): 483–485. https://doi.org/10.1370/afm.787.

68  Jenkins, Rachel, Robert Kydd, Paul Mullen, Kenneth Thomson, James Sculley, Susan Kuper, Joanna Carroll, Oye Gureje, Simon Hatcher, Sharon Brownie, Christopher Carroll, Sheila Hollins, and Mai L. Wong. "International Migration of Doctors, and its Impact on Availability of Psychiatrists in Low and Middle Income

Countries." *PloS One* 5, no. 2 (2010): e9049–e9049. https://doi.org/10.1371/jour
nal.pone.0009049.

69  Dementia Australia. "New Report Reveals Two Thirds of People Think Dementia is
a Normal Part of Ageing, Rather Than a Medical Condition." September 20, 2019.
https://www.dementia.org.au/about-us/media-centre/media-releases/new-report-
reveals-two-thirds-people-think-dementia-normal.

70  Dementia Australia. "Dementia and Discrimination Survey Results." Accessed
January 7, 2023. https://www.dementia.org.au/dementia-action-week/survey-
results.

71  United Nations, "CRPD."

72  Smith, S.E. "The 'Inspiring' Narrative Restricts and Fetishizes Disabled." bitch-
media. March 3, 2022., https://www.bitchmedia.org/article/paralympic-disabled-
athletes-pay-to-play.

73  Cations, Monica, Samantha Loi, Brian Draper, Kate Swaffer, Dennis Valakoulis, and
Anita Goh. "A Call to Action for the Improved Identification, Diagnosis, Treatment,
and Care of People with Young Onset." *Australian and New Zealand Journal of
Psychiatry* 55, 9 (2021). https://doi.org/10.1177/00048674211037542.

74  Cole-Whittaker, Terry. *What You Think of Me Is None of My Business.*
New York: Penguin Putnam Inc., 1988.

75  Aitkenhead, Decca. "Russell Brand: It's irrelevant What Other People Think Of
You." *The Guardian.* February 13, 2013. https://www.theguardian.com/cult
ure/2013/feb/03/russell-brand-irrelevant-what-other-people-think.

76  Howard, Robert. "Doubts About Dementia Diagnoses." *The Lancet* 4, no. 8
(2017): 580–581. https://doi.org/10.1016/S2215-0366(17)30150-5.

77  Hu, William T. "No Doubts About Dementia Advocacy." *The Lancet* 4, no. 11
(2017): 830. https://doi.org/10.1016/S2215-0366(17)30373-5.

78  Hu, "No Doubts."

79  Swaffer Kate. "The Reliability and Meaning of a Dementia Diagnosis." *Australian
Journal of Dementia Care.* 7, no. 6 (2019): 21–24.

80  The Practo Blog for Doctors. "The Hippocratic Oath: The Original and Revised
Version." Accessed October 30, 2022. https://doctors.practo.com/the-hippocra
tic-oath-the-original-and-revised-version/.

81  Talk of the Nation. "Read Martin Luther King Jnr's 'I Have a Dream' Speech
in its Entirety." January 18, 2010. https://www.npr.org/2010/01/18/122701
268/i-have-a-dream-speech-in-its-entirety.

82  Swaffer, Kate. "Disability Rights, Enabling Design and Dementia, In *The World
Alzheimer's Report: Design, Dignity, Dementia: Dementia-Related Design and the
Built Environment Vol 1*, edited by Richard Fleming, John Zeisel, and Kirsty Bennet.
London: Alzheimer's Disease International, 2020.

83  Swaffer, Kate. "The Behavioural and Psychological Symptoms of COVID-19 (BPSC-
19)." *Kate Swaffer, Creating Life with Words: Inspiration Truth and Love.* March 27,
2020. https://kateswaffer.com/2020/03/27/the-behavioural-and-psychological-
symptoms-of-covid-19/.

# 7. Mental Health, Physical Health, Older Age, and Oppression

LIAT AYALON

Shirly has been a compulsive shopper ever since she could remember. Born in a hideaway as a refugee in Russia just after World War II and raised in Israel as the only daughter of Holocaust survivors, she did not have much to shop with during her early years. She had many wishes, though they often remained unfulfilled. More than anything, she wanted to have a red bicycle on which she could ride to school every day and feel the wind in her hair. This never happened because her parents were too concerned for her safety and thus, never allowed her to learn how to ride a bicycle. At the same time, there were other things, of which she had too much. She had too much care and attention; too many worries surrounded her mere existence. She was not allowed to leave food on her plate and was always reminded that it was a good idea to leave her house with a piece of bread in her pocket, just in case.

When she grew up and had a family of her own, money became abundant due to her husband's successful business and so did time and the freedom that came with both. She never bought a red bicycle, but she started buying way too many clothes, some of which would have gone well with the red bicycle had she had one. She bought skirts and dresses; long pants and short pants; red, white, yellow, and green jackets; and more shoes than one could imagine. Just in case. For all four seasons and possible dress codes or occasions. As long as her husband and kids were still living at home, her time was somewhat occupied with housekeeping tasks and various other errands that came with the role of being a mother and a wife. The limited living space, shared by four additional souls ensured that clothes would accumulate only in certain parts of the apartment; other parts were left untouched. When her youngest son finally left the house following the unexpected death of her husband, Shirly had all the time, money, and space she needed to go on a shopping spree and fill the emptiness in her life and her apartment with concrete materials.

As long as she was still healthy, no one attempted to interfere with her compulsive shopping and hoarding behaviors. She was a respectable member of her community and a wonderful grandmother to her four grandchildren. However, exactly after she celebrated her 75th birthday, she had an unexplained fall that sent her to the hospital for a week. Upon her release from the hospital, she started experiencing increasingly frequent falls. Her concerned children decided that their mother could no longer live independently on her own. The transition to the nursing home was brutal because it forced Shirly to separate from the clothes, which she had actively accumulated for many decades in all rooms and closets that were available to her in her spacious apartment. Due to her functional decline, she also needed a home care worker to ensure her safety and assist her in everyday tasks. As a result, things became even worse, when Shirly had to give one of the two closets in the single-room nursing unit to a home care worker, who moved in with her upon her transition to the nursing home.

Despite her growing physical disability due to the frequent unexplained falls and the remote location of her nursing home, Shirly continued to spend most of her time shopping and looking for bargains. Accompanied by her home care worker, she would leave early in the morning with a few plastic bags, looking for sales and deals she should not leave unattended. Returning to the nursing home in the afternoon with bags full of goodies no one was asking for, she would leave her shopping bags on the floor, secretly hoping for them to disappear in the morning, yet being always negatively surprised by the fact that indeed, the bags had been taken away by her home care worker who was instructed by her children to toss away as many of the new purchases as possible to keep her unit free of obstacles and prevent falls.

This new practice of clearing the unit from her new purchases was experienced very negatively by Shirly, who felt her autonomy and independence were being compromised. Shirly felt deprived of her free will and as if her wishes and interests did not matter anymore. She lacked the energy to fight with the home care worker and with her children, her sense of control had diminished, and her interest in other activities had declined. She became depressed and withdrawn with little interest in any of the activities the nursing home had to offer.

Shirly's life experiences are well explained by the theory of cumulative advantages and disadvantages.[1,2] The theory postulates that over time, the effects of negative events and hurdles in our lives add up and become increasingly more noticeable and influential. Consistently, advantages, which were acquired early in life, also become more prominent in old age. Cumulative advantages and disadvantages are largely responsible for the wide variability among older people and for the fact that older people are more heterogenous than any other age group.

Reflecting on Shirly's life experiences, one question that arises concerns her ability to stay off the radar and to so-called function "normally" for so many years against the "requirement" to give up her freedom and independence once physical and functional impairments became more pronounced and physical assistance became a necessity. This illustrates the intersection between mental health conditions, physical and functional impairments, and ageing and the possible impact each of these conditions has on one's physical health, mental health, and ability to live independently and exert autonomy.

We are all allowed to make inadequate decisions, even decisions that may compromise our health, mental health, and well-being. However, at a certain age, within a certain constellation of abilities, disabilities and challenges, our liberty can be compromised. This intersection between mental health conditions, physical illness, and functional impairment in old age may expose people to multiple vulnerabilities, which can result in the oppression of liberty and autonomy. The ease with which liberty is taken away can be attributed to three prominent "isms," namely mentalism, ableism, and ageism.

## Mental Health Conditions and Mentalism

The prevalence of mental health conditions is high in the general population.[3] For instance, during the first half of 2020 in the context of the COVID-19 pandemic, the global prevalence of depression was estimated at 28.0 percent, 26.9 percent for anxiety, 24.1 percent for post-traumatic stress disorder, 50.0 percent for psychological distress, and 27.6 percent for sleep problems. These estimates were derived from a pooled analysis of 32 countries.[4] The prevalence of mental health conditions among older people was also high. In a European study of 3,142 people over the age of 65, one in two people had experienced mental health condition/s in their life, one in three within the past year, and one in four had a mental health condition at the time of evaluation.[5] These conditions are not necessarily more prevalent in old age when we consider older people in the general community. In fact, some research shows that older people are somewhat less likely to experience mental health conditions.[6] Older people are considered to be more resilient compared with younger adults, especially with regard to emotional regulation and problem-solving.[7] Similar findings, attesting to the resilience of older people compared with younger people also were reported during the COVID-19 pandemic.[8]

Nevertheless, it is important to note that in some settings, mental health conditions among older people are extremely prevalent. Older people are particularly likely to experience high levels of depression and anxiety in institutional settings.[9] In institutional settings, the prevalence of depression can be as high as 61 percent according to some estimates.[10] This has been partially attributed to being placed in an institutional environment, which often deprives the individual of their individuality. Among the reasons for depression given by nursing-home residents were loss of independence and autonomy, limited privacy, social isolation, and the prominent presence of illness and death at the institute.[11]

In 1958, Goffman coined the term "total institutions" to describe settings in which people spend their entire time, including both leisure activities and basic human activities such as eating or sleeping. In such institutions, the borders between sleeping, playing, and working are nonexistent, yet people are disconnected from the outside world. People are often deprived of their identity and personal characteristics and become part of a collective.[12] It often is easier for staff to deal with the collective in total institutions. All meals are served at the same time, bedtime takes place at the same time, and there is limited need to address individual requests and desires. The negative ramifications of total institutions outweigh their supposed benefits as they violate the autonomy, liberty, and desires of the residents.

The term "learned helplessness" represents an aversive situation that the individual is unable to avoid and as a result, fails or stops attempting to escape negative situations. Learned helplessness is attributed to the uncontrollability of the original event.[13] As a result of learned helplessness, one's sense of self-efficacy declines and one's sense of depression and hopelessness increases.[14] Depression is considered an undesired consequence of learned helplessness. Although certainly not all nursing homes operate within the total institution framework and there are many different reasons for the high levels of depression among nursing home residents, living in a total institution, deprived of liberty and autonomy, could be one of the reasons.[15]

It also is important to note that certain conditions, such as cognitive impairment or dementia, are more common in old age and certainly are more common in nursing homes or other institutional settings.[16] Whereas the prevalence of Alzheimer's disease (the most common type of dementia) is 5 percent at the age of 65, its prevalence is more than 30 percent among those 85 and older. In institutional settings such as nursing homes, the prevalence of dementia can be as high as 53 percent.[17] The fact that depression, agitation, apathy, and other neuropsychiatric symptoms often accompany dementia may also explain the high prevalence of depression in nursing homes.[18]

Mentalism is defined as discrimination or oppression against a mental trait or condition manifested in discrimination against people who received psychiatric treatment, for instance.[19] People with mental health conditions often are subject to the stigma, prejudice, and discrimination that accompany these conditions. In contrast with having a physical condition, which can be seen as "bad luck," genetics, or purely physiological in nature, mental health conditions are often seen as one's fault and as being within one's control. Hence, people with mental health conditions often are seen as dangerous and irresponsible.[20]

The stigma of mental illness has many ramifications for one's health, well-being, and mental health.[21] One major problem is the internalization of the stigma by the person who experiences mental health conditions. This may result in negative self-perceptions, low self-esteem, a sense of failure, shame, and even the avoidance of much-needed treatment.[22] At the interpersonal level, the stigma of mental illness often results in the social isolation of people who experience mental health conditions, a general sense of fear and resentment toward them, and a general disinclination to hire them for a job, rent them an apartment, or simply engage in social interactions with people with mental health conditions.[23] People with mental health conditions might be regarded as incapable of making their own decisions and this argument might be used to justify coercive treatment, for instance. Research also has shown that people with mental health conditions are more likely to be incarcerated, less likely to receive adequate medical treatment and even less likely to receive adequate insurance,[24] all of which can be examples not only of interpersonal stigma and discrimination but also of discriminatory systemic policies.

In conjunction with the literature on stigma and discrimination toward mental health conditions, there also is a large body of literature specifically on stigma toward dementia.[25] People with dementia often are excluded from decisions that concern their health and well-being because they are considered incompetent to make their own decisions. The literature suggests that the stigma of dementia often generalizes to the entire family and affects not only the individual who experiences dementia but also their relatives and family caregivers.[26] Caregivers often report reduced support and limited social contact because of the stigma associated with dementia. This type of stigma is referred to as "stigma by association."[27]

One major hurdle that prevents adequate treatment of people with mental health conditions concerns the fact that physicians are not well-trained in working with people with mental health conditions.[28] Nonetheless, primary care physicians represent the primary gatekeepers and the most preferred service option for most people with mental health conditions.[29] As such, many people, of any age, with mental health conditions do not receive the adequate treatment they require. Coupled with self-stigma and limited knowledge about mental health also among family members and friends, access to adequate and effective mental health treatments often is limited.[30]

## Physical Functioning, Physical Disability, Physical Illness, and Ableism

Having a disability or disabilities is very common and it is expected that most of us will experience at least one type of disability throughout our life. In fact, at the age of 65, men in the United Kingdom had a total life expectancy of 15.3 years, but their disability-free life expectancy was 12.1 years. For women over 65 in the United Kingdom, on the other hand, the average total life expectancy is 19.4, but only 11.0 years are disability-free.[31] Both life expectancy and disability-free life expectancy are highly dependent on education, income, geographic location, and other socioeconomic indications. For instance, in the United States, there was a 6.7-year gap in disability-free life expectancy across states.[32]

Like mentalism, ableism also has three components, namely stereotypes, prejudice, and discrimination toward people with disabilities. Disabilities can be physical, sensory, or intellectual, but also can be invisible in the form of chronic health or psychiatric conditions.[33] Ableism also reflects the positive sentiment toward certain abilities. Ableism toward people with disability or functional impairments represents a preference toward people with normative abilities. Ableism is considered an umbrella term for many other forms of "ism" as all other forms of "ism" also, to some degree, reflect a valuation of one group's abilities over the other. Ableism is used to reflect the superiority of the majority group over other groups, which are seen as inferior in their ability. Instead of accepting and accommodating the needs of people with a disability, ableism views people with a disability as inferior and advocates the medicalization of such people or the prevention of their existence because of their disabilities.[34]

The World Health Organization (WHO) report on disability highlighted some of the barriers faced by people with disabilities. These barriers were identified as environmental in nature and include inadequate policies and standards, which either fail to consider people with disabilities or do not enforce policies that are geared to ensure the rights of people with disabilities.

Ableism in the form of negative attitudes, prejudice, and discrimination of people based on their disabilities also is considered to be quite prevalent and certainly plays a role as a major barrier throughout the life course of people with disabilities. Problems with service delivery, lack of services, and accessibility issues also were identified as important obstacles.[35]

Ageing with disabilities has been contrasted with disabilities with ageing. Whereas the former represents disabilities that occur early in life, the latter represents disabilities that occur in middle age or late life. This distinction also results in very different services allocated to each of the groups.[36] It has been argued that older people often are overlooked by the disability movement. Disability programs cater to a younger population and concentrate on education, employment, and residential services. Ageing services, on the other hand, do not emphasize rehabilitation and/or involvement in the community, but rather are more focused on disease management or social well-being. Hence, this artificial distinction represents the expectation that our life course is divided by chronological age. Whereas at younger age periods, people are expected to focus on education, raising a family, and work, at an older age, people are expected to retire. Following this logic, disability policy measures and services target younger people with disability, but people who acquire their disabilities later in life often are excluded from rehabilitation and support services.[37]

## Old Age, Ageing, and Ageism

The past century has seen a revolution in the percentage of older people in the population and the average number of years one is expected to live. Nevertheless, instead of celebrating this revolution, the media, policy stakeholders, researchers, the public, and older people themselves at times, view these changes as a challenge rather than as an opportunity.[38] Ageism, defined as stereotypes, prejudices, and discrimination toward people because of their age is more common than the other two big "isms," namely sexism and racism.[39] In fact, one in two people in society reports exposure to ageism.[40]

Ageism can occur at the structural/societal level through laws and policies that disregard older people or that actively discriminate against them.[41] Institutional ageism was widely evident during the early stages of the COVID-19 pandemic when people were instructed to stay at home or not to return to their job simply because of their chronological age. Similarly, not providing people with emergency care simply because of their age is considered ageism and often is dictated by policy either at the national or structural level.[42]

Ageism does not occur only at the structural level though and certainly is not limited to the healthcare system. Ageism is manifested in varied settings including the media, the workforce and the digital world and can manifest in interpersonal interactions and at the individual level.[43] For instance, there is research as well as a theoretical rationale for a relationship between ageism and loneliness. Older people may refrain from having relationships with other older people simply because of their age. Consistently, society at large may push older people toward disengagement from general society by viewing older people as irrelevant or as not contributing to society.[44] A common categorization of older people, found in different cultures and countries views them as incompetent but warm. Hence, they might be subject to pity, but not to admiration and this may also result in their social exclusion.[45]

At the individual level, ageism can be directed internally.[46,47] Past research has shown that the negative stereotypes of old age and ageing are so pervasive that they are being internalized at a very young age. When people grow older, these stereotypes become self-relevant and impact their thinking, behaviors, and feelings about themselves as well as about other older people.[48] Older people who hold negative self-perceptions of ageing are more likely to die before those who hold positive self-perceptions, are less likely to engage in health behaviors, and are more likely to report poorer physical and mental health.[49,50,51]

## Oppressions and "Isms" in Intersection

Shirly's life story illustrates well the intersection between different "isms." As a younger, functionally independent woman, Shirly was able to engage in self-destructive behaviors that negatively impacted her life and probably the lives of her loved ones. However, as an older woman with physical and functional disabilities, accompanied by mental health conditions, she had minimal control over her residential alternatives and life habits. As a younger and "healthier" person, Shirly was able to engage in self-destructive behaviors with no interference. Obviously, obsessive shopping and hoarding are problematic and can harm the individual, but under most circumstances, the person who engages in these behaviors is left alone out of respect for their autonomy. As an older person with a disability, this autonomy was taken away from her.

It is clearly not the same to be a younger woman with mental health conditions or an older woman with the exact same conditions, accompanied by physical and functional impairments. In Shirly's case, physical and functional impairments in old age shone the spotlight on her mental health conditions.

This of course is not the only relevant intersection. Compared with men, women are more likely to live longer and to experience chronic health conditions; they also are more likely to find themselves in caregiving positions but are less likely to have available carers.[52,53,54] As such, just like Shirly, more women than men are likely to spend the last years of their lives in institutional care.[55] Hence, the experience of ageing as a woman and experiencing mental health conditions and physical and functional impairments is likely quite different from the experiences of men of comparable functioning.

There are several commonalities in the different types of "isms." The first one concerns the use of language. There is a growing understanding that language constructs reality.[56] As such, over the years there have been attempts to change the terminology concerning people with mental health conditions, people with physical and/or functional impairments, and older people. For instance, it is no longer acceptable to use terms such as mentally ill or disabled people as these terms place the condition rather than the person in the center. Automatically associating illness with suffering also is unacceptable given the unsupported assumptions such a reference makes. It also is unacceptable to use belittling terms such as the elderly or the ageing tsunami when talking about older people. The assumption is that once the terminology is changed, public attitudes will also change.[57]

Another common feature is the tendency to institutionalize people with mental health conditions, people with physical and/or functional impairments, and older people. Some psychiatric institutions and some nursing homes have been characterized as total institutions. Moreover, given the de-institutionalization processes that have taken place in the mental health field, nursing homes are now considered a product of de-institutionalization as they often cater to older people with mental health conditions.[58] One approach to shifting away from the total features of institutional living is that of person-centered care.[59] The rationale is that the person is in the center and their wishes and needs should be respected. Following such an approach, some nursing homes tend to change their features and become more home-like. Staff are trained to view the individual as a person, rather than as a patient. Research has supported this model of care by demonstrating improved quality of life and well-being among residents and staff alike.[60]

Invisibility and social exclusion are additional features associated with all three isms.[61,62] Social exclusion might be intentional but, at times, might be unintentional, resulting in increased isolation and loneliness among older people with mental illness, for instance. Combined, the different isms result in even greater exclusion from everyday life and in a disruption of one's access to goods and services among other things. For example, there are very few healthcare professionals who specialize or wish to specialize in old age and even fewer with an interest in mental health conditions and old age. Hence, older people with mental health conditions and/or physical and functional disabilities may receive substandard treatment by people who are not necessarily qualified to treat their conditions and/or by providers who prefer to serve other population groups.

## Conclusions and Future Steps

Acknowledging intersectionality is essential to better capture the experiences associated with different "isms" and their impact on our physical and mental health. The intersections between various forms of disability likely change over a lifespan and have different characteristics and implications for men and women, for young and old, and for people of different ethnic groups.

I have highlighted the need to move forward and change the way we think, feel, and act toward people because of their age, mental health conditions, and/or disabilities. Such a change is needed to live in an inclusive society that accepts people, regardless of their age and or functional level. In the field of ageism, four possible interventions were identified as a means to combat ageism. Educational interventions and intergenerational contact are thought to be effective in changing attitudes toward older people. Legal interventions that ban age discrimination also have shown to be effective as they not only dictate what is right or wrong, but they also set societal norms concerning appropriate behaviors versus discriminatory ones. Finally, social campaigns do not have enough evidence to support their use as a tool to combat ageism, but they too have the potential to change public attitudes, if done in a way that is guided by a comprehensive theory of change.[63]

In the case of mental health conditions and physical and or functional disabilities, research also has shown that intergroup contact has the potential to change attitudes.[64] Educational interventions as well have shown to reduce both public and self-stigma among people with mental health conditions.[65] A recent review has found that in addition to social contact, social marketing at the population level can reduce stigma and discrimination toward people with mental health conditions.[66]

Legally, there is no UN Convention for the rights of older people. Such a convention is highly needed to guide anti-age discrimination at the local and sub-regional levels. A UN Convention would set clear guidelines as to what constitutes age discrimination. Such a Convention would form public norms and sway public attitudes and behaviors. It is important to acknowledge that in contrast to the lack of a UN Convention for the rights of older people, a UN Convention for the rights of people with disabilities has existed for more than a decade now. This Convention advocates the view of people with disabilities as people with rights who are capable of making decisions for themselves. The Convention takes a broad lifespan perspective and addresses all types of disability.[67] However, not all older people experience disabilities, and we should ensure the protection of the rights of older people, regardless of their physical and/or mental functioning. Therefore, ensuring a legal reinforcement of older people's rights at the international level and subsequently at the national level is expected to have a positive impact on people's mental health and well-being and ensure that older people, regardless of their mental health or physical/functional level, will fully enjoy the rights granted to all other members in society.

## Notes

1 O'Rand, Angela M. "The Precious and the Precocious: Understanding Cumulative Disadvantage and Cumulative Advantage Over the Life Course." *The Gerontologist* 36, no. 2 (1996): 230–238. https://doi.org/ 10.1093/geront/36.2.230.

2 Crystal, Stephen, Denis G. Shea, and Adriana M. Reyes. "Cumulative Advantage, Cumulative Disadvantage, and Evolving Patterns of Late-Life Inequality." *The Gerontologist* 57, no. 5 (2017): 910–920. https://doi.org/10.1093/geront/gnw056.

3 Nochaiwong, Surapon, Chidchanok Ruengorn, Kednapa Thavorn, Brian Hutton, Ratanaporn Awiphan, Chabaphai Phosuya, Yongyuth Ruanta, Nahathai Wongpakaran, and Tinakon Wongpakaran. "Global Prevalence of Mental Health Issues Among the General Population During the Coronavirus Disease-2019 Pandemic: A Systematic Review and Meta-Analysis." *Scientific Reports* 11, no. 1 (2021): 10173. https://doi.org/10.1038/s41598-021-89700-8.

4 Nochaiwong et al., "Global Prevalence."

5 Andreas, Sylke, Holger Schulz, Jana Volkert, Maria Dehoust, Susanne Sehner, Anna Suling, Berta Ausín, et al. " Prevalence of Mental Disorders in Elderly People: The European MentDis_ICF65+ Study." *British Journal of Psychiatry* 210, no. 2 (2017): 125–131. https://doi.org/10.1192/bjp.bp.115.180463.

6 Karlin, Bradley E., Michael Duffy, and David H. Gleaves. "Patterns and Predictors of Mental Health Service Use and Mental Illness Among Older and Younger Adults in the United States." *Psychological Services* 5, no. 3 (2008): 275. https://doi.org/10.1037/1541-1559.5.3.275.

7 Gooding, Patricia A., Amanda Hurst, Judith Johnson, and Nicholas Tarrier. "Psychological Resilience in Young and Older Adults." *International Journal of Geriatric Psychiatry* 27, no. 3 (2012): 262–270. https://doi.org/ 10.1002/gps.2712.

8 Varma, Prerna, Moira Junge, Hailey Meaklim, and Melinda L Jackson. "Younger People Are More Vulnerable to Stress, Anxiety and Depression During COVID-19 Pandemic: A Global Cross-Sectional Survey." *Progress in Neuro-Psychopharmacology and Biological Psychiatry* 109 (2021): 110236. https://doi.org/ 10.1016/j.pnpbp.2020.110236.

9   Teresi, Jeanne, Robert Abrams, Douglas Holmes, Mildred Ramirez, and Joseph Eimicke. "Prevalence of Depression and Depression Recognition in Nursing Homes." *Social Psychiatry and Psychiatric Epidemiology* 36, no. 12 (2001): 613–620. https://doi.org/ 10.1007/s127-001-8202-7.

10  Jongenelis, K., Anne M. Pot, Annemieke M. H. Eisses, Aartjan T. F. Beekman, Herman Kluiter, Wijnand van Tilburg, and Miel W. Ribbe. "Depressie bij oudere verpleeghuispatiënten: Een review" [Depression Among Older Nursing Home Patients. A Review]. *Tijdschrift voor Gerontologie en Geriatrie* 34, no. 2 (2003): 52–59. https://www.researchgate.net/publication/10765358_Depression_among_older_nursing_home_patients_A_review.

11  Choi, Namkee G., Sandy Ransom, and Richard J. Wyllie. "Depression in Older Nursing Home Residents: The Influence of Nursing Home Environmental Stressors, Coping, and Acceptance of Group and Individual Therapy. *Aging & Mental Health* 12, no. 5 (2008): 536–547. https://doi.org/10.1080/13607860802343001.

12  Goffman, Erving. "Characteristics of Total Institutions." In *Symposium on Preventive and Social Psychiatry*. Washington, D.C.: Walter Reed Army Institute of Research, 1958.

13  Maier, Steven F. and Martin E. Seligman. "Learned Hlplessness: Theory and Evidence." *Journal of Experimental Psychology: General* 105, no. 1 (1976): 3. https://doi.org/10.1037/0096-3445.105.1.3.

14  Alloy, Lauren B. and Lyn Y. Abramson. "Learned Helplessness, Depression, and the Illusion of Control." *Journal of Personality and Social Psychology* 42, no. 6 (1982): 1114. https://doi.org/ 10.1037//0022-3514.42.6.1114.

15  Choi, Ransom, Wyllie, "Depression," 536–547.

16  Fagundes, Daniel F., Marcos Túlio Costa, Bárbara Bispo da Silva Alves, Maria Madalena Soares Benício, Lanna Pinheiro Vieira, Lara S. F. Carneiro, Osvaldo José Moreira Nascimento, and Renato Sobral Monteiro Junior. "Prevalence of Dementia in Long-Term Care Institutions: A Meta-Analysis." *Jornal Brasileiro de Psiquiatria* 70 (2021): c https://www.scielo.br/j/jbpsiq/a/m4ZRhqjgMk5w7LwqyzHs6Cm/.

17  Fagundes et al., "Prevalence of Dementia," 59–67.

18  Brodaty, Henry, Michael H. Connors, Jing Xu, Michael Woodward, David Ames, and PRIME Study Group. "The Course of Neuropsychiatric Symptoms in Dementia: A 3-Year Longitudinal Study." *Journal of the American Medical Directors Association* 16, 5 (2015): 380–387. https://doi.org/ 10.1016/j.jamda.2014.12.018.

19  Rabheru, Kiran and Margaret Gillis. "Navigating the Perfect Storm of Ageism, Mentalism, and Ableism: A Prevention Model." *The American Journal of Geriatric Psychiatry* 29, no. 10 (2021) 1058–1061. https://doi.org/ 10.1016/j.jagp.2021.06.018.

20  Gaiha, Shivani M., Tatiana Taylor Salisbury, Mirja Koschorke, and Usha Raman. "Stigma Associated With Mental Health Problems Among Young People in India: A Systematic Review of Magnitude, Manifestations and Recommendations." *BMC Psychiatry* 20, no. 1 (2020): 538. https://doi.org/ 10.1186/s12888-020-02937-x.

21  Link, Bruce. G., Joe C. Phelan, and Greer Sullivan. "Mental and Physical Health Consequences of the Stigma Associated with Mental Illnesses." In *The Oxford Handbook of Stigma, Discrimination, and Health*. Oxford: Oxford University Press, 2018.

22 Livingston, James D. and Jennifer E. Boyd. Correlates and Consequences of Internalized Stigma for People Living with Mental Illness: A Systematic Review and Meta-Analysis. *Social Science & Medicine* 71, no. 12 (2010): 2150–2161. https://doi.org/10.1016/j.socscimed.2010.09.030.

23 Kurzban, Robert and Mark R. Leary. "Evolutionary Origins of Stigmatization: The Functions of Social Exclusion." *Psychological Bulletin* 127, no. 2 (2001): 187. https://doi.org/10.1177/1745691615583132.

24 Corrigan, Patrick .W., Amy Kerr, and Lissa. Knudsen. "The Stigma of Mental Illness: Explanatory Models and Methods for Change." *Applied and Preventive Psychology* 11, no. 3 (2005): 179–190. https://doi.org/10.1016/j.appsy.2005.07.001.

25 Herrmann, Lynn K., Elisabeth Welter, James Leverenz, Alan J. Lerner, Nancy Udelson, Cheryl Kanetsky, and Martha Sajatovic. "A Systematic Review of Dementia-Related Stigma Research: Can We Move the Stigma Dial?" *The American Journal of Geriatric Psychiatry* 26, no. 3 (2018): 316–331. https://doi.org/ 10.1016/j.jagp.2017.09.006.

26 Werner, Perla and Jeremia Heinik. "Stigma by Association and Alzheimer's Disease." *Aging and Mental Health* 12, no. 1 (2008): 92–99. https://doi.org/10.1080/13607860701616325.

27 Lopez, Ruth P., Karen M. Kenney, Lauren Sanborn, Victoria Davis, and Jennifer Duncan Davis. "Managing Shame: A Grounded Theory of How Stigma Manifests in Families Living with Dementia." *Journal of the American Psychiatric Nurses Association* 26, no. 2 (2020): 181–188. https://doi.org/10.1177/1078390319832965.

28 Ayalon, Liat, Khaled Karkabi, Igor Bleichman, Silvia Fleischmann, and Margalit Goldfracht. "Barriers to the Treatment of Mental Illness in Primary Care Clinics in Israel." *Administration and Policy in Mental Health and Mental Health Services Research* 43, no. 2 (2016): 231–240. https://doi.org/ 10.1007/s10488-015-0634-0.

29 Gum, Amber M., Liat Ayalon, Jared Matt Greenberg, Balint Palko, Emily Ruffo, and Patricia A Areán. "Preferences for Professional Assistance for Distress in a Diverse Sample of Older Adults. *Clinical Gerontologist* 33, no. 2 (2010): 136–151. https://doi/org/ 10.1080/07317110903551901.

30 Pepin, Renee, Daniel L. Segal, and Frederick L. Coolidge. "Intrinsic and Extrinsic Barriers to Mental Health Care among Community-Dwelling Younger and Older Adults." *Aging & Mental Health* 13, no. 5 (2009): 769–777. https://doi.org/ 10.1080/13607860902918231.

31 Jagger, Carol, Ruth Matthews, Fiona Matthews, Thompson Robinson, Jean-Marie Robine, Carol Brayne, and Medical Research Council Cognitive Function and Ageing Study Investigators. "The Burden of Diseases on Disability-Free Life Expectancy in Later Life." *The Journals of Gerontology: Series A* 62, no. 4 (2007): 408–414. https://doi.org/10.1093/gerona/62.4.408.

32 Farina, Mateo P., Anna Zajacova, Jennifer Karas Montez, and Mark D. Hayward. "US State Disparities in Life Expectancy, Disability-Free Life Expectancy, and Disabled Life Expectancy Among Adults Aged 25 to 89 Years." *American Journal of Public Health* 111, no. 4 (2021): 708–717. https://doi.org/10.2105/AJPH.2020.306064.

33 Bogart, Kathleen R. and Dana S. Dunn. "Ableism Special Issue Introduction." *Journal of Social Issues* 75, no. 3 (2019): 650–664. http://onlinelibrary.wiley.com/doi/10.1111/josi.2019.75.issue-3/issuetoc.

34  Wolbring, Gregor. "The Politics of Ableism." *Development* 51, no. 2 (2008): 252–258.
35  World Health Organization. *Summary: World Report on Disability 2011.* Geneva: WHO, 2011.
36  Verbrugge, Lois M. and Li-Shu Yang. "Aging with Disability and Disability with Aging." *Journal of Disability Policy Studies* 12, no. 4 (2002): 253–267. https://doi.org/10.1177/1044207302012004.
37  Jönson, Hakan and Annika.T. Larsson. "The Exclusion of Older People in Disability Activism and Policies—A case of Inadvertent Ageism?" *Journal of Aging Studies* 23, no. 1 (2009): 69–77.
38  Ayalon, Liat and Clemens Tesch-Römer. "Taking a Closer Look at Ageism: Self- and Other-Directed Ageist Attitudes and Discrimination." *European Journal of Ageing* 14 (2017): 1–4. https://doi.org/10.1007/s10433-016-0409-9.
39  Ayalon, Liat. "Perceived Age, Gender, and Racial/Ethnic Discrimination in Europe: Results from the European Social Survey." *Educational Gerontology* 40, no. 7 (2014): 499–517. https://doi.org/10.1080/03601277.2013.845490.
40  Officer, Alana, Mira Leonie Schneiders, Diane Wu, Paul Nash, Jotheeswaran Amuthavalli Thiyagarajan, and John R. Beard. "Valuing Older People: Time for a Global Campaign to Combat Ageism." *Bulletin of the World Health Organization* 94, no. 10 (2016): 710–710A. https://doi.org/10.2471/BLT.16.184960.
41  Ayalon, Liat and Clemens Tesch-Römer. *Contemporary Perspectives on Ageism.* Berlin: Springer Nature, 2018.
42  Ayalon, L. "There Is Nothing New Under the Sun: Ageism and Intergenerational Tension in the Age of the COVID-19 Outbreak." *International Psychogeriatrics* 32, no. 10 (2020: 1221–1224. https://doi.org/ 10.1017/S1041610220000575.
43  Ayalon and Tesch-Römer, *Contemporary Perspectives.*
44  Shiovitz-Ezra, Sharon, Jonathan Shemesh, and Mary McDonnell/Naughton. "Pathways from Ageism to Loneliness." In *Contemporary Perspectives on Ageism,* edited by Liat Ayalon and Clemens Tesch-Römer, 131–147. Berlin: Springer, 2018.
45  Cuddy, Amy J. C., and Susan T. Fiske. "Doddering, but Dear: Process, Content, and Function in Stereotyping of Older Persons." In *Ageism: Stereotyping and Prejudice Against Older Persons,* edited by Todd Nelson, 3–26. Boston: MIT Press, 2002.
46  Ayalon and Tesch-Römer, "Taking a Closer Look," 1–4.
47  Nelson, Todd D. "Ageism: Prejudice Against Our Feared Future Self." *Journal of Social Issues* 61, no. 2 (2005): 207–221. https://doi.org/10.1111/j.1540-4560.2005.00402.x.
48  Levy, Becca. "Stereotype Embodiment: A Psychosocial Approach to Aging." *Current Directions in Psychological Science* 18, 6 (2009): 332–336. https://doi.org/10.1111/j.1467-8721.2009.01662.x.
49  Sargent-Cox, Kerry A., Karin J. Anstey, and Mary A. Luszcz. "Longitudinal Change of Self-Perceptions of Aging And Mortality." *Journals of Gerontology Series B: Psychological Sciences and Social Sciences* 69, no. 2 (2014): 168–173. https://doi.org/10.1093/geronb/gbt005.
50  Levy, Becca R. and Lindsey M. Myers. "Preventive Health Behaviors Influenced by Self-Perceptions of Aging." *Preventive Medicine* 39, no. 3 (2004): 625–629. https://doi.org/10.1016/j.ypmed.2004.02.029.
51  Brothers, Allyson, Anna E Kornadt , Abigail Nehrkorn-Bailey, Hans-Werner Wahl, and Manfred Diehl. "The Effects of Age Stereotypes on Physical and Mental Health

are Mediated by Self-Perceptions of Aging." *The Journals of Gerontology: Series B* 76, 5 (2021): 845–857. https://doi/org/ 10.1093/geronb/gbaa176.

52 Rodríguez-Madrid, María Nieves, María Del Río-Lozano, Rosario Fernandez-Peña, Jaime Jiménez-Pernett, Leticia García-Mochón, Amparo Lupiañez-Castillo, and María Del Mar García-Calvente. "Gender Differences in Social Support Received by Informal Caregivers: A Personal Network Analysis Approach." *International Journal of Environmental Research and Public Health* 16, no. 1 (2019): 91. https:// doi.org/ 10.3390/ijerph16010091.

53 Dahlberg, Lena, Sean Demack, and Claire Bambra. "Age and Gender of Informal Carers: A Population-Based Study in the UK. *Health & Social Care in the Community* 15, no. 5 (2007): 439–445. https://doi.org/ 10.1111/j.1365-2524.2007.00702.x.

54 Luppa, Melanie, Tobias Luck, Siegfried Weyerer, Hans-Helmut König, and Steffi G. Riedel-Heller. "Gender Differences in Predictors of Nursing Home Placement in the Elderly: A Systematic Review." *International Psychogeriatrics* 21, no. 6 (2009): 1015–1025. https://doi.org/ 10.1017/S1041610209990238.

55 Luppa et al., "Gender Differences," 1015–1025.

56 Okun, Sarit and Liat Ayalon. "Ageism: The Importance of the Linguistic Concept for the Construction of the Experience." *Ageing and Society*, Under revision.

57 Peisach., C.e.a., *Your Words Matter: Combating Ageism in the Lexicon for Mental Health Clinicians Caring for Older Persons.* Under review.

58 Salime, Samira, Christophe Clesse, Alexis Jeffredo, and Martine Batt. "Process of Deinstitutionalization of Aging Individuals with Severe and Disabling Mental Disorders: A Review." *Frontiers in Psychiatry*, 13 (2022). https://doi.org/ 10.3389/ fpsyt.2022.813338.

59 Morgan, Stephanie and Linda H. Yoder. "A Concept Analysis of Person-Centered Care." *Journal of Holistic Nursing* 30, no. 1 (2012): 6–15. https://doi.org/ 10.1177/0898010111412189.

60 Brownie, Sonya and Susan Nancarrow. "Effects of Person-Centered Care on Residents and Staff in Aged-Care Facilities: A Systematic Review." *Clinical Interventions in Aging* 8 (2013): 1. https://doi.org/ 10.2147/CIA.S38589.

61 Donovan, Nancy J. and Dan Blazer. Social Isolation and Loneliness in Older Adults: Review and Commentary of a National Academies Report." *The American Journal of Geriatric Psychiatry* 28, no. 12 (2020): 1233–1244. https://doi.org/ 10.1016/j.jagp.2020.08.005.

62 Boardman, Jed. "Social Exclusion and Mental Health–How People With Mental Health Problems are Disadvantaged: An Overview." *Mental Health and Social Inclusion* 15, no. 3 (2011): 112–121. https://doi.org/10.1108/2042830111 1165690.

63 Okun, Sarit and Liat Ayalon. "Eradicating Ageism through Social Campaigns: An Israeli Case Study in the Shadow of COVID-19." *Journal of Social Issues* 78, no. 4 (2022): 991–1016. https://doi.org/10.1111/josi.12540.

64 Pettigrew, Thomas F., Linda Tropp, Ulrich Wagnew, and Oliver Christ. "Recent Advances in Intergroup Contact Theory." *International Journal of Intercultural Relations* 35, no. 3 (2011): 271–280. https://doi.org/10.1016/j.ijintrel.2011.03.001.

65 Waqas, Ahmed, Salma Malik, Ania Fida, Noureen Abbas, Nadeem Mian, Sannihitha Miryala, Afshan Nax Amray, Zunairah Shah, and Sadiq Naveed. "Interventions to Reduce Stigma Related to Mental Illnesses in Educational Institutes: A Systematic

Review. *Psychiatric Quarterly* 91, no. 3 (2020): 887–903. https://doi.org/10.1007/s11126-020-09751-4.

66  Thornicroft, Graham, Elaine Brohan, Aliya Kassam, and Elanor Lewis-Holmes. "Reducing Stigma and Discrimination: Candidate Interventions." *International Journal of Mental Health Systems* 2, no. 1 (2008): 3. https://doi.org/10.1186/1752-4458-2-3.

67  UNDESA. "Convention on the Rights of Persons with Disabilities (CRPD)." Accessed January 7, 2023.
    https://www.un.org/development/desa/disabilities/convention-on-the-rights-of-persons-with-disabilities.html.

# 8. *Human Rights of Older Persons: Wishful Thinking or Reality?*

CLAUDIA MAHLER

Let me begin with some personal remarks. I want to share with you why I think it is time to provide older persons with the well-deserved protection of their human rights for today and the next generations. I will show how my passion and desire to improve the human rights of older persons started and what kind of improvements I see over time.

I started to work in the field of older persons' human rights after I read a report in 2010. A colleague from the Advisory Committee of the Human Rights Council analyzed the human rights framework and came to the conclusion that older persons were invisible in the human rights discussion, and that most of the existing relevant documents were not legally binding and specific measures on the national level were missing.[1] The analysis brought to light that older persons' human rights have not been as well protected as the rights of others, and raised awareness about, for example, ageism and age discrimination as gaps, since the specificity of the human rights of older persons had not been included in other treaties.

At this time, I was very fortunate because I had started a new position as a senior researcher on economic, social, and cultural rights at the German Institute of Human Rights (GIHR), the national human rights institution in Germany with A status in regard to the Paris Principles.[2] I suggested that I could work on the human rights of older persons as a new topic. With this specific focus in my work plan, I wanted to change the injustice that people in the latter part of their lives could not benefit from the system that they had built for all of us—the human rights framework. It became obvious that there was almost no specific focus on older persons in the field of human rights in Germany or Europe.

During my first year, the Office of the High Commissioner for Human Rights (OHCHR) launched a questionnaire on the human rights of older persons and the GIHR submitted their views. I remember that it was hard to find any resources. In the same year at the United Nations General Assembly, a resolution was negotiated that initiated the UN Open-Ended Working Group on Ageing (OEWG-A),[3] which was established at the UN by General Assembly Resolution 67/182 in December 2010. The OEWG-A held its first session in 2011[4] and its twelfth session in 2022. It is a state-driven process and non-governmental organizations (NGOs), and national human rights institutions (NHRIs) can participate. In 2012, a new resolution changed the mandate slightly. Now, the OEWG-A was expected to suggest dedicated measures to strengthen the international protection regime for older persons without further delay, including a new dedicated legally binding international instrument.[5] The working group discussed themes and normative key elements, but no agreed outcomes or specific proposals were released. Everything began with one report, which was followed by many reports, and today the amount of available material is enormous.[6]

The next milestone for me was the development of the mandate of the UN Independent Expert on the Enjoyment of all Human Rights by Older Persons in 2013.[7] Some said it was a side track, but in my opinion, we needed more key stakeholders to raise awareness, because the voices of older persons were not as loud as they should have been. The unequal treatment was not fully understood and was still viewed as something normal. During these first years of work on the topic, I had difficulty finding allies on the national level, because few people found it necessary to focus on older persons' human rights and even fewer wanted to join me on this specific topic.

It was good to know that a handful of people around the globe were, however, eager to work on the human rights of older persons and I met them frequently in discussions at the Council of Europe (CoE) or the UN. But the pace at which the work elaborated was very slow and it felt more and more like a "delaying process" and a gerontological and geriatric discussion and not as a discussion about rights.

Some new developments took place around the world including in the regional frameworks. I joined the newly established working group of the Steering Committee for Human Rights (CDDH) at the CoE to discuss and draft an instrument to frame human rights in light of the needs and views of older persons. The working group consisted of CoE member states, NGOs, and NHRIs. When the non-binding recommendations of the Ministers of the Council of Europe were finalized,[8] I hoped that this would be a game changer for European states. The document shows clearly that the human rights of older persons needed a different shape and member states like France and Germany were very active members of the working group and agreed among themselves on the content. In my naiveté, I could not believe that nothing would change and that governments would not see this as a step in the direction of strengthening the protection of the human rights of older persons. This part of the story was completed in 2014 and we are now in 2022. Not much happened during this time in the European region,[9] which was influenced by the non-binding CoE's ministerial recommendations from 2014.

The discussion at the OEWG-A continued for a decade without much progress. After the COVID-19 crisis, which highlighted many shortcomings, some governments requested the identification of gaps in the current human rights framework.

In 2012, the office of the UN High Commissioner produced an analytical paper,[10] which determined that there were existing gaps and that better implementation of the existing conventions would not close all the identified protection gaps. In the tenth session of the OEWG-A, member states asked for an update on the analytical paper of 2012. Furthermore, they wanted to officially discuss the outcome of the analytical updated paper at the next session. Unfortunately, the COVID-19 pandemic caused the postponement of the 11th session. There was no session in 2020. After this break, member states, NHRIs and NGOs, met in a hybrid format in 2021. The analytical update paper was only discussed in a side event.[11] During this exchange, several gaps were identified and the additional value of a specific convention on the rights of older persons was highlighted. The study exhibited evidence that the current human rights framework is insufficient, but no official decision at the OEWG-A was made.

Member states asked to officially discuss the study of the OHCHR at the 12th session in order to move forward, but the members of the bureau of the OEWG-A (Argentina, Slovenia, Canada, and the Philippines) which planned the session in 2022, did not take up the request. The twelfth session was a hybrid session and had panel discussions on two thematic issues and two normative elements. On the last day, Argentina made a proposal to install an informal cross-regional core group, to draft a proposal for a working group which would prepare the material during the time between sessions. This proposal received a lot of support, but the proposal was not as strong and forward-looking as many had hoped for. The proposal for the working group should be presented at the next session of the OEWG-A in 2023.

Why does it take so long to get the political will to draft a convention on the human rights of older persons? Many key stakeholders asked this question after the 12th session.

I want to add that I was part of the working group as a member of the GIHR till 2021 and because I was appointed the second mandate holder as UN Independent Expert on the enjoyment of all human rights by older persons,[12] I took part in the OEWG-A as part of the mandate of the Independent Expert. It was a great honor to speak at the High-Level Panel on the impact of the COVID-19 pandemic on the human rights of older persons in 2021 and the thematic panels at the twelfth session in 2022, but I had hoped for more progress because the COVID-19 pandemic highlighted the gaps and shortcomings in the protection of older persons.

## *Invisibility*

Older persons are entitled to the same rights as everybody else, but there are many barriers which hinder them in fully enjoying their human rights. The older part of the population is still more or less invisible in the existing international human rights framework because the current system is fragmented and does not focus specifically on older persons' human rights, except through the mandate of the Independent Expert on the full enjoyment of all human rights by older persons. Till today the global human rights framework lacks a specific prohibition on age discrimination, which is one reason why older persons are not considered in the human rights system. Another issue that is not discussed very widely is ageism, which is a main factor that explains why the violations of the human rights of older persons are overlooked. The missing acknowledgment of ageism leads to further age discrimination. This lack of awareness and recognition leads to fast justifications for age discrimination.

Older persons deserve better protection for their human rights. They should not be left behind in a system that they developed when they were part of the younger generation. Older persons care a lot for other parts of society but do not speak up loudly to raise awareness of the injustices of the current system. Another aspect which is often overlooked is that we speak about contemporary older persons but there are a lot of new generations of older persons to come. The older generation might increase their presence from one or two decades to three or four decades in the life course. Furthermore, the younger generation of today is the older generation of tomorrow! This is, why I cannot understand why older persons are frequently overlooked and not included as valuable participants.

During the COVID-19 pandemic, the whole world witnessed that older persons had to cope with the biggest negative impact.[13] They had to bear the brunt and were left behind.[14] All age groups are at risk of contracting COVID-19, but older persons are at a significantly higher risk of mortality and severe disease following infection.[15] Adults at a higher age may also face age discrimination in decisions on medical care, triage, and life-saving therapies. It was visible that the emergency health plans did not take their specific needs into account. Emergencies like the pandemic led to a decrease in critical services and support unrelated to COVID-19, further increasing risks to the lives of older persons. These shortcomings led to a high number of human rights violations and shone a spotlight on the gaps in the current human rights framework.

## *A Big Diverse Group Which Is Oppressed*

In 2022, there were 771 million persons aged 65 years or older worldwide. The ageing population has a female face. On average women tend to live longer than men; they comprise the majority of older persons, especially at advanced ages. Globally, the number of older persons aged 65 or above is expected to more than double, which means that during the next three decades, we will reach over 1.6 billion in 2050.[16] This phenomenon will be visible in all regions.[17]

Older people are the fastest-growing part of the population worldwide. They are women. They are persons with migrant backgrounds. They are living in rural areas and have the highest poverty risk. These intersecting characteristics show that older adults are a very diverse group. I also would like to stress that inequalities get aggravated in older age.

Unfortunately, people in older age are very often invisible in the different debates. Their experience, contribution, and participation are not acknowledged. Older persons are less included as stakeholders and are not recognized as experts of their lived realities. They are regularly described with many stereotypes and viewed as frail and unproductive, which demonstrates already ageist approaches that are deeply rooted in our societies. These are grounds why policymakers very often overlook them, and these large groups of the population are not a priority on the national, regional, or international levels.

There is no doubt that older people are entitled to the same human rights as everybody else, but in reality, there are many barriers that hinder older persons in the full enjoyment of their human rights. I would like to emphasize that they are rights holders not only beneficiaries, and it is time to change the narrative in this regard. A lot needs to be done to make older persons a priority. Furthermore, we must question stereotypes and biases and update images of older persons to make our societies age-inclusive. An inclusive living space would be an environment where we all enjoy our human rights in later life and on an equal basis as others.

## *Who Is an Older Person?*

I am very often asked, who is an older person? At which age does a person belong to the older persons age group?

From my point of view, one answer is clear, the question cannot be answered with a single age limit! As mentioned before, we are talking about decades, not only a few years and the circumstances around the world are diverse and dependent on social factors. Therefore, I am not fully convinced that the definitions of the Interamerican Convention on the Human Rights of Older Persons[18] and the African Protocol[19] are fit for purpose because both include age limits.

Age discrimination occurs for different rights at different stages in the life course. Regarding the right to work, a person in their 50s might already be an older worker in Europe, but when it comes to care, we might consider the diverse needs of persons in their 70s, 80s, and 90s. When we discuss the right to education, the focus for older persons might be lifelong learning or vocational training in the workforce. Furthermore, in tribal and indigenous communities, older persons may be viewed as "elders" who may enjoy higher status and power and be valued for their wisdom. They are the ones who preserve the culture and languages. Older adults are treated differently, and each right would also have an impact on various lived realities in combination with the different stages of the life course and might be highly diverse around the globe. But still today age is widely used to structure society and our own lives. Chronological age is often used to define older persons in domestic, regional, and international policies and legislation. It is easier to understand and contextualize topics for governments to have a clear age limit, but it does not do justice to the different stages of life. In countries with lower life expectancies, older age starts earlier than in those with higher life expectancies.

From my point of view, it is necessary to challenge the common perception that a typical life trajectory comprises three distinct phases: childhood with education, adulthood with work, and old age with retirement. This model is outdated and does not reflect the additional years we gained because of improved health care and living conditions. There should be parts of work in interchange or intervals with education, which would seem more appropriate in our globalized world to adjust to diverse realities.

Because of the increased life expectancy and evolving life choices and opportunities, age is not synonymous with decline and inactivity. The current systems are still working with age limits. For example, mandatory retirement ages that exclude older persons from the labor market based on old age can be found in many countries. Some governments have already realized that a more flexible system would work better for older persons and the economy, but these examples are still rare.

In current policymaking, the concept of biological age is generally in use. It emphasizes the state of older persons, both in terms of the functioning of their bodies and their remaining abilities. Certain groups, such as indigenous people, refugees and internally displaced persons, persons deprived of their liberty, or patients living with HIV, may face biological signs of ageing earlier than others, owing to adverse life conditions. This includes older persons who have endured conditions of war, conflict, and natural disasters.

Perceptions of old age can also depend on cultural and other factors, such as the demographic characteristics of a community. In this context, ageing is viewed and constructed primarily as a medical problem warranting medical intervention. Very often the discussions are opened with the negative notion that the ageing population is a problem for policymakers and the potential of longevity is not considered in these exchanges. Hence the medical model continues to permeate policy thinking on ageing. Illness and frailty are often, wrongly, attributed to all older persons. This is very often combined with weakened abilities, lack of adaptability, and dependency, without considering that these qualities are not intrinsic to old age. This assessment leads to the assumption that older persons need to be *looked after* and policy decisions are taken "in the best interest of older persons" assuming they all experience mental and physical decline because of their older age.

Therefore, I propose that age be seen as a social construct whereby social, economic, and political contexts determine whether individuals are considered or consider themselves as old or older.

## *Why Is There a Need For Better Protection of Human Rights?*

One major question often asked is "What do human rights have to do with older persons?" The short answer is "Everything." Human rights are the basis for an inclusive society. But when the Universal Declaration on Human Rights (UDHR) was designed and drafted in 1948, older persons and their specific needs and contributions were not considered. Age as a factor of discrimination was not the focus of the mothers and fathers of the UDHR. Because of this gap, the binding conventions especially the International Covenant on Economic, Social and Cultural Rights (ICESCR) and the International Covenant on Civil and Political Rights (ICCPR), which enshrine the rights of the UDHR, do not mention age as a ground for discrimination. Hence, the drafters of the ICESCR and the ICCPR seemed to be aware that there might be more grounds a person could be discriminated against in the future, and this might be why they included the notion of *other status* in the non-discrimination clauses in the two covenants. Having said that, one could argue that everything is perfect because age as a specific aspect of discrimination is covered. But we have realized that age discrimination is treated differently because age is not directly stated. In the cases of older age discriminatory behavior, the regularly reported practice seems to ignore, or too easily justify, discrimination based on older age.

The international human rights covenants and several human rights conventions–with the exception of the Convention on the Rights of the Child—apply to people of all ages.[20] This would include older persons, but we have witnessed that the current human rights framework is not specific enough to fully protect the human rights of older persons. This is why an international and regional debate has been ongoing regarding the recognition of the human rights of older persons, with a view to developing a new International Convention on the Human Rights of Older Persons to close the gaps in the remaining human rights framework. It has been argued that these developments reflect a paradigm shift in the ageing discourse, in which older people are considered active holders of human rights rather than "objects of charity" or "beneficiaries." The overall findings of analytical studies show that the current human rights framework is not comprehensive; it is fragmented and does not address the diverse needs of older persons. We also have to recognize that emerging issues, which are crucial for the full protection of older persons, have not been considered. To name two examples: digitalization and climate change.

## *Age Discrimination*

As mentioned before, age discrimination as a specific clause is missing in the current human rights framework. The absence of age as a clear ground for discrimination reveals a gap in the international human rights framework.[21] As a result, many national anti-discrimination laws fail to address age-related discrimination holistically.

Discriminatory provisions, such as age limits are visible in laws and policies and lead to unequal treatment. Because of the long history of unequal treatment in older age, older persons themselves very often assume that it is justified and should not be discussed in the broader public.

## Ageism

During the COVID-19 pandemic, ageist attitudes have become visible in various forms. We had to witness triage procedures as well as forms of verbal abuse and negative images targeting older persons in the media and public debates around the globe. The pandemic has drastically amplified prevalent ageism, which results also from the portrayal of older persons as unproductive and burdens on societies.[22] Regarding some responses of authorities, older adults were viewed as dispensable and not worthy of intensive care treatment. It was assumed because of ageist approaches, that life at a later stage was not worth living and couldn't have a high quality. These intergenerational resentments, which became evident during the pandemic, often result in a breach of basic human rights and attacks against the human dignity of older persons.[23] It seems that the difficulty of defining the target group or victims of ageism adds an additional layer of complexity to studying and combating ageism.

Ageism is not a new phenomenon. The term was coined by Robert Butler in 1969,[24] at a time when the two Covenants came to light. The term and the concept of ageism are still missing in the UN human rights framework.[25] This is in contrast to several UN human rights treaties, which oblige States Parties to take steps to combat racism, sexism, and ableism. In my report on ageism and age discrimination, I define ageism as stereotypes, prejudice, and/or discriminatory actions or practices against older persons that are based on their chronological age or on a perception that the person is "old."[26] I was very pleased that the UN Decade on Healthy Ageing focused on ageism in one of the first reports, and brought a lot of evidence that ageism is visible around the world.[27] I welcomed the WHO campaigns and took part in different events to raise awareness that structural and internal ageism are hindering older persons to enjoy their human rights. The Human Rights Council Resolution 48/3 adopted on October 7, 2021, included ageism for the first time.[28]

## Digitalization

The new digital world with its myriad different tools might be a perfect solution to connect with loved ones who are living far away or could not be reached because of distancing rules. On the other hand, they can also pose a serious threat to some people.[29] But as said before, older persons are a diverse group. Some older persons use their digital tools on an everyday basis and others might be digitally illiterate. Older persons who are familiar with digital tools use their smartphones as often as their grandchildren and know how to communicate and get sufficient information. Hence, they use services to support their independence. There is no specific reference to the right to assistive technology in the current human rights framework except in the Convention on the Rights of Persons with Disabilities (CRPD) which gives guidance. It recognizes the importance of access to assistive technology.[30] The United Nations Principles for Older Persons, the ICCPR, and the ICESCR do not include a specific reference, which can be seen as another gap in the human rights framework.

In this context, the infrastructure in the respective living situation is always very important. Older adults living in rural areas, without enough resources or access to the world wide web might not be in a position to benefit from any service, which would be available via digital avenues. Another aspect is the educational basis or the inclusion of digital technology during work life. Older women especially have less contact with and insights into digital tools via their time in the labor market, often because of their educational and professional background. These markers increase the digital divide. The digital divide is another form of exclusion because older persons might not participate in the community, or get their needed medical appointments, or have been unable to make vaccination appointments, or have not been informed about the protection measures in place in armed conflicts. Access to information and to ways to book services are vital for older persons. Hence, if they are only provided via digital communication channels, this can increase the risks of reduced enjoyment or violations of human rights by older persons.

Digitals tools on the other hand can be an asset to increase opportunities for independent living. Smart solutions in smart homes or emergency buttons or virtual visits by nurses and doctors can be a wonderful support to obtain services and feel safe in one's home. Many smart solutions are still very expensive, which already excludes a high proportion of older persons. Private companies should invest more in age-friendly solutions, and I hope that they will consider Universal Design when designing new technical tools and include older persons as the experts of their needs. I am confident that this will improve and the next generations of older persons may be more willing to try and use new virtual and digital supports.

The whole legal framework does not include the right to access to the digital world. Digital tools and assistive technology for older persons are a must for them to take part in society and ensure independent living.[31]

## Climate Change

Regarding climate change, the debate is very often dedicated to the next generation, which means children and young people. I am still surprised that in the notion of next-generation, older persons are not included, because we all know the youth of today is the next generation of older people, with a much longer timeframe to belong to the older person cohorts. But climate change is not only a topic for future generations. There is enough evidence that the current global warming causes damage, especially to older persons. For example, the heat waves of 2003 and 2012 had a devastating impact on the lives of older persons, especially older women. Mortality during the heat waves heavily increased. As I am writing these lines, we hear reports about another heatwave in Western Canada (2021). Older women reported that they could not get enough protection through ventilation to have a dignified life because of the high temperatures. The number of deaths increased significantly, mostly older adults living alone without sufficient ventilation.[32]

The voices of older persons get louder. The case of KlimaSeniorinnen in Switzerland is a prominent one. In 2016, KlimaSeniorinnen and four individual plaintiffs came to the federal government and asked for increased climate protection to protect their fundamental rights to life and health.[33] Their complaints were dismissed and they went to the European Court of Human Rights in Strasbourg.[34] The case is now pending at the grand chamber of the European Court of Human Rights and this shows that the court is taking this question seriously.[35] Relevant stakeholders and European governments are expecting the decision to have far-reaching consequences.

Unexpected extreme rainfalls have caused devastating damage to infrastructure and support systems. The floods in Great Britain disturbed the support system for care homes and other facilities like schools, etc. The horrible pictures where houses were floating away and residents had to wait for evacuation on top of their roofs were broadcast and showed that these extreme weather conditions need to be tackled in emergency schemes. These schemes must have specific precautions for older persons with or without disabilities or in need of care. Most governments realized that they were not prepared to assist and support older adults in these circumstances but rearranging for new developments is time-consuming.

During all these climate change crises, it is evident that older persons' human rights are not well protected.[36] Older persons have not been considered when it comes to preventive measures or evacuation plans. Their right to participation is often neglected because they are not seen as targets of climate change, or the impact on older people is not considered.

## Armed Conflict

Other emergencies where older persons have been left behind are armed conflicts and accommodation as displaced persons inside and outside the country of origin. Older persons are very often those who stay in their homes because they feel bound to their land and home or fear that they will not manage to start from scratch in a different place or country.[37] There might be many other grounds for why older women and men tend to leave the war zones at a very late stage. Life-saving information may not reach them because they do not have access to digital channels, or they may not want to be a burden on family members who have decided to flee. The lack of mobility and lack of support to move out of the conflict zone can cause delays in evacuation.

Humanitarian aid support does not always have older persons and their specific needs on their minds. Older persons in rural areas are especially hard to reach and it is difficult to provide sufficient medical treatment as well as food and water. Regarding persons in need of care during a conflict, the care and medical personnel are either at the front or leaving the country. For people who live in institutions, assistance and support are vital. Their right to life is dependent on support and effective protection during armed conflicts. Evacuation for large numbers of persons who live in care facilities must have specific preparations and precautions.

## Data

Regularly collected data is insufficient with regard to age aggregation.[38] Very often it tends to exclude older cohorts of their sets, which leads to invisibility regarding indicators and measures. Data is significant for the realization of the human rights of older persons; it is a prerequisite for evidence-based and informed decision-making and normative action. There is evidence that the current data on older persons is inconsistent and includes gaps. These data gaps are barriers and have negative impacts on the enjoyment of all human rights by older persons. The lack of data also consists of risks in this context. In all discussions I attended for the last 10 years, missing data was always mentioned as a reason why the protection of older persons is not as sufficient and accurate as possible. We do not see the whole picture without the data; we miss the evidence that would allow us to implement the right measures.

For example, when it comes to specific violations of sexual violence, it is assumed that sexual violence does not occur in later life.[39] This assumption is based on the idea that after a certain age or after menopause older women or older persons are no longer sexually active or attractive enough to be a target of sexual violence.[40] The assumption is wrong in every respect and these stereotypes lead to wrong decisions and gaps in data collection.

## Conclusion

Older persons deserve the full enjoyment of their human rights. The current human rights framework needs to be improved and for this reason, I showed from my perspective that political will is needed to take the next step. Furthermore, I wanted to highlight why the current human rights framework is not sufficient and that only better implementation of the existing framework would not be enough to close the remaining protection gaps. The pandemic highlighted human rights violations of older persons and I shed light on some of the new phenomena, like digitalization or climate change, which need to be considered when strengthening the human rights of older persons. Older adults are overlooked in data and are not part of the emergency plans, which has devastating consequences for their lives. It is time, right now, to change the narrative toward one that older persons are rights holders and the experts in their lived realities and not only beneficiaries of social security systems. We could achieve much better protection of the human rights of older persons through a comprehensive legally binding international human rights treaty. I will work to achieve this goal, overcome barriers, and show with my reports and speeches that the current and the next generation of older persons must enjoy their human rights on an equal basis with others.

## Notes

1 Chung, Chinsung. *Advisory Committee Expert paper on the issue of the human rights of elder persons.* Geneva: OHCHR, 2010. https://www.ohchr.org/en/press-releases/2010/01/advisory-committee-discusses-working-paper-human-rights-elderly..

2 Office of the High Commissioner (OHCHR). "Principles relating to the Status of National Institutions (The Paris Principles)." Accessed January 6, 2023. https://www.ohchr.org/en/instruments-mechanisms/instruments/principles-relating-status-national-institutions-paris.

3 United Nations Department of Economic and Social Affairs (UNDESA). " Open-Ended Working Group on Ageing." Accessed May 13, 2022. https://social.un.org/ageing-working-group/index.shtml.

4 UNDESA. "First Working Session." Open-Ended Working Group on Ageing. Accessed May 13, 2022. https://social.un.org/ageing-working-group/firstsession.shtml.

5 UNGA. "Towards a Comprehensive and Integral International Legal Instrument to Promote and Protect the Rights and Dignity of Older Persons." Resolution adopted

by the General Assembly UN Doc A/RES/67/139. Accessed May 13, 2022. https://
documents-dds-ny.un.org/doc/UNDOC/GEN/N12/486/94/PDF/N1248694.
pdf?OpenElement.

6  Byrnes, Andrew and Titti Mattsson. "Background Paper: The Human Rights of Older
   Persons." Seoul: 20th Informal ASEM Seminar on Human Rights, 2021. https://
   asef.org/wp-content/uploads/2021/02/ASEMHRS20-Background-paper.pdf.

7  OHCHR. "About the Mandate." Accessed May 13, 2022. https://www.ohchr.org/
   en/special-procedures/ie-older-persons/about-mandate.

8  Council of Europe. "Promotion of Human Rights of Older Persons." Accessed May
   13, 2022. https://rm.coe.int/1680695bce.

9  Council of Europe. "Promotion of Human Rights of Older Persons." Accessed May
   13, 2022. https://rm.coe.int/promotion-of-human-rights-of-older-persons/168
   09fb9bf. Including a report on a practical Workshop, organised by the CDDH 2018.

10 OHCHR. "Analytical Paper on Older Persons." Accessed January 6, 2023.
   https://www.ohchr.org/en/documents/outcome-documents/analytical-outc
   ome-paper-normative-standards-international-human-rights.

11 OHCHR. "Working Paper: Update to the 2012 Analytical Outcome Study on the
   Normative Standards in International Human Rights Law in Relation to Older
   Persons." Accessed May 13, 2022. https://social.un.org/ageing-working-group/
   documents/eleventh/OHCHR%20HROP%20working%20paper%2022%20
   Mar%202021.pdf.

12 OHCHR. "Independent Expert on the Enjoyment of All Human Rights By Older
   Persons." Accessed May 13, 2022. https://www.ohchr.org/en/special-procedures/
   ie-older-persons.

13 United Nations Sustainable Development Group. "Policy Brief: The Impact of
   COVID-19 on Older Persons." Accessed May 13, 2022. https://unsdg.un.org/
   resources/policy-brief-impact-covid-19-older-persons.

14 UNDESA. "Unacceptable" – UN expert urges better protection of older persons facing the highest risk of the COVID-19 pandemic." Accessed May 13, 2022. https://
   www.un.org/development/desa/ageing/news/2020/03/covid-19/. A   powerful
   statement by the former UN Independent Expert on the enjoyment of all human
   rights by older persons Rosa Kornfeld Matte .

15 OHCHR. "Impact of the Coronavirus Disease (COVID-19) on the Enjoyment
   of All Human Rights By Older Persons."Accessed May 13, 2022. https://doc-
   uments-dds-ny.un.org/doc/UNDOC/GEN/N20/189/73/PDF/N2018973.
   pdf?OpenElement.

16 UNDESA, Population Division. "World Population Prospects 2022: Summary of
   Results." UN DESA/POP/2022/TR/NO. 3.

17 UNDESA, Population Division. "World Population Prospects 2022: Summary of
   Results."

18 Organization of American States. "Inter-American Convention on Protecting the
   Human Rights of Older Persons." Accessed May 13, 2022. https://www.oas.org/
   en/sla/dil/inter_american_treaties_A-70_human_rights_older_persons.asp.     In
   force since 2017.

19 African Union. "Protocol to the African Charter on Human and Peoples' Rights
   on the Rights of Older Persons in Africa." Accessed May 13, 2022. https://au.int/
   sites/default/files/treaties/36438-treaty-0051_-_protocol_on_the_rights_of_olde
   r_persons_e.pdf.

20 Doron, Israel and Benny Spanier. "International Elder Law, The Future of Elder Law." In *Beyond Elder Law*, edited by Israel Doron and Ann M. Soden, 125–148, 128. Berlin, Heidelberg: Springer, 2012.

21 De Pauw, Marijke, Bridget Sleap, and Nena Georgantzi. "Ageism and Age Dscrimination in International Human Rights Law." In *Ageing, Ageism and the Law*, edited by Israel Doron and Nena Georgantzi, 174–194, 182. Cheltenham: Edward Elgar, 2018.

22 OHCHR, "Impact of the Coronavirus."

23 Age Platform Europe. "COVID-19 and Human Rights Concerns for Older Persons." Accessed May 13, 2022. https://www.age-platform.eu/sites/default/files/Human_rights_concerns_on_implications_of_COVID-19_to_older_persons_updated_18May2020.pdf.

24 Butler, Robert. "Age Ism: Another Form of Bigotry." *The Gerontologist* 9, no. 4 (1969): 243.

25 Doron, Israel and Nena Georgantzi. *Ageing, Ageism and the Law, European Perspectives on the Rights of Older Persons.* Cheltenham: Edward Elgar, 2018.

26 OHCHR, "Independent Expert," A/HRC/48/53 para 21.

27 World Health Organization. *Global Report on Ageism.* Geneva: WHO, 2020.

28 UNGA. "Human Rights of Older Persons." October 14, 2021. A/HRC/RES/48/3. https://undocs.org/Home/Mobile?FinalSymbol=A%2FHRC%2FRES%2F48%2F3&Language=E&DeviceType=Desktop&LangRequested=False.

29 UNECE. "Ageing in the Digital Era." Policy Brief no. 26. Accessed May 13, 2022. https://unece.org/sites/default/files/2021-07/PB26-ECE-WG.1-38_0.pdf.

30 OHCHR. "Report of the Independent Expert on the Enjoyment of All Human Rights by Older Persons." 2017. UN Doc A/HRC/36/48. Accessed May 13, 2022. https://documents-dds-ny.un.org/doc/UNDOC/GEN/G17/219/52/PDF/G1721952.pdf?OpenElement.

31 OHCHR. "Working Paper: Update to the 2012 Analytical Outcome Study on the Normative Standards in International Human Rights Law in Relation to Older Persons." Accessed May 13, 2022. Para 183-191. https://social.un.org/ageing-working-group/documents/eleventh/OHCHR%20HROP%20working%20paper%2022%20Mar%202021.pdf.

32 Cecco, Leyland. "Record Heatwave May Have Killed 500 People in Western Canada." *The Guardian,* July 2, 2022. https://www.theguardian.com/world/2021/jul/02/canada-heatwave-500-deaths.

33 Klimaseniorinnen. "Senior Women for Climate Protection Switzerland to Sue Switzerland before the European Court of Human Rights." Accessed May 13, 2022. https://en.klimaseniorinnen.ch/.

34 " Verein KlimaSeniorinnen Schweiz et. al. v. Switzerland." Amicus curiae by 3 UN Special Rapporteurs Marcos A. Orellana, David R. Boyd, Claudia Mahler, 2021. https://www.ohchr.org/sites/default/files/Documents/Issues/ToxicWaste/AmicusKlimmaECtHR.pdf.

35 ECHR. "Grand Chamber to Examine Case Concerning Complaint by Association that Climate Change is Having an Impact on their Living Conditions and Health." April 29 2022. https://hudoc.echr.coe.int/app/conversion/pdf/?libr ary=ECHR&id=003-7322460-9989782&filename=Relinquishment%20in%20fa vor%20of%20the%20Grand%20Chamber%20of%20the%20case%20Verein%20K limaSeniorinnen%20Schweiz%20and%20Others%20v.%20Switzerland.pdf.

36 OHCHR. "Analytical Study on the Promotion and Protection of the Rights of Older Persons in the Context of climate Change." UN Doc A/HRC/47/46. Accessed May 13, 2022. https://documents-dds-ny.un.org/doc/UNDOC/GEN/G21/099/23/ PDF/G2109923.pdf?OpenElement.

37 Human Rights Watch. "No One is Spared: Abuses Against Older People in Armed Conflict." Accessed May 13, 2022. https://www.hrw.org/sites/default/files/med ia_2022/02/global_olderpeople0222_web.pdf.

38 Kornfeld-Matte, Rosa. "Report on the Human Rights of Older Persons: The Data Gap Conundrum." UN doc A/HRC/45/14. Accessed May 13 2022. https://www. ohchr.org/en/documents/thematic-reports/data-gap.

39 OHCHR. "Human Rights of Older Women: The Intersection Between Ageing and Gender." UN Doc A/76/157. Accessed May 13, 2022. https://documents-dds-ny. un.org/doc/UNDOC/GEN/N21/193/82/PDF/N2119382.pdf?OpenElement.

40 OHCHR. "UN Advocacy Brief on Older Women." Accessed May 13, 2022. https://www.ohchr.org/sites/default/files/2022-03/UN-Advocacy-Brief-Older-Women.pdf.

# 9. "Viva La Nannalution!" Overcoming Ageist Sexism in Environmental Activism: The Australian Older Women's Knitting Nannas Against Gas and Greed

LARRAINE J. LARRI

## Introduction

Becoming 50, I was eligible for lower premium insurance from Australian Seniors. Being called "senior" was strange since I certainly did not feel old enough. Through its monthly magazine, *Dare*, Australian Seniors promotes ageing well. One article caught my eye, "Silver Lining: It's Time to Embrace Your Silver Hair." It was about ageism in the workplace and how that keeps women covering up our ageing by coloring our hair. I went grey early and colored my hair for years to maintain an image of youthful employability. When I gained a management position in the NSW Department of Ageing, Disability and Home Care, expecting a more inclusive workplace I reverted to my natural silver. The hardest people to convince were my partner and my hairdresser. "Oh my heavens, you can't do that, you'll look so old!" they said.

And when we do grey, it's not just our hair that shades; our whole beings seem to disappear from public view. Anecdotally, women talk about this sudden onset of invisibility, which also includes condescension (such as calling us "dearie," "sweetie," or "pet"). Australian writer Helen Garner attributes this to the withdrawal of the erotic gaze since older women, "are no longer, in the eyes of the world, a sexual being."[1] In "This Chair Rocks: A Manifesto Against Ageism" American Ashton Applewhite challenges all ages to overcome the negative, discriminatory, and limiting effects of ageism.[2]

The Australian Knitting Nannas Against Gas and Greed (a.k.a. KNAG or the Nannas) are a group of older women who have challenged the conventional view that environmental activists are young, unemployed, and scruffy. On their website, the Nannas assert "Anyone can be an activist and contribute to change. Any type of action can be strong. If we get together and use our strengths, we can make change."[3]

The Nannas evolved from events in the Northern Rivers Region (NSW, Australia) when communities began fighting against coal seam gas (CSG) extraction, also called "fracking."[4] This was very much a "not in my back-yard" rural grassroots movement where many people were thrown into pro-test by circumstance rather than being lifelong activists.[5]

I will describe the ageist and sexist nature of oppression these older women faced and overcame in becoming twenty-first-century environmen-tal activists. KNAG broke through an ageist deficit model that views older women as "old bags," "useless nobodies,"[6] and "digitally disengaged."[7]

Part of a larger dissertation into "Nannagogy" or older women's environ-mental activist Social Movement Learning (SML), the research identified a knowledge gap and gender blindness toward older women. Data was collected through primary sources including a written online survey (n=67); interviews (n=10); and document analysis of social media in the public domain (purpo-sive sample of Facebook posts, digital videos, e-mails, and e-news bulletins). All informants were active members of the movement and drawn from several KNAG loops (or groups) in approximately 40 locations. Interviewees were de-identified by choosing pseudonyms based on women they admired. The research was approved by the James Cook University Human Research Ethics Committee (2017–2021).

I will continue with a brief literature review contextualizing what we know about ageist sexism affecting older women in social movements. Following that is an overview of the challenge confronting Australian anti-CSG activists, such as the Knitting Nannas, due to climate change denialism. Next are examples of pivotal transformative experiences for the Nannas in overcoming the oppression of ageist sexism and becoming accepted as envi-ronmental activists. These are grouped into three themes: (1) Disengaging from denigration—discovering empowerment; (2) Strategic essentialism as activist identity; and (3) Claiming virtual space—collective and connective action. The chapter concludes with implications for the inclusion of older women in environmental activist movements.

### *Ageist Sexism in Social Movements—The Literature*

Sexism in social movements is a recurring and underresearched theme as is older women's use of digital media in activism.[8,9,10] Roy describes examples where women in mainstream peace movements left due to sexism and formed Women Strike for Peace in the United States (from 1961 onwards), the Greenham Common Women's Peace Camp in the United Kingdom (from 1987 to 2000), and the Raging Grannies initially in Canada spreading across North America (1987 to present).[11] Investigating women's environmentalism in extractive mining in the Peruvian and Ecuadorean Andes, Jenkins documents how women had protested alongside men but formed women-specific groups as a way of combating sexism and marginalization within the broader anti-mining movement.[12] When Velasquez researched the emergence of Ecuador's Andean rural women's anti-mining movement, she found that sexism within the existing movement sparked a gendered critique, ultimately leading to the establishment of the anti-mining women's group, *Frente de Mujeres Defensoras de la Pachamama* (Women's Front for the Defence of Mother Earth).[13] Agrarian women from anti-mining struggles across the country came together through this movement and became publicly visible and vulnerable to violence from the pro-mining state. The women shared their experiences about the negative impacts of mining on food production and their concerns for future generations through the loss of livelihoods and ecological, and environmental values. Despite compensation from the mining companies, many had lost their sources of income and sustenance through increasingly unproductive lands.

A common thread of women's environmental activism is strategic essentialism. Essentialism is the practice of assuming the nature of things is fixed rather than culturally defined. Women are often essentialized as being close to nature, earth mothers, and nurturers, and therefore more likely to be concerned with environmental issues and planetary well-being.[14,15] This is "descriptively false in that it denies the real diversity of women's lives and social situations."[16]

Sexism and ageism are examples of the negative effects of essentializing.[17] Groups like the Raging Grannies use this strategically as an "oppositional discourse in which women assume the characteristics assigned to them by a phallocentric culture to challenge phallocentrism and its description of and prescription for women."[18] Numerous feminist scholars look at the intersection of motherhood and activism but fewer have extended this to include an analysis of grandmotherhood and activisms.[19,20] Sawchuk critiques the ageist and sexist narratives of grandmotherhood, finding the Raging Grannies' "strategic deployment" of the grandmother identity is disarming and efficacious.[21] Police were reluctant to move them on or arrest them and they claimed it was easier to get their message across using humor and parodying the image of essentialized older women.[22] Humorous performative activism has become their identity brand, which they use to engage and educate audiences in understanding issues such as the toxic impacts of CSG. Similarly, Ecuadorian anti-mining women drew on their Pachamama (Mother Earth Inca goddess) mythology to "present a more cohesive identity and narrative around their activism."[23]

## Climate Change Denialism and Fighting Fracking in Australia

The larger background for the existence of the Nannas is explained in this overview. Australia's commitment to action on global warming and climate change has waxed and waned over the last 40 years. We have shifted from accepting the anthropogenic causes of climate change in the 1980s and 1990s to becoming sceptical and confused in the late 1990s and early 2000s. From 2007 to 2013, we adopted a stance of concerted action which was followed by almost two decades of lack of consensus and political inertia dubbed the *Energy Wars*. In 2021, we are seen as an international pariah lagging in addressing decarbonization.[24,25] The causes of such shifts are attributed to divisive political leadership, the economic power of fossil fuel industries, vested interests, and media disinformation campaigns.[26,27,28,29]

Not only have fossil fuels been linked to climate change, but unconventional CSG extraction is also known to be environmentally toxic.[30,31,32,33] In Australia, CSG is an environmental concern because much of the land targeted for exploration is in farming and rural communities. This has implications for food security (the exploration of CSG mines are located in Australia's richest food production areas); biodiversity (diverse and rare natural environments are threatened); water security and purity (as one of the driest continents, Australia relies on its precious water resources much of which are held in natural geological formations of aquifers and artesian reservoirs); human health issues (due to the impact of polluting gases on both air and water quality); First Nations cultural ancestral connection to Country; and community cohesion (where fracking is contentious and communities are divided, newcomers "fly in/fly out" for work, and the added potential for "boom town" mentalities leading to increases in violence).[34,35,36]

## Pivotal Transformative Experiences in Overcoming Ageist Sexism

*Disengaging from Denigration—Discovering Empowerment.* Many older women were among the thousands of people mobilised by the Gasfield Free Northern Rivers Alliance (GFNR) anti-fracking awareness-raising campaign that began in 2010. The women who started KNAG had no concept of forming a separate identity group until they encountered ageist sexism. After attending a 700-strong public meeting in the town of Lismore (early March 2012), eight older women joined an action group offering training in non-violent direct action (NVDA). The women, not previously known to one another, were attracted to learning this form of activism as a safe and positive way for older women to protest. Driven by concern for the environment and climate change they were committed to fighting fracking by using their professional and life skills for purposeful retirement. They sought intergenerational climate justice protecting the planet now for future generations.

The expert leaders of the NVDA "community of practice" were left-leaning men from the North Eastern Forest Alliance (NEFA) conservation group and The Greens political party.[37] In the group of around 25 people, half were non-aligned, mostly men and some younger women in their 30s and 40s. During their weekly meetings, the older women became frustrated by "a lot of talk but didn't lead to much action" (according to a survey respondent and interviewees). There was also animosity from some men. Nanna Joy (pseudonym) explained to me:

> ... some of the men involved in the NVDA group were not treating the women, especially the older women, as if we had any agency. Pretty much putting us in our little pigeonhole ... [with] suggestions that we provide catering, tea and bickies and that we could do paperworkey bits and pieces. Which is certainly not why we joined the NVDA ...we were pretty much stereotyped and there were quite a few sweet little old ladies there, I suppose they didn't expect us to be on the cutting edge. It's a particular type of sexism that suddenly, once you reach menopause, you've never had sex, you've never used your brain, you haven't heard half the words in the English language and you're deaf. Yeah—and they speak slowly and loudly to you!

This quotation shows how the women felt undervalued, undermined, and ignored, realizing other activists saw them as inconsequential grannies. They were keenly aware of being stereotyped as frail, of diminished importance, and lacking in agency and coherent brain function. After several meetings, tensions escalated and they realized their efforts to use their own initiative were not welcome. Nanna Joy described the events to me:

> There was a meeting where some of the men from the Greens and NEFA kind of picked on us. We were doing things on our own initiative; I think that was one of the biggest things. And so, it was particularly targeted, especially targeted towards the [older] women who had shown the most initiative. So after the meeting, we went downstairs, had a coffee and it was just like, 'what the fuck just happened there?' I guess that happened within the couple of months

leading up to the start of the Nannas. We kept going to the NVDA after that
and tended to sit in a group and support each other.

The women reacted to the disorienting denigration by going to a nearby
café and forming a subgroup. Talking through their experience, they unin-
tentionally did what many feminist consciousness-raising groups have done
before, which was to support one another, critically reflecting on the dynamics
of the oppression they were encountering. They had not expected left-leaning
men to be both sexist and ageist. This was a pivotal moment of transformative
learning that led to emancipatory decision-making, setting a core value for
KNAG.[38] Determined to be activists, they promoted confidence in their own
judgment and from then on refused to ask permission before acting. They
freed themselves from insubstantial support roles. This learning was critical
to the establishment of a community of practice by older women in environmental activism that drew on situated experiential social learning.[39]

Despite few Nannas having been feminist activists during the "second
wave" of feminism in the 1970s and 1980s, interviewees confirmed most
were aware of counteracting sexism in their daily lives. "Everyday feminism" describes seeing one's life through a "gendered lens" with a feminist
awareness in one's everyday activity.[40] The women intuitively began critically
reflecting on their oppression and empowerment to overcome the "double
jeopardy of old age," ageism and sexism.[41] Their solution was to disengage
from denigration in order to take meaningful action. Highly motivated and
not wanting to waste time fighting for equality, they side-stepped the issue by
banding together, eager to make a start.

Even though angered by their treatment in the NVDA group, they con-
tinued going to meetings wanting to learn non-violent protest strategies.
They were also mindful of not being a disruptive element within the cohesive
GFNR Alliance, which was gaining social and political momentum.

Without knowing it, the soon-to-be Knitting Nannas were implementing
learning later in life along critical feminist geragogy (or educational gerontology) principles. This challenges ageism showing how older people's education should attend to issues of knowledge, power, and control as opposed to
functionalist, medical, or deficit models of gerontology casting older adults
on a trajectory of disengagement, decline, decreased capacities, and ultimate
frailty of both body and mind. Elder education should be "a collective and
negotiated enterprise, as well as assuming a liberating and transforming
notion which endorses principles of collectivity and dialogue as central to
learning and teaching."[42]

No longer asking permission, two of the women began touring the
Metgasco mining company sites noticing one location with a waste pond

and earth-moving equipment, an activity that indicated exploratory wells. They decided to undertake "guerrilla surveillance" of Metgasco truck movements.[43] Knowing they would be in position for some time, on June 8, 2012, they took their chairs, a thermos of tea, and knitting to pass the time productively. The women were able to share their information with the NVDA group. This led to the first GFNR weeklong blockade by 60 peaceful protesters where the nascent Nannas were first reported by media using their novel knit-in, rather than sit-in, form of protest.[44,45] The movement grew as new members were attracted to this passive protest.

The women experienced a range of reactions to their activism from family and friends. Not only did they have to convince colleague activists of their determination, but they also dealt with the opinions of others summed up by one survey responden: "Some are confused, some think I'm nuts, some really admire me." Another survey respondent experienced those who were supportive, "to having Facebook friends block me as they don't want to hear." Family members were mentioned as either being wholeheartedly supportive (admiring, proud) or less supportive (interested, amused). It seems activism has skipped a generation with granddaughters being more engaged in climate change activism than daughters. A third survey respondent wrote her granddaughter was "her biggest fan" whom she felt is politically astute, as this quote shows: "My daughter was originally embarrassed, warning me not to get arrested, but eventually she became very supportive, but she's not politically motivated in any way. My granddaughter has been my biggest fan, standing alongside me at many gatherings."

Women overcame their husband's hesitancy by enlisting their help and recognized their children held varying attitudes. One survey respondent wrote:

> My husband helps out as a 'roadie' so he comes along to most things that we do. He has never been involved in anything like this before and is still rather hesitant. My children range in feeling very proud of what I do down to not being sure if I am being too radical.

Another survey respondent experienced her family's shift from amusement to encouragement: "At first there was amusement, then with consistent nagging, a change of attitude and encouragement, on their part." Some Nannas experienced hostility or condescension in the form of mild denigration such as "most just nod and smile" or "they thought it was a harmless activity," or being called "looney" and "a little crazy." One woman wrote:

> The menfolk are a little less tolerant than the womenfolk. My husband and two sons (in their 20s) support me but aren't too interested in WHAT I actually do.

So I just have that part of my life as mine. It doesn't bother me. In fact, I think
it's healthy for people to be free to do what is important to them and for others.

Overall, women's motivation to join KNAG was not influenced by the
disparate range of sentiments from their significant others–from admiration
and encouragement to benign hostility and denigration. This indicates the
novelty and challenges faced by early KNAG in stepping out from invisibility
and voicelessness. The camaraderie they found in the community of practice
empowered them to get on with their activist lives. In the least supportive
environments, women chose to interpret negativity as a form of freedom to
express their authentic selves.

*Strategic Essentialism as Activist Identity—An Older Woman's Way of
Protesting.* In the first six months of KNAG, the women learned about forming their collective social movement identity.[46] Initially, they cast themselves
as fearless "elder Jane Bonds." They then realized the subversive and humorous potential of playfully using the stereotype they had originally railed
against. The persona of little old ladies stealthily knitting appealed to their
collective sense of humour. Interviewees confirmed they did not know that
the Canadian Raging Grannies had made a similar choice some 25 years
earlier.[47]

Initially, knitting was a way of productively spending time but it quickly
became a way of expressing a form of environmental activism in which older
women could engage.[48] As founding member Liz Stops, reported, "The name
. . . was purposefully devised. 'knitting' and 'Nannas' are words that immediately conjure a nostalgic image of older women exuding trust and love."[49]
"Nanna-ness" is a form of strategic essentialism that communicates identity
and purpose with great clarity. Collectively, these Northern Rivers women
began to refer to themselves as a "determination of Nannas," drawing inspiration from the French Revolution *Les Tricoteuses*, who sat knitting at the
base of the guillotines in silent protest at being disenfranchised.[50] A founding
Nanna, Clare Twomey is quoted saying, "We're like the iron fist inside the
velvet glove; we sit and we knit and we bear witness."[51] Enjoying the camaraderie of group humor and creativity, the women had begun to see themselves
as part of a revolution, devising a "Nannafesto,"[52] and printing "Viva La
Nannalution" on protest buttons, conference agendas, banners, and T-shirts
(Figure 9.1).

By January 2014, within around 18 months, the women had taken on a
strong visual identity. The decision-making process around identity was part
of creative discussions during knit-ins. Nanna Joy said:

*Figure 9.1:* Viva La Nannalution conference agenda cover. (Source: Clare Twomey, reproduced with permission.)

> We would just sit around in a circle and knit and come up with these amazing ideas. And we just bounced off each other. It was us talking amongst us, ourselves . . . we had lots of fun playing with the word Nanna. I think it was quite early . . . I came up with using the word *Nannafesto* just because it fits.

For their uniform, Nannas chose yellow and black as a way of showing solidarity with the pre-existing anti-fracking farmer-based Lock the Gate Alliance.[53] The women later added red to be inclusive of Australia's First Nations people who use red, yellow, and black in their flag. In a process they call "Nannafying" or "Nanna-ing Up," women playfully combine aprons, dresses, T-shirts, protest buttons, and yellow-and-black revolutionary berets. Much of their clothing and adornments is upcycled from second-hand shops. Each Nanna chooses how she applies this uniform contributing to the "loop" (meaning group) identity. This can be seen in their many Facebook posts, such as, "Needling our MP Thomas George yet again" where women wear the signature outfits with a knitted yellow-and-black beret.[54] KNAG is careful to protect its brand, which has now become well-known for focusing on environmental issues, particularly the fight against CSG and fossil fuels. Nanna Vida told me she felt this gives women ownership of a courageous identity:

> Getting Nannafied gives you a certain heroic persona. It also reminds us that we have expectations to live up to—what we expect of ourselves and what we expect to project out there . . . we need to just keep reminding each other to stay on message about what we're about.

Another woman (survey data) further confirmed the KNAG community of practice ethos of collective identity embodies qualities of persistence, positivity, relentlessness, camaraderie, empathy, and gentleness in their educative approach which she described as an awakening of awareness:

> . . . the camaraderie and empathy of the Knitting Nannas give strength and hope as a group. With our persistent, positive, relentless but gentle way of protesting against the assault on our environment and other injustices, we are helping to wake up awareness in our communities.

Having fun as activists has been a strong motivating factor for the Nannas. One survey respondent described the knit-in tactic as, "great fun and an effective way" of showing concerns. Another survey respondent was clearly enthused and stimulated by being in KNAG and summed up her feelings of engagement in the community of practice as, "being with an incredibly diverse and creative bunch of women is the most inspiring and fun thing I have ever experienced." In KNAG, older women feel safe to explore new identities and activities. A third survey respondent valued "opening myself to experiences that I would never have thought I would be in 20 or so years ago" and considered that NVDA was instrumental in promoting "a peaceful empowerment that, as individuals and in groups, we can make a difference." A fourth survey respondent was relieved to find a way of drawing on her extensive life experience post-retirement by engaging in a liberating, collective, and enjoyable negotiated learning enterprise within KNAG. For her, the determination to not let physical limitations constrain involvement in a purposeful retirement was important, as was being able to use her professional skills:

> I've always been involved in social justice issues as a result of being a teacher of adults. It's helped me come to terms with retirement. I have worthwhile causes and feel passionate about making a difference. Didn't think I'd be able to make much of a difference when I stopped working. Nannas have the time, the passion and the staying power because their families have grown, and they no longer have work pressures to deal with.

Compatibility with active ageing and the freedom to choose preferred ways of protesting were reiterated by Nanna Elsie, a lifelong activist and Queensland-based loop originator, involved since 2014. Elsie was motivated by KNAG's use of strategic essentialism, embodied in "Nannahood" and the ethos of inclusivity:

> Who argues with a Nanna? It's just so brilliant! It's so clever. I also like the idea, as another Nanna said to me, you could be 80 years old and bedridden, and you can still be a Knitting Nanna because you can still go online and do stuff. So you don't have to be out in the streets running around. If you don't want to be, you can if you want to be … and there's the peaceful element to it – the calm, the peaceful supportive, the nurturing … and you don't have to knit. But I am a Nanna. I like the freedom of the Nannas. If you follow the Nannafesto, you can't do anything wrong.

Data indicated the atmosphere of knit-ins embodies a milieu that is motivational, respectful of diversity and individuality, engaging, challenging, and empowering. The Nannas community of practice is consistent with critical feminist geragogy.

The women delight in challenging the stereotype of a non-descript older woman. They recognize this draws attention and stirs curiosity, which creates the opportunity for conversation. Diversity and individuality among Nannas are celebrated and contribute to ageing well.

Appreciating one another's individuality and strengths is paramount for Nannas. KNAG rejects a universalized identity for women, preferring to find strength in diversity. The women feel empowered in their KNAG identities and have noticed gaining greater self-confidence. Inclusion fosters involvement and is considered a motivational condition of sustained engagement in learning, along with enjoying learning, which is evident in the fun and positivity Nannas report when they Nannafy.[55] This view was supported by a survey respondent who wrote she was "… becoming more positive in myself about being 'out there,' basically on show, if you like." KNAG members generally receive positive comments, are affirmed for what they are doing, and feel a sense of safety in numbers. Another woman wrote: "When I wear my Knitting Nanna outfit, people acknowledge me in a positive way. Love, love, love being a Nanna." And a third woman was surprised to learn how powerful the KNAG outfit was because it provokes both attraction of passers-by and anxiety in politicians:

> The power they have! Even politicians are nervous of us and hate us sitting outside their offices. We are visible, colourful, approachable, and provide so many photo opportunities. We are a novelty and people talk about us and pass the info on.

Nannas intentionally craft their empowerment culture and incorporate it as an essential activist skill for their community of practice. Nanna Joy described how she encouraged women to use their life experiences and talents. She compared this with wasting women's abilities by falling into ageist stereotyping where older women are "wrinkly, invisible, useless drudges, drains on the public purse." Joy explained her rationale for KNAG's approach to empowering members:

> . . . you'd sit with six women knitting-in, and so you've got 300 years of experience and you've got graphic designers and nurses and managers and academics and people who have brought up a million children. Yeah, all of these incredible talents that are wasted making cups of tea and pushing petitions under people's faces. This is, I guess, one of the strong points of the Nannas: to find people's strengths and to utilize those strengths within each loop and then within the larger movement. So some people are very good at organizing. There are some people who are good with public speaking. We make a point of acknowledging each other as valuable members of society.

The Nannas are known and admired for their courage, determination, and wisdom in their defence of environmental sustainability by challenging ageist sexism. Under the camouflage of Nannafying and knitting-in, KNAG connects with individuals, communities and networks to amplify their anti-fracking messages. They reclaim and reframe public spaces by shifting from the private domestic to footpaths, roadsides, and community markets. Engaging in performative educative activism through their bold visual statements of quiet, persistent acts of rebellion and resistance has become their trademark. In the process, KNAG has learned more about the power of their grandmotherly identity in garnering support. They realized that authority gained through a collective identity is transformative and empowering.

## Claiming Virtual Space—Collective and Connective Action

This research challenges the conventional wisdom that older women are caught behind a digital divide. Findings show they are a cohort who lived through the knowledge economy transition and experienced first-hand, in workplaces and homes, the upskilling involved in the digital revolution of the late twentieth and early twenty-first centuries. As a result of their KNAG identities, many moved from Web 1.0 to Web 2.0 technologies. While Facebook and email remain staple platforms of choice, the women have become active users of Messenger and Zoom. Contemporary SML includes becoming digitally savvy in order to be more capable activists fluent in connective action.

Having social media visibility has contributed to building the KNAG identity and strengthened this activist community with added social benefits of increasing older women's well-being adding value, purpose, and connection to their lives. KNAG survey (2017) data emphasized the importance of networking for maintaining friendships and supporting one another in both protesting and personal lives. As described by a survey respondent, social media connectedness engenders understanding and cooperation amongst their community of practice and enhances purposeful ageing. She wrote:

> I feel part of the group and valued when networking through Messenger and emails. My life, though busy, has taken on more purpose with the work we are doing. We can only be effective if everyone in the group understands each other and can cooperate willingly.

Messenger has proved beneficial as a more private channel within loops compared to Facebook, which presents the public persona or brand of KNAG activism. Nanna Jessie told me how women in her loop have different daily routines for checking their smartphones for messages and emails which they call "Nannachat". According to Nanna Jessie, her loop uses Messenger more than Facebook for keeping in touch:

> [Messenger] happens more than Facebook now for our loop. And it's sort of like Nannachat. A lot of it is interpersonal stuff as well as organisational stuff – someone's sick or someone's been away and come back. They're welcomed back home or catch up with things. It just goes on sometimes. I don't check my phone until I stop at night and sometimes there's ten messages on it.

KNAG loops upskill members in using Facebook and smartphones so that they can network across the movement. Journalist Nanna Jeanette had only just begun to use social media when she joined the Nannas. Through being a Nanna, her online competence and confidence increased. Similarly to many Nannas, she lives outside a regional town, is somewhat geographically isolated, and has found Facebook invaluable in creating a sense of community and collective identity through in-group communication:

> I think they've been great on the uptake of social media. I was only really starting to use social media not long before I joined up with the Nannas myself. And so we've all made good use of it. It's really essential for keeping us in touch with each other and also with loops nationwide. It's really valuable. I don't think we'd function so well without it, especially because we're all quite scattered geographically, even my loop. There's people coming from an hour or more away in all different directions. So having Facebook ... really helps keep us together and just share information.

KNAG has become progressively skilled in translating their real-world collective actions into online connective action and in strengthening their followers' engagement with their messaging. Online visibility enables followers to affirm their relationship to the cause and legitimizes the cause for both followers and others.[56] When loops engage in peaceful actions, they make sure they take photos and videos documenting their activities for use as content in social and traditional media. There are 31 active loops on Facebook and a total of over 40,300 followers or members, some of whom may be active on multiple sites (analysis conducted in January 2021). Even though the 40,300 followers may not be unique individuals, this is a substantial following that significantly amplifies the collective voice of KNAG, aiding women's identification with the movement.[57] By comparison, Australia's two major political parties, Labor and Liberal, each claim membership of around 60,000.[58]

Thematic analysis of comments from Facebook posts in 2016 about the KNAG vigils challenging the NSW newly introduced anti-protester legislation thanked Nannas for their peaceful protest in defence of people's democratic rights to protest and characterized them as brave, courageous, and inspiring. The posts generated a significant social media reaction, including a total of 3,951 likes, 680 comments, 907 shares, and 69,559 views.[59,60,61] In another example, the Lismore loop coal cleaning experiment initially gained 119 likes, 16 comments, and 170 shares and continued to be reprised with around 23,000 views by September 2021.[62,63]

The online connective action draws positive reactions to the Nannas indicating brand awareness of, and engagement with the Knitting Nannas' form of activism. KNAG is a media movement having proved its expertise in presenting a clearly articulated media profile using digital online tools to complement its offline environmental activism. They have proven their ability to gain attention and social media engagement.

## Conclusion

The under-researched double jeopardy of ageist sexism exists in social movements. Through the case study of the Australian Knitting Nannas, this chapter has shown how older women with everyday feminist consciousness, identified and challenged oppressive stereotyping to assert their right to be vocal and visible environmental activists. Disengaging from denigration was the first pivotal transformation of a small group of older women who went on to create an alternative older women's way of non-violent environmental protesting. Embodied in this was the passive knit-in, a means of bearing witness and drawing attention to unsustainable fossil fuel use in the face of climate change. Emboldened by adopting the humorous, performative, and educative strategic essentialism of a Nannalution, these women proved their claim that you are never too old to be an activist. In doing so, they have crafted their special niche in a galaxy of environmental activist organizations where they are admired for their bravery and courage—a far cry from their beginnings.

Women and older women have always been activists. What has been lacking is the acknowledgement and recognition of women's capabilities. In Australia, KNAG has broken the older women's environmental activist glass ceiling. So much of how they have done this seems serendipitous and intuitive. In actuality, it was predictable once these women's extensive capabilities were recognized by themselves, by one another, and by those observing and interacting with them. These are women of consequence because they have come to believe in their agentic selves. It is no longer acceptable for social movements to exclude or denigrate the vital contribution of older women.

## Notes

1  Garner, Helen. *Everywhere I Look*. Melbourne: Text Publishing, 2016.
2  Applewhite, Ashton. *This Chair Rocks: A Manifesto Against Ageism*. New York: Celadon Books, 2019.
3  Knitting Nannas Against Gas. *Nannafesto – Knit the Dream*. https://knitting-nan nas.com/about-us/what-we-do/.
4  Acosta, Carlos .L., Dusty Horwitt, Avery Kelly, and Amanda Lyons. *A Guide to Rights-Based Advocacy: International Human Rights Law and Fracking*, edited by Rita Parks and Elizabeth Wilmott-Harrop, 73. New York Sisters of Mercy (NGO), Mercy International Association: Global Action, 2015.
5  Ollis, Tracey. "Learning in Social Action: The Informal and Social Learning Dimensions of Circumstantial and Lifelong Activists." *Australian Journal of Adult Learning* 51, no. 2 (2011): 248–268. https://files.eric.ed.gov/fulltext/EJ951 996.pdf.
6  Cecil, Vanessa, Louise Pendry, Jessica Salvatore, Hazel Mycroft, and Tim Kurz. "Gendered Ageism and Gray Hair: Must Older Women Choose Between Feeling Authentic and Looking Competent?" *Journal of Women & Aging* (2021): 1–16. https://doi.org/10.1080/08952841.2021.1899744.
7  Trentham, Barry, Sandra Sokoloff, Amie Tsang, and Sheila Neysmith. "Social Media and Senior Citizen Advocacy: An Inclusive Tool to Resist Ageism? *Politics, Groups, and Identities* 3, no. 3 (2015): 558–571. https://doi.org/10.1080/21565 503.2015.1050411.
8  Tosh, Jemma and Maya Gislason, "Fracking is a Feminist Issue: An Intersectional Ecofeminist Commentary on Natural Resource Extraction and Rape." *Psychology of Women Section Review* 18, no. 1 (2016): 54–59.
9  Jenkins, Katy. "Unearthing Women's Anti-Mining Activism in the Andes: Pachamama and the 'Mad Old Women'." *Antipode* 47, no. 2 (2015): 442–460. https://doi. org/10.1111/anti.12126.

10  Trentham et al., "Social Media."

11  Roy, Carole. "The Raging Grannies: Meddlesome Crones, Humour, Daring, and Education." PhD diss. University of Toronto, 2003, 345.

12  Tosh and Gislason, "Fracking is a feminist issue."

13  Velásquez, Teresa A. "Enacting Refusals: Mestiza Women's Anti-Mining Activism in Andean Ecuador." *Latin American and Caribbean Ethnic Studies* 12, no. 3 (2017): 250–272. https://doi.org/10.1080/17442222.2017.1344263.

14  Murray, Suellen. "Taking the Toys from the Boys." *Australian Feminist Studies* 25, no. 63 (2010): 3–15. https://doi.org/ 10.1080/08164640903499893.

15  Bartlett, Alison. "Feminist Protest and Maternity at Pine Gap Women's Peace Camp, Australia 1983." *Women's Studies International Forum* 34, no. 1 (2011): 31–38. https://doi.org/10.1016/j.wsif.2010.10.002.

16  Stone, Alison. "Essentialism and Anti-Essentialism in Feminist Philosophy. *Journal of Moral Philosophy* 1, no. 2 (2004): 135–153. https://brill.com/view/journals/jmp/1/2/article-p135_2.xml?language=en.

17  McHugh, Nancy A. "Strategic Essentialism." In *Feminist Philosophies A-Z*. Edinburgh: Edinburgh University Press, 2007.

18  McHugh, "Strategic Essentialism," 35.

19  Chazan, May and Stephanie Kittmer. "Defying, Producing, And Overlooking Stereotypes? The Complexities of Mobilizing 'Grandmotherhood' as Political Strategy." *Journal of Women & Aging* 28, no. 4 (2016): 297–308. https://doi.org/10.1080/08952841.2015.1017428.

20  Chazan, May and Melissa Baldwin. "Granny Solidarity: Understanding Age and Generational Dynamics in Climate Justice Movements." *Studies in Social Justice* 13, no. 2 (2019): 244–261. https://doi.org/10.26522/ssj.v13i2.2235.

21  Sawchuk, Dana. "The Raging Grannies: Defying Stereotypes and Embracing Aging Through Activism." *Journal of Women & Aging* 21, no. 3 (2009): p. 171–185. https://doi.org/10.1080/08952840903054898.

22  Sawchuk, "The Raging Grannies," 180–181.

23  Tosh and Gislason, "Fracking is a Feminist Issue."

24  Rudd, Kevin and Thom Woodroofe. "A Foreign Policy for the Climate." *The Saturday Paper*. April 3–9, 2021. https://www.thesaturdaypaper.com.au/opinion/topic/2021/04/03/foreign-policy-the-climate/161736840011370#hrd.

25  Seccombe, Mike. "US Climate Summit to be a Reckoning for Morrison." *The Saturday Paper*. April 17–23, 2021. https://www.thesaturdaypaper.com.au/news/politics/2021/04/17/us-climate-summit-be-reckoning-morrison/161858160011469.

26  Taylor, Maria. *Global Warming and Climate Change: What Australia Knew and Buried... Then Framed a New Reality for the Public*. Canberra: ANU Press, 2015.

27  Krien, Anna. "The Long Goodbye: Coal, Coral and Australia's Climate Deadlock." *Quarterly Essay* 66 (2017). https://www.quarterlyessay.com.au/essay/2017/06/the-long-goodbye/extract.

28  Bacon, Wendy and Arunn Jegan. "Lies, Debates, and Silences. How News Corp Produces Climate Scepticism in Australia. GetUp Australia, 2020. https://www.getup.org.au/lies-debates-and-silences.

29  Wilkinson, Marian. *The Carbon Club: How a Network of Influential Climate Sceptics, Politicians and Business Leaders Fought to Control Australia's Climate Policy.* Sydney, Australia: Allen & Unwin, 2020.

30  IPCC. "Summary for Policymakers." In *Climate Change 2022: Mitigation of Climate Change. Contribution of Working Group III to the Sixth Assessment Report of the Intergovernmental Panel on Climate Change,* edited by P.R. Shukla et al. Cambridge, UK and New York, NY, USA: CUP 2022.

31  Acosta et al., *A Guide to Rights-Based Advocacy.*

32  Tosh and Gislason, "Fracking is a Feminist Issue."

33  *Fracking.* Merriam-Webster.com dictionary [online]. Accessed January 6, 2023. https://www.merriam-webster.com/dictionary/fracking.

34  Ollis, Tracey and Michael Hamel-Green. "Adult Education and Radical Habitus in an Environmental Campaign: Learning in the Coal Seam Gas Protests in Australia. *Australian Journal of Adult Learning* 55, no. 2 (2015): 204–221. https://www.proquest.com/docview/1702098802.

35  Hirsch, Jameson K., K. Bryant Smalley, Emily M. Selby-Nelson, Jane M. Hamel-Lambert, Michael R. Rosmann, Tammy A. Barnes, Daniel Abrahamson, Scott S. Meit, Iva GreyWolf, Sarah Beckmann, and Teresa LaFromboise. "Psychosocial Impact of Fracking: A Review of the Literature on the Mental Health Consequences of Hydraulic Fracturing." *International Journal of Mental Health and Addiction* 16, no. 1 (2018): 1–15. https://doi.org/10.1007/s11469-017-9792-5.

36  Grubert, Emily and Whitney Skinner. "A Town Divided: Community Values and Attitudes Towards Coal Seam Gas Development in Gloucester, Australia." *Energy Research & Social Science* 30, Supplement C (2017): 43–52. https://doi.org/10.1016/j.erss.2017.05.041.

37  Lave, Jean and Etienne Wenger. *Situated Learning: Legitimate Peripheral Participation.* Cambridge: Cambridge University Press, 1991.

38  Mayo, Peter. "Synthesizing Gramsci and Freire: Possibilities for a Theory of Radical Adult Education." *International Journal of Lifelong Education* 13, no. 2 (1994): 125–148. https://doi.org/10.1080/0260137940130204.

39  Merriam, Sharan B. and Lisa M. Baumgartner. *Learning in Adulthood: A Comprehensive Guide.* Hoboken: John Wiley & Sons, 2020.

40  Schuster, Julia. "Why the Personal Remained Political: Comparing Second and Third Wave Perspectives on Everyday Feminism." *Social Movement Studies* 16, no. 6 (2017): 647–659. https://doi.org/10.1080/14742837.2017.1285223.

41  Findsen, Brian and Marvin Formosa. *Lifelong Learning in Later Life: A Handbook on Older Adult Learning.* Rotterdam: Sense Publishers, 2011, 95.

42  Findsen and Formosa, *Lifelong Learning,* 105.

43  Ngara-Institute. "Ngara Institute's 2018 Annual Lecture and Australian Activist of the Year Award." December 6, 2018. YouTube. https://www.youtube.com/watch?v=OI-k1DYsg1c.

44  Harlum, Scott. "CSG Pond 'Dozer Rally Ends." *The Daily Telegraph.* June 27, 2012. https://www.dailytelegraph.com.au/news/nsw/lismore/csg-pond-dozer-rally-ends/news-story/825f1c2c9ac95ddae56c9cc417d01b4b.

45  Hargraves, Melissa. "Lock the Dozer Action 'a Success'." *The Echo.* June 21, 2012. https://www.echo.net.au/2012/06/lock-the-dozer-action-a-success/.

46  Della Porta, Donatella and Mario Diani. *Social Movements: An Introduction,* 2nd ed. Carlton, Victoria, Australia: Blackwell Publishing Ltd, 2006.

47  Roy, "The Raging Grannies," 345.

48  Larri, Larraine J. and Hilary Whitehouse. "Nannagogy: Social Movement Learning for Older Women's Activism in the Gas Fields of Australia." *Australian Journal of Adult Learning* 59, no. 1 (2019): 27–52. https://eric.ed.gov/?id=EJ1225530.

49  Schuster, "Why the Personal."

50  Stops, Liz. "Les Tricoteuses: The Plain and Purl of Solidarity and Protest." *Craft Design Enquiry* 6 (2014): 7–8. https://doi.org/10.22459/CDE.06.2014.02.

51  Northern Star. "No Gas Nannas." *The Northern Star.* June 28, 2012.

52  Knitting Nannas Against Gas. "Nannafesto – Knit the Dream." November 17, 2018.        https://www.facebook.com/KnittingNannasAgainstGasKyogleLoop/posts/the-nannafesto-knit-the-dream-we-peacefully-productively-protest-agai nst-the-des/2244988438864809/.

53  Lock the Gate Alliance. "Working Together to Stop Coal and Gas." Accessed June 1, 2022. https://www.lockthegate.org.au/.

54  Knitting Nannas Against Gas. "Needling our MP Thomas George Once Again." November 13, 2014. https://www.facebook.com/KnittingNannasAgainstGas/pho tos/a.393583890678354/745194468850626.

55  Wlodkowski, Raymond J. and Marjorie B. Ginsberg. *Enhancing Adult Motivation to Learn: A Comprehensive Guide for Teaching All Adults.* San Francisco: Jossey-Bass, 2017.

56  George, Jordana J. and Dorothy E. Leidner. "From Clicktivism to Hacktivism: Understanding Digital Activism." *Information and Organization* 29, no. 3 (2019): 100249. https://doi.org/10.1016/j.infoandorg.2019.04.001.

57  George and Leidner, "From Clicktivism to Hacktivism."

58  Davies, Anne. "Party Hardly: Why Australia's big Political Parties are Struggling to Compete with Grassroots Campaigns." *The Guardian,* December 12, 2020. https://www.theguardian.com/australia-news/2020/dec/13/party-hardly-why-austral ias-big-political-parties-are-struggling-to-compete-with-grassroots-campaigns.

59  Knitting Nannas Against Gas. "Today Nanna Clare Took the Step of Locking on to the Gates of NSW Parliament." April 1, 2016. https://www.facebook.com/Knitt ingNannasAgainstGas/posts/971687049534699.

60  Lock the Gate Alliance. "70 Year Old Nannas Sleeping Out to Protest the Anti-Protest Laws." May 3, 2016. https://www.facebook.com/Lock.The.Gate.Alliance/posts/1119260468146019.

61  Lock the Gate Alliance. "Nannas 24 Hours into 48 Hour Vigil Outside NSW Parliament." May 4, 2016. https://www.facebook.com/Lock.The.Gate.Alliance/videos/1120015351403864.

62  Knitting Nannas Against Gas. "Knitting Nannas Put Coal to the Test Today." March 2, 2017. https://www.facebook.com/KnittingNannasAgainstGas/posts/12547 05284566206.

63  Lee, Rosie. "#Nannas #nowaternolife #protectourwater #InternationalWomensDay #WILPF." February 18, 2019. https://www.facebook.com/rosie.lee.35325/vid eos/2164387183582634.

# 10. The Silver Tsunami, the Ticking Time Bomb and Other Demographic Imaginaries: Moving from Demographic Threat to Demographic Resilience

ALANNA ARMITAGE

> Describing the demographic shift with a term that connotes terror and destruction can have powerful, even tragic, consequences for the elderly.[1]

On November 15, 2022, the world reached 8 billion people, a global success story. Advances in health care and reductions in global poverty mean people around the world are living longer. According to the United Nations Department of Economic and Social Affairs (UNDESA) report—*World Population Prospects 2022*—life expectancy in 2019 increased to 72.8 years, a nearly nine-year increase over 1990. By 2050, a further drop in mortality could increase life expectancy to an average of 77.2 years. The number and percentage of older persons are increasing in virtually every country. In 2022, there were 771 million people aged 65 years or over, three times more than in 1980 (258 million). This older population could reach 994 million by 2030 and 1.6 billion by 2050.[2]

The fact that people are living longer and healthier lives than at any time in human history should be seen as a major accomplishment. Why, then, are the media, politicians, and even social scientists so apocalyptic in their warnings about the impact of ageing populations? Headlines like these are common: *The Demographic Cliff,*[3] *Ageing is the Real Population Bomb,*[4] *The Silver Tsunami,*[5] *The Pensions Time Bomb,*[6] or *Old Age is the Next Global Economic Threat.*[7] Is population ageing truly a major peril to economies and societies? Any demographic change, including population ageing, requires preparation. But could the "problem" of population ageing be based more on imagination and ideology than on actual evidence? This chapter summarizes some of the popular narratives related to population ageing and looks at how the meaning we give to certain demographic trends, what I call *demographic imaginaries*,[8] affect the way we collect and understand statistics, measure economic impact, and design public policy. It calls for re-imagining demographic change, particularly population ageing, moving away from *apocalyptic demography*[9] toward *demographic resilience*[10] grounded in evidence and human rights.

## Demographic Imaginaries Around Population Ageing

How a problem is imagined and defined can lead to radically different solutions. Political demographer Michael Teitelbaum claims that fears around population ageing are one of the "most popular foci of exaggeration in current discussions on demographic trends."[11] Several other practitioners and scholars have produced robust studies on the detrimental impact of non-neutral language associated with population ageing.[12,13,14,15,16] Building on this scholarship, in an earlier work, I put forth the concept of *demographic imaginaries*. According to this concept, the "crisis" of population ageing and responses to it are based on far more than purely technical considerations around demographic data. In fact, imagination and ideology have played a major role in the meaning given to demographic indicators and to demographic change. We could describe the demographic imaginary as the stories being told "to justify the exercise of power by those who possess it, situating these individuals within a tissue of tales that recapitulate the past and anticipate the future."[17] Based on the literature, I would argue that three common themes—part doctrine, part metaphor—constitute the demographic imaginary around population ageing: the *natural order*, the silver *tsunami*, and the *time bomb*, which, taken together, help fuel the construction of the "crisis" of population ageing.

*The Natural Order.* Let's begin with what we consider a normal, natural, or optimal age. When my grandmother was born in Canada in 1918, life expectancy was around 55 years. Today, the average Canadian woman can expect to live to 85—a gain of 30 years in three generations. What do those additional 30 years mean? Renowned physician and ageing activist, Alexandre Kalache, argues that the world maintains out-of-date assumptions about the life course and that the longevity revolution forces us to rethink previously held notions about ageing and old age. "Life has stopped being a 100-meter dash, and has become a marathon, for which we must prepare both individually and socially."[18]

Kalache explains that people still see life as segmented into three broad phases. In the first phase, we learn, go to school, and sometimes further our studies; in the second phase, usually the longest, we are employed. For women, this middle phase often involves raising children and taking on other caring roles. Finally, in the third phase, we rest for a growing number of years before dying. This is viewed as the "natural order" and much of our social policy and our individual expectations within the life course remain tied to this simplistic model. For most of us, the ages of 60 or 65 are an artificial threshold, which shapes the way we live, the services to which we are entitled, and eligibility for certain health and financial benefits.[19]

This may have made sense a few generations ago, but today's life expectancy rates have transformed this reality. Today, older persons are a diverse group, and age is "a relative concept which varies across time and space."[20] Age is not just a number, but a social construct based on custom, practice, and the perception of a person's role in their community. The so-called vulnerability of older persons must be defined differently. Older persons can be vulnerable not only because of physical and mental conditions, but also because of the way society perceives them and their interaction with their environment. While some older persons are dependent, economically or otherwise, most continue to be actively engaged and often support their families until late in life.[21]

In addition, there is evidence to suggest that older age is not correlated with one's ability to be innovative. In a study of 2.7 million company founders, economists at MIT, the U.S. Census Bureau, and Northwestern University found that the most successful entrepreneurs are middle-aged. In fact, 50-year-old entrepreneurs were nearly twice as likely to build a successful company as a 30-year-old, and industry experience was a significant positive in predicting success.[22] The "natural life course" as it has been portrayed has evolved dramatically and its original definition no longer applies.

As outlined in UNFPA's submission to the report of the Independent Expert on the rights of older persons, "defining older persons as a single large wave of 60+ or 65+ [and] aggregating all data into a single large age group at the end of life, or not collecting data for smaller age groups towards the end of life disguises the diversity among older persons."[23] It ignores the physical and social environments in which we live, which according to the World Health Organization (WHO), are powerful influences on how we age, including the cumulative impact of advantage and disadvantage across our lives, shaped by factors such as the family we were born into, our sex, our ethnicity, and income and other financial resources.[24]

*The Silver or Gray Tsunami.* The silver or gray tsunami is a common metaphor used to describe the unprecedented increase in the number of older people in the world, an "intentional as a shorthand description of the burden that will befall the country when millions of people grow old, get sick and need care."[25] The notion that a tsunami of "grey haired, cane carrying", over 60s is about to strike, is embedded in the symbols and metaphors we use to depict population ageing.[26] The symbols of frailty associated with the gray tsunami implicitly suggest that older adults are not capable of contributing to society or to meeting their own needs. Perhaps even more concerning is that the notion of a gray or silver tsunami informs economic theory. It is "an economic term based in calculations of increasing cost. On the nation's balance sheet, the great silver tsunami rests squarely in the liability column. This drain on financing is coming. Be aware. Be warned. Plan ahead."[27] However, the diversity of experiences in older age is much more complex than the stereotypical view of this stage of life and the silver or gray tsunami metaphor not only fuels the notion of ageing as a threat, it also seriously "dulls our ability to assess the quite different kinds of policy challenges that affect older people with widely varying characteristics."[28]

Much of the demographic panic related to ageing is associated with what is considered an unnatural or "unbalanced population age-structure."[29] Although no demographic trend is inherently good or bad, since the early 1920s, economists have argued for the existence of an optimum population.[30] Although mentioned much less frequently, the concept still influences the way we think about demographic change, whether "the demographic dividend"[31] or the economic implications of demographic change. When there are demographic shifts, such as rapid population ageing, the notion that we are moving away from some optimum population size or structure, can raise anxiety levels. Like a tsunami that "strikes without warning and ... sucks everything out to sea ... we're supposed to believe old people are going to suck all our resources out with them."[32]

The notion of an optimum population is also reflected in the language and symbols used to describe age structures. The well-known *population pyramid,* a graphical illustration of the distribution of a population by age group and sex is a good example. The more a graph looks like a pyramid, the more it represents the historical norm. The more it looks like an inverted pyramid, the higher the proportion of older persons. The divergence from the traditional population pyramid is termed "morphed population pyramid" or "constricted population pyramid,"[33] words which combined with *the silver tsunami,* or *the ticking time bomb,* described in the next section, create an image of a large bulk of seemingly unproductive elderly people dependent on a shrinking cohort of productive young workers, fueling the notion of population ageing as a threat.

*The Ticking Time Bomb.* Closely associated with the tsunami metaphor is the notion of older people as a ticking time bomb of enormous economic and societal cost. Economists and demographers decry the "dramatic consequences" of population ageing:

> As sizeable populations of older adults retire and age out of the workforce, younger people are having fewer kids. It's setting up a ticking demographic time bomb, readying to explode when there aren't enough young people to care and pay for what the older generation needs.[34]

Editor of *MIT Technology Review,* David Rotman, argues that conventional wisdom is that an ageing population is toxic for economic growth.[35] Economists are concerned about how "dwindling workforce straining to support burgeoning numbers of retirees,"[36] will affect their countries' economies as well as their future capacity to finance their social security systems. A retrospective analysis done in 2009 of attitudes reported in *The Economist* confirms this view. It found that 64 percent of articles and stories portrayed population ageing as a liability, often depicting older people as frail non-contributors.[37] However, assumptions on the impact of population ageing have been debunked by several academics who underline that despite the panic about ageing, there is surprisingly very little evidence that ageing societies are worse economically.[38] As Teitelbaum argues, "Pundits and advocates forecast that demographic ageing will surely bankrupt economies by increasing the 'old-age dependency burden' of pension and healthcare expenditures."[39] Similarly, demographer Phil Mullan views the so-called ageing time bomb as "a kind of mantra for opponents of the welfare state and for a collection of alarmists."[40]

The assumption that a large number of retirees will be dependent on a relatively smaller generation of traditional working-age people between 15 and 64 is in fact the heart of the problem. For example, the demographic dependency ratio which measures the size of the "dependent" population in relation to the "working-age" population who theoretically provides social and economic support to the population too old (or too young) to have a job [41] are increasingly seen as aged biased. The concept of age dependency excludes such important trends as increasing employment of women or longer education for young people. The Council on Ageing of Ottawa suggests that changes in employment among older workers and among women have increased employment over the past 20 years. It also argues that continued employment growth among people in their 60s, including new technologies and new business policies, might keep talented people working longer and will greatly ease if not eliminate any "tsunami threat" in the coming decades.[42]

Further evidence of the bias in the concept of "dependency is offered by National Transfer Accounts, which are available for an increasing number of countries. National Transfer Accounts use labor income and consumption expenditures to define dependencies, rather than employment status" and show transfers between people of different ages.[43] The results are telling. Older persons are not only recipients—they often provide financial support, child care or other types of in-kind support to younger generations. "At an aggregate level, National Transfer Accounts help to dispel the myth that population ageing necessarily implies a net economic cost."[44]

This is also supported by WHO data that states that only a small proportion of older people are actually dependent on others for care, and that older people make substantial contributions to their families and societies. In Kenya, for example, the average age of smallholder farmers is 60 years, making them critical for ensuring food security.[45] Research from the United Kingdom in 2011 showed that the contributions older people made through taxation, consumer spending, and other economically valuable activities were worth nearly £40 billion more than expenditure on them through pensions, welfare, and health care combined.[46]

"Furthermore, even in countries that have mandatory retirement ages, a notable share of older persons continue to work in formal or informal employment [...] In countries that offer small or no retirement benefits, almost all older persons continue to work for as long as they can."[47]

The notion that population ageing will bankrupt the economy fails to reflect the reality of older persons' contribution to the economy. Looking at gross domestic product (GDP) data from 1990 to 2015, Acemoglu and Boston University's Pascual Restrepo found no correlation between ageing demographics and slowed economic growth.[48] Economist Phil Mullen suggests that a modern society's normal capacity to grow economically provides more than adequate resources to sustain an ageing society and allow continued growth in living standards for all.[49]

Imagining old age as unnatural, as a gray tsunami, or as a ticking time bomb of economic catastrophe, sabotages the way older persons are considered and counted, subtly undermining our ability to promote more sophisticated policies based on evidence and human rights. "As noted by the *Report of the Independent Expert of the UN*, it is essential to portray older persons as active participants in society rather than as passive receivers of care and assistance or an impending burden on welfare systems".[50] In summary, the language we use and the images we construct, such as the old-age dependency ratio are "not only simplistic but also misleading and stigmatizing and can unwittingly perpetuate the notion of older persons as a burden."[51].

## *The Consequences of Viewing Ageing as a Threat*

The *Global Report on Ageism*, published by WHO in 2021, outlines the many consequences of ageism and calls for building a movement to change the narrative around age and ageing.[52] Part of that movement is to recognize the role that we can all play as practitioners to re-imagine the way we think and talk about population ageing. This is particularly important for economists and demographers. Anthropologist Susan Greenhalgh argues that because demography and its methods are rooted in science and empirical research (statistics, quantitative data), demographic data takes on a veneer of truth that transcends the social.[53] The next section looks at some of the consequences of these demographic imaginaries: They can lead to age bias in data collection and analysis, they can ignite intergenerational conflict, and, more seriously, they can endanger lives.

*Age Bias in Statistics.* As noted, most of our data on older persons has focused on "chronological age, defining older persons as those aged 60 or 65 years or over."[54] This is the easy way out: It provides a simple, clear, and easily replicable way to measure and track various indicators of population ageing. However, there has also been increasing recognition that the mortality risks, health status, type and level of activity, productivity, and other socioeconomic characteristics of older persons have changed significantly in many parts of the world, particularly in the last few decades.

This is just one example of age bias in data collection, and data disaggregation; another is the serious gap in data available to capture the lived realities of older persons. In her report to the 45th session of the Human Rights Council, the Independent Expert on the enjoyment of all human rights by older persons, stressed the importance of addressing these gaps. The report noted: "This lack of significant data and information on older persons is, in itself, an alarming sign of exclusion and renders meaningful policymaking and normative action practically impossible."[55]

Reliable data, disaggregated by age, sex, and other relevant characteristics, is key to predicting demographic shifts, understanding their implications and developing inclusive policy responses that are based on evidence and human rights.[56] On the positive front, alternative concepts and measures have been introduced, which provide a more nuanced perspective of what population ageing means in different contexts. For example, the concepts of "perspective age" rather than "chronological age," and "economic dependency ratios" rather than "demographic dependency ratios," help to "put the spotlight on the contributions of older persons."[57] These new measures and concepts offer more sophisticated ways of "assessing the living conditions and living arrangements of older persons, their productive and other contributions to society, and their needs for social protection and health care."[58]

*Intergenerational Conflict.* The UN defines intergenerational solidarity as social cohesion between generations. The notion of solidarity speaks to how people of different generations relate to each other and help and depend on one another in their daily lives. In today's world, unfortunately, we hear more about intergenerational conflict than about solidarity. A fair amount has been written on rising intergenerational battles, and we get the impression that generations are pitted against each other, with the young resenting the old for monopolizing scarce resources, depleting pensions, or voting the wrong way. I was shocked recently in a meeting when a young university student proposed this solution for a rapidly ageing world: He would base the right to vote on average life expectancy rates. In other words, the more time you are expected to live on this earth, the more your vote should be worth. The vote of an 18-year-old would be worth 100 percent, that of an 80-year-old would be worth 50 percent and so on.

A culture of ageism had taken hold in many societies, with older people facing pervasive discrimination in health care, employment. and other spheres of their lives. As populations age, we may witness growing intergenerational conflict and increased perceptions of "generational inequity." Ageism and negative stereotyping may continue as technological advances become ever more ingrained in our personal lives, with those who cannot or will not adapt at risk of being left behind.[59] According to Professor Andrea Charise at the University of Toronto, one of the deficits of an ageist society is lack of intergenerational communion. In households with multi-generational interaction, memories can be handed down and shared freely. Strong and meaningful relationships between people of different generational cohorts help mitigate the isolation and loneliness which affect both older and younger people.[60] In light of today's global challenges, connecting the generations improves the well-being of both groups.

*Endangering Lives.* Finally, and most seriously, negative metaphors related to population ageing have the potential to endanger the lives of older persons, supporting the idea that "if the *elderly* are like a dangerous tsunami, then why would we work to prolong or improve quality of life for this threatening population?"[61] The COVID-19 pandemic was a heartbreaking example of the impact of ageism on older adults. We heard shocking claims during the COVID-19 pandemic that many older people dying from the virus "would have died anyway." Yet many of these deaths were preventable. This also ignores the unimaginable pain and suffering these deaths caused affected people and their families, as the pandemic ripped through older populations. Ageism did not start with COVID-19, but the pandemic brutally exposed existing fault lines in society. Often neglected and out of sight, older people living in care homes were among the most vulnerable of all. We heard haunting stories of people dying alone, without their loved ones, subjected to minimal care by overwhelmed and underfinanced facilities. The tragedies in nursing homes are just one, albeit extreme, expression of how we failed older people, a failure the pandemic put into stark relief. Yet COVID-19 cannot be blamed exclusively. Even before the pandemic, many older people experienced neglect, poverty, social exclusion, and isolation. It is this structural condition that must be refashioned, along with the pervasive messages society communicates subtly through its cultural cues – that older persons are a burden, less valuable, even expendable.

## *The Way Forward: From a Focus on Demographic Threat to a Focus on Demographic Resilience*

Existing policies are letting older people down, and worse—are letting societies down. By refusing to recognize the contribution of older persons, governments are ignoring a vital source of experience, income, and contribution. It is important that all of us, especially professionals committed to the human rights of older persons in different domains, be aware of language and images, which are so often used in a way that subtly undermines our older populations.[62] The good news is that initiatives are underway to do just that. Organizations involved in reframing ageing[63] have proven that the use of positive metaphors reduces people's implicit (or unconscious) bias against older people. The ability of these positive demographic imaginaries to move unconscious, deeply entrenched attitudes suggests advocates can use them to reduce unintentional bias.[64]

Partly as a reaction to the potential negative impact of apocalyptic demography on the rights of people, including older people, the concept of demographic resilience has emerged. Demographic resilience recognizes that a seismic shift in thinking will be needed to create new narratives on demographic change. Demographic resilience is an aspiration that involves the ability to predict demographic shifts, understand their implications, and develop policy responses that are based on evidence and human rights, rather than imagination and ideology. They move beyond narrow quick-fix approaches to population ageing focused on older people as a burden, toward comprehensive population and social policies aimed at ensuring prosperity and well-being for all.[65]

Demographically resilient societies see expenditure on older populations as an investment, not a cost. These investments can yield significant dividends, both in the health and well-being of older people and for society as a whole through increased participation, consumption and social cohesion.[66] Demographically resilient societies understand and anticipate the population dynamics they are experiencing. They have the skills, tools, political will, and public support to manage them so that they can mitigate potentially negative effects for individuals, societies, economies, and the environment, and harness the opportunities that come with demographic change.[67]

Politicians, social scientists, and the media need to be aware of how the demographic imaginary affects how we see ageing, how we collect data, and how we design policy. The Council of Ageing of Ottawa reminds us: "The real world of policy consists of shades of grey, of transitions, of pathways – not arbitrary all-or-nothing static cross-classifications."[68] The hope is that by speaking to demographic resilience, we can build a vibrant community of practice among national policymakers, academics, civil society, and the UN that addresses demographic change in a way that is comprehensive, grounded in evidence, and based on human rights. This will help move from a narrow and ultimately futile focus on silver tsunamis and ticking time bombs toward comprehensive population and social policies aimed at ensuring prosperity and well-being for all. Demographic imaginaries do not stand still; they are an act of creation. Understanding and navigating these imaginaries, and cultivating new ones, will allow us to produce a vibrant approach and more robust policymaking, ensuring rights and choices for all.

## Disclaimer:

The views expressed herein are those of the author and do not reflect the views of UNFPA or the United Nations. Any information that may be contained in this chapter does not imply recognition by the United Nations of the validity of the views in question and is included without prejudice to the position of any Member State of the United Nations. The author's contributions are made in her personal capacity and do not reflect the view of UNFPA or the United Nations or their own institutions.

# Notes

1 Charise, Andrea. Cited in "Stop Dehumanizing Old People by using the Phrase 'Grey Tsunami.'" *The Sunday Magazine*. October 13, 2017. https://www.cbc.ca/radio/sunday/the-sunday-edition-october-15-2017-1.4353223/stop-dehumanizing-old- people-by-using-the-phrase-grey-tsunami-1.4353251.

2 United Nations Department of Economic and Social Affairs, Population Division. "World Population Prospects 2022: Summary of Results." UN DESA/POP/2022/TR/NO. 3.

3 Dent, Harry. *The Demographic Cliff: How to Survive and Prosper During the Great Deflation Ahead*. Canada: Penguin Random House, 2015.

4 Bloom, David E. and Leo M. Zucker. "Aging is the Real Population Bomb." Accessed January 6, 2023. https://www.imf.org/en/Publications/fandd/issues/Series/Analytical-Series/aging-is-the-real-population-bomb-bloom-zucker.

5 "The Silver Tsunami." *The Economist*. February 20, 2010. http://www.economist.com/node/15450864.

6 "The Pensions Time Bomb." *The Economist*. November 19, 2000. https://www.economist.com/unknown/2000/11/19/the-pensions-time-bomb.

7 Smith, Noah. "Old Age Is the Next Global Economic Threat. Japan's Deflation is a Warning to Other Countries with Swelling Elderly Populations." *Bloomberg Opinion*. October 20, 2020. https://www.bloomberg.com/opinion/articles/2020-10-20/old-age-is-the-next-global-economic-threat?leadSource=uverify%20wall.

8 Armitage, Alanna. "From Demographic Security to Demographic Resilience: Towards an Anthropology of Multilateral Policymaking in Eastern Europe." PhD Thesis, Graduate Institute, Geneva, 2021. Drawing on scholarship on ideology, "imagined communities," and the "social imaginary," I argue that the meaning given to demographic indicators and to demographic change are very much a reflection of the emerging social imagination underscoring the biopolitical logics of the state.

9 Bytheway, Bill and Julia Johnson. "An Ageing Population and Apocalyptic Demography." *Radical Statistics* 100 (2010): 4. https://www.radstats.org.uk/no100/BythewayJohnson100.pdf.

10 The concept of demographic resilience was adopted by UNFPA's Eastern Europe and Central Asia Regional Office in 2021 as an attempt to provide a new framework for addressing rapid population change in the region.

11 Teitelbaum, Michael S. (2014). "Political Demography: Powerful Forces Between Disciplinary Stools." *International Area Studies Review* 17, no. 2 (2014): 99–119.

12 Applewhite, Ashton. *This Chair Rocks: A Manifesto Against Ageism*. New York: Celadon Books, 2020.

13 Barusch, Amanda. "The Aging Tsunami: Time for a New Metaphor?" *Journal of Gerontological Social Work* 56, no. 3 (2013): 181–184. https://doi.org/10.1080/01634372.2013.787348.

14 Calasanti, Toni. "Brown Slime, the Silver Tsunami, and Apocalyptic Demography: The Importance of Ageism and Age Relations." *Social Currents* 7, no. 3 (2020). https://doi.org/10.1177/2329496520912736.

15 Charise, Andrea. "Let the Reader Think of the Burden": Old Age and the Crisis of Capacity." *Occasion: Interdisciplinary Studies in the Humanities* 4, May 31, 2012.

16 Mullen, Phil. *The Imaginary Time Bomb: Why an Ageing Population is Not a Social Problem*. London: I.B. Tauris Publishers, 2000.

17 Thompson, John B. *Studies in The Theory of Ideology*. Berkeley, CA: University of California Press, 1984, 11.

18 Kalache, Alexandre. "An Education Revolution in Response to the Longevity Revolution." *Revista Brasileira fe Geriatria e Gerontologia* 22, no. 4 (2019). https://doi.org/10.1590/1981-22562019022.190213.

19 Kalache, "An education."

20 UNFPA. "Measure What you Treasure: Ageism in Statistics." https://www.ohchr.org/sites/default/files/Documents/Issues/OlderPersons/AgeismAgeDiscrimination/Submissions/UNs/UNFPA-2.pdf.

21 UNFPA, "Measure."

22 Rotman, David. "Why you Shouldn't Fear the Gray Tsunami." *MIT Technology Review*. August 21, 2019. https://www.technologyreview.com/2019/08/21/133311/why-you-shouldnt-fear-the-gray-tsunami/.

23 UNFPA submission to A/HRC/48/53: Report on Ageism and Age Discrimination, 5 August 2021, https://www.ohchr.org/en/documents/thematic-reports/ahrc4853-report-ageism-and-age-discrimination.

24 World Health Organization. "Misconceptions on Ageing and Health." October 30, 2015. https://www.who.int/news-room/photo-story/photo-story-detail/ageing-and-life-course.

25 Greenlee, Kathy. "Overcoming the Silver Tsunami." *Generations Today*. July-August 2020. https://generations.asaging.org/silver-tsunami-older-adults-demographics-aging.

26 UNFPA, "Measure."

27 Greenlee, Kathy. "Overcoming the Silver Tsunami." *Generations Today*. July-August 2020. https://generations.asaging.org/silver-tsunami-older-adults-demographics-aging.

28 Council of Ageing of Ottawa. "The Grey Tsunami Threat: A Failure of Evidence to Drive Policy. A Discussion Paper by the COA Experts Panel on Income Security." October 2017. https://coaottawa.ca/wp-content/uploads/2017/11/2017-10-income-security-Tsunami-paper.pdf.

29 Striessnig, Erich. "What is the Optimal Fertility Rate?" *Nexus: The Research Blog Of IIASA*. February 27, 2014. https://blog.iiasa.ac.at/2014/02/27/what-is-the-optimal-fertility-rate/.

30 Wolfe, A. (1936). "The Theory of Optimum Population." *The Annals of the American Academy of Political and Social Science* 188 (1936): 243–249. For Wolfe, the optimum size of population "will be that which furnishes the labor supply which, fully utilized, is necessary to operate the total resources of land, materials, and instrumental capital at the point of least (labor) cost per unit of product or income" (246).

31 The Demographic Dividend is defined as the economic growth potential that can result from shifts in a population's age structure, mainly when the share of the working-age population (15 to 64) is larger than the non-working-age share of the population (14 and younger, and 65 and older). UNFPA 2016.

32 Applewhite, *This Chair Rocks*.

33 The Oxford Institute of Population Ageing. "Global and Regional Population Pyramids." Accessed January 6, 2023. https://www.ageing.ox.ac.uk/population-horizons/data/gpt.

34 Brueck, Hilary. "Japan is Reversing a Dangerous Demographic Time Bomb—But Now the US is in the Danger Zone. *Business Insider.* July 13, 2018. https://www.businessinsider.com/japan-demographic-time-bomb-reversing-but-us-is-in-danger-2018-7.

35 Rotman, "Why you Shouldn't Fear."

36 Bloom and Zucker, "Ageing is."

37 Martin Ruth, Caroline Williams, and Donal O'Neill. "Retrospective Analysis of Attitudes to Ageing in the Economist: Apocalyptic Demography for Opinion Formers." *BMJ* 8, no. 339 (2009): b4914. https://doi.org/10.1136/bmj.b4914.

38 UNFPA, "Measure."

39 Teitelbaum, "Political Demography," 108.

40 Mullan, Phil. *The Imaginary Time Bomb: Why an Ageing Population is not a Social Problem.* London: Tauris, 2000, 215.

41 Council of Ageing of Ottawa. "The Grey Tsunami Threat: A Failure of Evidence to Drive Policy." October 2017. https://coaottawa.ca/wp-content/uploads/2017/11/2017-10-income-security-Tsunami-paper.pdf.

42 Council of Ageing of Ottawa, "The Grey Tsunami Threat."

43 UNFPA. "Measure."

44 UNFPA, "Measure."

45 World Health Organization. *World Report on Ageing and Health.* Geneva: World Health Organization, 2015. https://apps.who.int/iris/handle/10665/186463.

46 WHO, "Misconceptions on Ageing."

47 UNFPA, "Measure."

48 Acemoglu, Daron, and Pascual Restrepo. 2017. "Secular Stagnation? The Effect of Aging on Economic Growth in the Age of Automation." *American Economic Review,* 107 (5): 174–79. DOI: 10.1257/aer.p20171101

49 Mullan, *The Imaginary Time Bomb.*

50 Office of the High Commissioner for Human Rights (OHCHR). "Human Rights of Older Persons: The Data Gap Conundrum." July 9, 2020. A/HRC/45/14. Cited in UNFPA, "Measure."

51 UNFPA, "Measure."

52 WHO, *Global Report.*

53 Greenhalgh, Susan. *Cultivating Global Citizens: Population in the Rise of China.* Cambridge, Massachusetts; London: Harvard University Press, 2010.

54 UNFPA, "Measure."

55 OHCHR. "Human rights." Cited in UNFPA, "Measure."

56 UNFPA. "Demographic Resilience Programme for Europe and Central Asia." 2020. https://eeca.unfpa.org/sites/default/files/pub-pdf/104_demographic_resilience_brochure_updated_2023_r1.pdf.

57 UNFPA, "Measure."

58 UNFPA, "Measure."

59 WHO, *Global Report.*

60 National Association of Federal Retirees. "Rewriting Ageing: In Conversation with Andrea Charise." October 1, 2020. https://www.federalretirees.ca/en/news-views/news-listing/october/rewriting-aging-in-conversation-with-dr-andrea-charise.

61 Gordon, Michael. "Gray Tsunami: A Dangerous Metaphor in Aging Discourse?" *Annals of Long-Term Care.* July 28, 2014. https://www.hmpgloballearning network.com/site/altc/blog/gray-tsunami-dangerous-metaphor-aging-discourse?key=gray+tsunami&elastic%5B0%5D=brand%3A37427.

62 Gordon, "Gray Tsunami."

63 Fulmer, Terry and Drew Volmert. "Reframing Aging: Growing 'Old at Heart.'" *Stanford Social Innovation Review.* June 12, 2018. https://doi. org/10.48558/DMTS-WM48.

64 Fulmer and Volmert, "Reframing Aging."

65 UNFPA. "Demographic Resilience Programme for Europe and Central Asia: Pathways for Societies to Thrive in a World of Rapid Demographic Change. Accessed January 6, 2023. https://eeca.unfpa.org/sites/default/files/pub-pdf/104_demographic_res ilience_brochure_r6.pdf.

66 WHO, "Misconceptions on Ageing."

67 UNFPA, "Demographic Resilience Programme."

68 Council of Ageing of Ottawa, "The Grey Tsunami."

# About the Authors

**Michael Adams**

Michael Adams is the Chief Executive Officer of SAGE—Advocacy and Services for LGBT Elders, the world's largest and oldest organization dedicated to transforming the LGBT ageing experience. In partnership with SAGE affiliates countrywide in the U.S.A., SAGE serves countless LGBT older people nationally via technical assistance, training, and services as well as advocacy at every level of government. Adams, a graduate of Stanford Law School and Harvard College, previously was the Director of Education and Public Affairs and Deputy Legal Director for Lambda Legal and Litigation Director for the American Civil Liberties Union (ACLU) LGBT Rights Project.

**Alanna Armitage**

Alanna Armitage, Ph.D., is the United Nations Population Fund (UNFPA) Representative in Mexico and Country Director for Cuba and the Dominican Republic. She is the former Regional Director for Eastern Europe and Central Asia where she and her team developed the concept of Demographic Resilience to help support countries address rapid demographic change from a rights-based perspective. She has championed women's health and rights over the past three decades as UNFPA Representative in several countries. As Director of UNFPA's Geneva Office, Armitage led the Fund's Geneva-based multilateral interactions on global health, human rights, and humanitarian response. She holds degrees in Cultural Anthropology and International Development Studies and a postgraduate degree in Health Systems Management. She holds a Ph.D. from the Geneva Graduate Institute of International and Development Studies, on the impact of demographic anxiety on gender equality in Eastern Europe. Armitage was featured in *Apolitical's 100 Most Influential People in Gender Policy 2021*, honoring people working on gender through policymaking, public service, research, philanthropy, advocacy, and activism.

## Liat Ayalon

Liat Ayalon, Ph.D., is a Professor in the School of Social Work at Bar Ilan University, Israel. Ayalon is the Israeli Principal Investigator (PI) of the EU-funded MascAge program to study ageing masculinities in literature and cinema. She was the coordinator of an international EU-funded Ph.D. program on the topic of ageism (EuroAgeism.eu; 2017–2022). Between 2014 and 2018, Prof. Ayalon led an international research network on the topic of ageism, funded through COST (Cooperation in Science and Technology; COST IS1402, notoageism.com). She consults for both national and international organizations concerning the development and evaluation of programs and services for older adults. In recognition of her work, Prof. Ayalon was selected by the UN Decade of Healthy Ageing as one of 50 world leaders working to transform the world into a better place in which to grow older.

## María Soledad Cisternas Reyes

María Soledad Cisternas Reyes is the Special Envoy of the Secretary-General of the United Nations on Disability and Accessibility. She was Chairperson of the Committee on the Rights of Persons with Disabilities of the United Nations (2009–2016) and recipient of the Chile National Prize of Human Rights (2014–2015). She was an expert for the ad hoc committee that developed the United Nations Convention on the Rights of Persons with Disabilities, for which she has also been the rapporteur for individual complaints. She is the director of several legal and interdisciplinary projects, as well as the author of various publications and an exhibitor at national and international conferences. Cisternas Reyes has a degree in Law and a Master's degree in Political Science. A lawyer, law professor, and researcher, she was awarded the 2022 International Human Rights Award by the American Bar Association.

## Alexandre Kalache

Alexandre Kalache is the President of the International Longevity Centre-Brazil (ILC-BR). He is a medical gerontologist and a member of the Brazilian

National Academy of Medicine and the U.K. Royal College of Physicians. Dr. Kalache has been a protagonist on worldwide ageing policy issues for more than four decades as both an academic (at the University of London and the University of Oxford) and as an international civil servant, (directing the WHO global department on ageing and health). He routinely advises governments at the national, state, and municipal levels, as well as private foundations and businesses worldwide. He is a long-standing human rights advocate.

**Larraine J. Larri**

Larraine J. Larri is a Research Fellow in the Cairns Institute at James Cook University, Queensland, Australia, and a member of the Australian Association for Environmental Education. She is an activist, researcher and program evaluation expert specializing in environmental adult education and environmental citizenship. She completed her Ph.D. (Education) in 2021 through James Cook University. Her research investigated the educative mechanisms for transformative action addressing political stasis on climate change within the Australian Knitting Nannas environmental activist movement. Using a transdisciplinary approach, the study addressed a lacuna in older women's environmental activist learning by identifying the dynamics of situated, experiential, and social transformative learning.

**Claudia Mahler**

Claudia Mahler, a national of Austria, assumed her role as the UN Independent Expert on the enjoyment of all human rights by older persons in May 2020. She has been a senior researcher in the field of economic, social, and cultural rights for the German Institute for Human Rights since 2010. She was also a visiting professor at the Alice Salomon Hochschule in 2020–2021.

From 2001 to 2009, Mahler conducted research at the Human Rights Centre of the University of Potsdam where her main fields were in human rights education, minority rights, and the law of asylum. In 2000, she was appointed as Vice-President of the Human Rights Commission for Tyrol and Vorarlberg. She has also worked as a lecturer in the field of human rights law and as a consultant to the Office of the High Commission for Human Rights in Geneva. From 1997 to 2001, she held the position of an assistant at the Leopold-Franzens-University Innsbruck, Austria, in the field of Criminal Law and Criminal Procedures. Mahler received her doctoral degree, from University Innsbruck, in 2000.

## Bette Ann Moskowitz

Bette Ann Moskowitz, a native of New York, U.S.A, is the author of six books and many essays and short stories. Her subject is often ageing, and as she has become older, she realizes that she is a native of Planet X, growing intellectually and emotionally stronger as the years go by. Her novel, *Three Legs in The Evening*, is about a woman who finds love in the shadow of her old age. She is a past recipient of a New York Foundation for the Arts Fellowship for Literary non-fiction, and a former teacher of writing at Queens College and Ulster County Community College. For several years she wrote a lifestyle column for a regional newspaper in the Hudson Valley, upstate New York, where she currently lives and has kept up her lifestyle blog, *Vinegar Mother*, posting once a week for four years.

## Silvia Perel-Levin

Silvia Perel-Levin is an advocate for the human rights of older persons. She has been working in the fields of human rights, ageing, and health for over 20 years at international organizations (IOs) including the World Health Organization (WHO) and the International Union for Cancer Control, and as a consultant with the United Nations Population Fund (UNFPA) and other IOs. At WHO, she managed the first multi-country study on elder abuse and produced, among other publications, the report *Missing Voices: Views of Older Persons on Elder Abuse*. Before that, she was a theatre and TV producer. In Geneva, Silvia represents the International Network for the Prevention of Elder Abuse (INPEA) and the International Longevity Centre Global Alliance (ILC GA). She chaired the NGO Committee on Ageing in Geneva for eight years until April 2022, advocating for the inclusion of ageing and older persons across the United Nations and promoting a UN Convention on the rights of older persons. She was born in Argentina and has also lived, studied, and worked in England, Israel, Hungary, and Switzerland. She has a B.A. in Social and Educational Theatre from Tel Aviv University and an M.Sc. in Inter-Professional Practice from the Institute of Health Sciences of City, University of London.

## Adolf Ratzka

Adolf Ratzka was born in 1943 and was raised in Bavaria, Germany, where he contracted polio in 1961, leaving him dependent on an electric wheelchair, ventilator, and assistance for the activities of daily living. After five years in hospitals, at age 22, he moved to the University of California, Los Angeles, where he completed his Ph.D. Since 1973, he has been based in Stockholm, where he was a research economist at the Royal Institute of Technology, working on architectural accessibility and its effects on the economy. He started the first European personal assistance user cooperative, STIL, which stood as the model for the Swedish LSS Act of 1993 (Swedish Act concerning Support and Service for Persons with Certain Functional Impairments)—the national direct payments scheme for personal assistance. He was the founding chairperson and director of the European Network on Independent Living (ENIL) (1989–1992), founding director of the Independent Living Institute (ILI) (1993–2017), and founding chairperson of Disability Rights Defenders (2015–2018). He has lectured on disability issues in over 30 countries.

## Kate Swaffer

Kate Swaffer is a highly published author, poet, international speaker, independent researcher, and an award-winning campaigner for the rights of people with dementia and older persons globally, and for dementia as a disability. She has an M.Sc. in Dementia Care, a Bachelor's in Psychology, a B. A. in Professional and Creative Writing, a graduate Diploma in Grief Counselling and is a retired nurse. Her incomplete doctorate uses autoethnography to investigate stigma, seeking to discover why it is still so prevalent for people with dementia and their families. Swaffer is an Honorary Associate Fellow in the Faculty of Science, Medicine, and Health at the University of Wollongong; an International Fellow in the Impact Research Group at the University of East Anglia; and a co-founder and human rights advisor to Dementia Alliance International, the global voice of dementia, providing support, including peer-support, and local, national, and international advocacy for all people with any type of dementia globally.

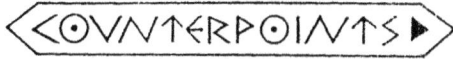

# Studies in Criticality

*General Editor*
*Shirley R. Steinberg*

Counterpoints publishes the most compelling and imaginative books being written in education today. Grounded on the theoretical advances in criticalism, feminism, and postmodernism in the last two decades of the twentieth century, Counterpoints engages the meaning of these innovations in various forms of educational expression. Committed to the proposition that theoretical literature should be accessible to a variety of audiences, the series insists that its authors avoid esoteric and jargonistic languages that transform educational scholarship into an elite discourse for the initiated. Scholarly work matters only to the degree it affects consciousness and practice at multiple sites. Counterpoints' editorial policy is based on these principles and the ability of scholars to break new ground, to open new conversations, to go where educators have never gone before.

For additional information about this series or for the submission of manuscripts, please contact:

Shirley R. Steinberg, General Editor
msgramsci@gmail.com

To order other books in this series, please contact our Customer Service Department:

peterlang@presswarehouse.com (within the U.S.)
orders@peterlang.com (outside the U.S.)

Or browse online by series:

www.peterlang.com

www.ingramcontent.com/pod-product-compliance
Lightning Source LLC
Chambersburg PA
CBHW050651280326
41932CB00015B/2868